A
Sharp
Left
Turn

A Sharp Left Turn

Notes on a life in
music, from Split Enz
to Play It Strange

Mike Chunn

ALLEN&UNWIN
SYDNEY • MELBOURNE • AUCKLAND • LONDON

First published in 2019

Cover photograph: Murray Cammick
Endpaper photograph (front left): Bruce Jarvis
Endpaper photograph (front right): Gijsbert Hanekroot via Getty Images

Allen & Unwin
Level 3, 228 Queen Street
Auckland 1010, New Zealand
Phone: (64 9) 377 3800
Email: info@allenandunwin.com
Web: www.allenandunwin.co.nz

83 Alexander Street
Crows Nest NSW 2065, Australia
Phone: (61 2) 8425 0100

A catalogue record for this book is available from the National Library of New Zealand.

ISBN 978 1 98854 713 8

Design by Megan van Staden
Set in Baskerville and Domaine
Printed in Australia by McPherson's Printing Group
10 9 8 7 6 5 4 3 2 1

MIX
Paper from
responsible sources
FSC® C001695
www.fsc.org

The paper in this book is FSC® certified.
FSC® promotes environmentally responsible,
socially beneficial and economically viable
management of the world's forests.

**To Brigid
and
to the memory of Von and Jerry**

Contents

Prologue

The Palmerston North Opera House had the 'Full House' sign out. It was 24 February 1975. We, Split Enz, stood on the stage bathed in coloured lights, and I plugged my bass guitar into an amplifier that was almost as tall as me. I was going to have power tonight. They call it bottom end. The bass. The instrument that no one knows is there until you stop playing and then the band sounds horrendous. Believe me.

The sound check is near finishing now. I see this band around me . . . and their happy faces. A full house does that. All the shows on our university tour have been full houses, just like this one. Our band is making moves, and we are bringing that energy to the stage, to the show. Tim, out front, is masterful, even here in an empty hall. He knows that he will rule the stage tonight. I know that too. I've been watching him onstage, with me, for eight years. And the others in their various shapes and sizes. Tonight we will assault them, these university students.

Our soundman, Murray Ward, calls out, 'Sound check over.' The band drifts away side-stage. I look up and the curtain, this ancient curtain, slowly comes down to cut me off. And I walk off-stage into a sheer, living hell.

It's happened.

Why?

Why here in this small, unexceptional town?

I am scared. No, I'm not scared. I am *terrified*. Of what? I don't know.

I can't go to the dressing room. They will look at me. They will see my wide eyes. I won't be able to speak. They might notice my heart rate, which has now zoomed up to 150 beats per minute. My thoughts are racing. I can't hold on to a thought. Give me a thought I can hold on to! It doesn't happen.

I look for shelter. I find a dark corner behind a black drape, far away from the well-worn corridors. No one can see me. I sit on the floor. When is the show beginning? How long do I have to sit here? What if someone finds me? Thoughts teem through my pathetic head. Thoughts that move so fast I don't know what they are. Thoughts. How long have I been here? A voice calls out.

'Chunn!' It's Wally. 'Where are you? Show is about to start!'

How long have I been here? Hours?

I race to the dressing room, avoid all eye contact and get into my costume. Wally and I have exactly the same costumes with polka-dot bow ties. Clowns. And all of a sudden I am in the shifting group, winding along past phantom stars of old and the echoes of opera music and onto the stage.

I put my bass on . . .

And the terror is gone.

Gone.

My heart rate drops to 75 beats per minute. I hold a thought. It stays. What is it?

I am crying for joy up here, on the boards, on the wooden

platform where our band will play a whole pile of glorious songs. Songs written by our own Juddsy and Tim.

I am happy.

And the curtain, the ancient curtain, lifts and hundreds of people start calling, clapping and whistling.

I am that child again. That young boy in south Auckland dreaming of the circus life. The escape. A platform on which to be someone who mattered. A stage.

I am back in that childhood world of excitement and hope. It wasn't that long ago. I hold that thought. I am back there.

Lift this curtain, this ancient curtain.

Chapter One
A Stake in the Ground

I n the late 1950s, Auckland, New Zealand, was a sprawl of skinny roads, scrawny trees and short-back-and-sides. The pace was sober and days rolled by. At the time, as the '60s loomed, New Zealand was in cultural isolation, still decades short of having some quantifiable presence on the global map. There was a World War II hangover and an increasingly anachronistic reliance on the United Kingdom to sustain and provide. This was ironic considering Britain's frugal attitude at the time. England's slow recovery post-war was in sharp contrast to the boom in the United States, where Elvis Presley, Marlon Brando and Jack Kerouac had merged from their divergent sources to forge an entertainment revolution, riding on the back of a massive commodity boom.

Through huffing and puffing, the British Empire had staved off the inevitable economic realities of the twentieth century and was yet to implode; in New Zealand, we all stood for the national anthem before movies (not 'God Defend New Zealand', but 'God Save The Queen'!), the radio was full of royalty reports and shopping specials, and there was no television. We marched to a textbook beat and no one seemed to go off on a tangent. The cinemas churned through British war movies in rapid succession, with John Mills on the bridge and moustaches on every lip.

For a boy with grazed knees and grey socks, the fantasy of battle was relived through stacks of war comics and guns made from firewood and suburban driftwood. Pieces of timber surfaced out of nowhere to become Bren guns, Sten guns and Lugers. I would attack the enemy in the undergrowth, under cover of the twenty fruit trees that dotted our half-acre backyard in the suburb of Otahuhu.

In moments of stealth and surprise I would pour red-hot bullets into the chest of my younger brother, Geoffrey. He was shorter than me but not by much, and would eventually tower over me. In more ways than one. He always had a busy mind; his original songs offered to the world many years later were testament to that. Geoffrey's focus when playing war games was survival. He tossed his skinny legs in the air and ran from the bullets. I shot him. He would refuse to die. I, on the other hand, threw myself onto the rotting fruit and muddy earth, all cadaver and carcass. Occasionally I would play alone and shoot myself. Then my mother would call me in and I would fade, exhausted, over a hot meal.

The branches of time in the Chunn family tree reached back to the late nineteenth century, when my grandfather Alfred was born in Greymouth. His father had emigrated from Wiltshire in England. Alfred was a mischief and a vagabond so it was no surpise when, in the collision of time and responsibility of which he took no notice, he became a bookie. He was called

Bunny, as he was always running from the police. A bookie is a wanted man unless he knows which cops to buy beer fotr. Fortunately, Bunny did. He always had a pile of pound notes in his back pocket, like fallen leaves of gold that he had cleverly picked from punters' pockets.

My grandmother was an Irishwoman called Babs, born and raised in Cork. She was born Mary but no one seems to know why she became known as Babs. Or how she got to Greymouth. She was Babs Chunn and that was that, and she was a barmaid. In time she became an alcoholic as she tried to cope with the tawdry behaviour of Bunny, who painted an invisible dotted line through the middle of their house. He lived in one half, and Babs and their two sons, Jerry and Jack, lived in the other. Bunny would appear in the evenings to eat dinner with them, say nothing, then go back across the dotted line. Gone. My father, Jerry, remembers his mother sitting in a chair weeping.

And then the war came. Bunny's slippery, clever nature ensured that his sons didn't go to Europe to fight. With his pocket full of money, he funded Jerry to attend Otago Medical School. Doctors were needed at home in a war, and that included med students. Farmers were also needed, to make sure that cows and sheep were plentiful. Meat in wartime is gold. So Bunny bought a farm and got Jack to run it.

Babs died in the late '60s. The kind, lush lawns of their house on 'Chunn's Hill' in Greymouth faded before her eyes. And, as much as she thought she might be going somewhere in life, the truth was a stationary wall of dead hours. Hopefully she would sit in the late-afternoon sun and watch the shadows of the boundary trees stretch and orchestrate the slow, methodical arrival of dusk.

Bunny staggered on, in the Kingseat psychiatric hospital in South Auckland. He died in 1976 after battling a mental disorder that no one seems to have a name for. He used to come to our Otahuhu home one Sunday a month in a striped three-piece suit and give each grandchild a half-crown. Maybe he was still taking bets on horses in Kingseat. He must have known his horses well.

My mother, Yvonne—Von for short—was also born in Greymouth, the daughter of Owen and Francie Williams. Her father was a peripatetic principal of primary schools, so it was by chance that Greymouth was Von's birthplace. She remembers nothing of it, as the Williams family moved on shortly afterwards. Small towns rolled off their car bonnet with the sea breezes. They always seemed to be close to the ocean as they drifted far and wide around New Zealand. Tokomaru Bay. Waitara. A few others lost in time.

The Williamses' marriage was also lost in time. It was failing, so Von was sent to boarding schools, where she forged a sense of place, a camaraderie with like minds.

At the end of the 1940s, after her parents divorced, Von's mother, Francie, married Sam Turner. He was different, old Sam. He had a large wooden Spitfire propeller on his study wall. When I was a kid I used to wonder what had happened to him in the war over there in England. Did he ever fly into a turbulent sky peppered with German bombers? His thumb on the trigger. His heart in his mouth.

Sam didn't want to talk about it. He was more of the present. He was on the board of companies like UEB and Craig's foodstuffs and things like that. He would hand out tins of baked beans. He had lines to stockbrokers and seemed to have a lot of shares. Whatever that was all about.

Von's father married Nell, a shopkeeper, and they lived in Katikati till the end of their lives. Brother Geoffrey and I would go there on the bus and stay a week or two. Their street never had any traffic driving down it. There was a sense of the stationary and the nameless. Did anyone wander? Did they ever take a different route to the dairy? How would one ever know?

Their house was drenched in silence. Nell didn't own a rack for putting wet dishes on. Every time I picked up a cup to dry it she would proclaim, 'That's the leaner!' Nell owned a bookshop, and every Christmas gave me a book. I still have one; it's called *Why Didn't They Ask Evans?* by Agatha Christie. I still don't know why.

Von went to nursing school in Auckland, which, as she looked very much like Elizabeth Taylor, was a means to an end. A young doctor there, Jerry Chunn, put two and two together and a match was made. They married in 1951. 'Twas a fairly lavish affair, with photographs taken at the Micky Savage Memorial above the sparkling Auckland harbour. Von was elegant, Jerry suave. It was a time-honoured union of a nurse and a doctor. Whoever their children might be, the future held for them a regime of cool medicines, free prescriptions and class A drugs—when necessary, and only to be administered by Jerry. More on that later.

In July 1951, Von and Jerry sailed out of Auckland's sparkling harbour and slid their way over six weeks to London on a merchant ship. Jerry took a job as the boat's doctor so he got a free trip. It was probably hellish. Drifting through the doldrums as a soft, hot rain mucked in with their sweat. Surging and grinding through the Atlantic's angry indolence with battleships, subs, U-boats and the thin, almost invisible remains of naval uniforms floating hundreds of metres beneath them. World War II had ceased only six years earlier. The thousands of bodies down in that deep blue tomb would have vanished by then, consigned to the history books, washed in the tears that fell all over the world.

The reason why these two New Zealanders were on this journey was so that Jerry could study for the MRCP(Ed)—Membership of the Royal College of Physicians (Edinburgh)—and the MRCPS (Membership of the Royal College of Physicians and Surgeons) in London. Things got off to a good start. Within a few weeks Von was pregnant with me.

A few years ago she gave me a photo in a tiny, neat envelope. I opened it and there was a picture of her standing on a footpath.

She said, 'See that window up there. Above me?'

'I do,' I said.

'Well, you were conceived in that room.'

'Well, well, well,' I said. And she had written the address on the back in case I ever went to Edinburgh and got around to visiting it (which I haven't yet).

Jerry passed his MRCP(Ed) and the next year, 1952, they drifted down to London. Before that, though, they drove a Morris 1000 on a European holiday, to Paris in the main. They went to Cologne, too, which was still in ruins from the war. For Von's whole life she would tell us, tell everyone, how Cologne was a shattered pile of rubble—*but!* the cathedral was in perfect condition. I thought that was a cool coincidence. She thought it was magical.

They caught the ferry back to London and I was born

in June at Hammersmith Hospital. Von grappled with prams weighing three stone (more than 19 kilos) and nappies that were impregnable flannel monsters.

The decision was made for the again-pregnant Von and me to return to New Zealand, leaving Jerry to complete his MRCPS. Tickets were bought and a date set, but there was a coronation to be had. Somehow Von and Jerry got tickets to a viewing stand managed by the New Zealand embassy, and saw Queen Lizzie roll past right in front of them. I had been dropped off at a Dickensian workhouse to be babysat, and when, in time, they picked me up, I was drenched in urine and there were splashes of gruel on my onesie.

A few weeks later Von and I were on the *Dominion Monarch* passenger ship heading for Cape Town. When we got there, the South African press came storming onto the ship to take photos of us. Yes, it would be natural for you, dear reader, to think 'That makes sense', seeing as Von was so pretty and I was so chubby. But no. Von and I were the first real humans to arrive in Cape Town who had been at the coronation! (Well, *she* was.) And that was news! The main Cape Town paper printed our photo. I still have it. And then we sailed to Auckland.

A few months later Jerry turned up. Once again he had been tortured on a merchant boat in exchange for a free trip as the on-board doctor. My parents didn't waste any time. Jerry looked up 'Doctors' Practices For Sale' in the *Trade & Exchange*, and there was one in Otahuhu, wherever that was. So we all went out there and Jerry bought it. It was in the Syd Handisides building on Great South Road, back when it was the main road between Auckland and Wellington. In the midst of this, my brother Geoffrey was born, in October 1953.

Coupled with this completed mission was the purchase of a house. Von and Jerry looked up 'Houses For Sale' in the *Trade & Exchange*, checked out a half-acre section with a two-storey house on it in Hutton Street, Otahuhu, and bought it for about five thousand quid. Voilà! Sorted. And in 1954, Von, Jerry, Geoffrey and I rolled into the big house in Hutton Street, Otahuhu, to start a life.

But back to dinnertime. Von had taken a Le Cordon Bleu cooking course in London in 1952, and brought back to New Zealand those fine cooking skills. It all seemed like a lot of work over there at the stove, but the stirring and straining and sifting and slopping all added up to things like pork Provençal or beef stroganoff. Dinner was quite a ceremony. Plates would be delivered to the table, usually by me, and the response was always positive. Grace before meals? I don't remember. I do recall her sneaking in things like Brussels sprouts and swedes, which we forced down. But she knew what it was all about, and now and then we had the sheer delight of sausages, mashed potato and peas!

Dinner was when we all happened to be in the same place at the same time. We didn't do a lot of talking round the table, mind you. To my pre-adolescent self it just seemed the way it should be. I know different now.

After dinner we collectively washed and dried the dishes, and this is where conversation rose to the surface. The details of life. Geoffrey and I would talk about movies and games, like pretending to have fatal crashes on our bicycles. (We would smear ourselves with mud as if it was dried blood from gaping wounds. In time, when a Kodak Brownie camera turned up, we would photograph these bloodthirsty scenes. That didn't last very long; I took a photo of Geoffrey with his pants down, and when Dad picked up the photos from the chemist the camera was confiscated.)

My sister, Louise, four years younger than me, would float about in a thoughtful, dreamy way. She was a girl of letters, reading books as often as she took breath. At the age of twelve, just before going to secondary school at Baradene College in Remuera, she actually put pen to paper and wrote one. It was set in the Victorian era. I wasn't aware of this until I heard Von and Jerry talking about how Louise had decided her book wasn't any good and had burned it. That seemed a fairly radical move.

Louise got her love of the written word from Jerry. As I write this, I look across at our bookshelves on which rest hundreds of books signed and dated by him. Orange Penguins—G.K. Chesterton, John Updike, Truman Capote et al. Hard covers by his favourite authors: F. Scott Fitzgerald, Graham Greene, P.G. Wodehouse, Evelyn Waugh. And then the books of poetry: T.S. Eliot, Dylan Thomas, Byron, Thomas Hardy.

In his fifties Jerry started writing verse, and over time wrote dozens and dozens of poems. This is one, about his father, Bunny. It's titled 'A Fragment'.

> *On the chalk-hill the earth was shallow*
> *Breeding gorse and blackberry—*
> *The two old rugged comrades of the Coast.*

For many years
Dad slashed at them
And kept them in their place

Then he grew old and died alone, suddenly,
In a great barn full of the mentally disturbed—
Grew old but never complained
As the new enemies he could not beat
Grew rampant on the thin layer of the brain.
He could not pick his slasher up
And hack at them with happy frenzy,
Could not follow with a bath
And shave
Before bouncing down the street
With his gold watch chain and sovereign case
And some old sentimental ditty in his eyes.

Jerry also wrote sixteen poems to Louise. She was his favourite. I didn't find them until the early '90s, when I was in my forties and Louise had lived overseas for ten years.

After the last washed—and dried—dish was put back in the cupboard, we drifted off to our bedrooms. Geoffrey and I shared one (and would do until I was twenty!). Jerry would come in, sit down and tell us a story, one of many oft-repeated but with spontaneous variations. The only one I can recall the title of was 'Slow Sammy'. I can see him: a man, gentle and patient, framed against the wallpaper, which is dark blue and boisterous, covered in sailing ships like the Spanish Armada. It seemed as if his words and soft voice had frozen those violent images so that they would never move again.

Louise would be in her large bedroom around the corner in a four-poster bed, reading *Anne of Green Gables* and flying through cosmic variations of plots, characters, imagery and imagination, all being sorted neatly for her coming adventures in adulthood with the written word. Our brother Derek was probably about to be born; the fifth Chunn child, Jeremy, was some way off conception. Then the lights went out and we all fell into dreams.

We would awake each dawn in clean, cold air often drenched in fog from the Tamaki Estuary. By midday it was gone and a blue sky would parade above us, if only for a short while. By mid-afternoon there were thunderclouds blacker than the night. These towering monoliths rolled in from the south and wiped the sun clean away from the now slate-coloured sky while sending my size-three feet scurrying down Hutton Street to number nine in a (usually vain) attempt to beat the downpour. If I clambered up the back steps five minutes too late it was thrilling, the cold water soaking slowly through the grey uniform and blue tie I wore every day to St Joseph's Convent School.

St Joseph's Convent was old and packed with white women in black habits, through which poked sour faces telling us about Ducky Lucky and Chicken Licken and Janet and John. More often than not, though, they told us about heaven (should that be Heaven?) and just where we all stood in regards to this invisible figment of fragmented fomentation. From my first day there, these grim females instilled a tenacious fear couched in Biblical references and social disciplines. The fear of God. The devil. (Should that be the Devil?) Self-loathing seemed a cool thing to them. And I liked the perfect symmetry of 666. They were devilishly good at strapping us, too. Thick, professional leather straps. Some factory must have made them from really tough Otahuhu bulls. But there were paradoxes and holes in their arguments, and each year led to more confusion. One moment, God was turning water into wine. (Presumably he could therefore turn tap water into lemonade? Such bliss.) The next, he was splashing black across our souls because we missed Mass on Sunday. And black souls were a one-way ticket to hell.

I needed to know more about this variance, as the thought of an eternity of scorched buttocks was more than I could bear. We had all been told about the two categories of sin—venial and mortal. Each type of sin was pegged to social and religious misdemeanours and resulted in the soiling of the soul, but was there a hierarchy of blackness?

Chunn: Sister Mary Carthage? How many venial sins does it take to earn one mortal sin?

Carthage: No number of venial sins could *ever* equal a mortal sin.

This was brilliant. All I had to do was make sure I got to Mass each Sunday and that I ate macaroni cheese on Fridays, and I could dream all day about the breasts on those McAuley High girls, pinch my classmates' pocket money and let crackers off in the girls' toilets. My punishment would only be a shortish period of flame-immersion in purgatory. (Should that be Purgatory?) Meanwhile, my old mate Jim Skinner from over the hill, in a careless moment, would let the communion Host touch his teeth and be guaranteed an infinite post-life in the fires of Satan. Poppycock.

Chapter Two
Toby Tyler and the Fab Four

With the clarity of purpose I gained at St Joseph's Convent School, I decided at the age of eight to be a petty thief and sneak into the movies for free. One day, I left Otahuhu at 5 a.m. on foot and arrived at Queen Street in downtown Auckland, 16 kilometres away, at midday, totally and utterly devastated by starvation. I'd forgotten to swipe some pennies from Jerry's coin box in his underpants drawer. No matter. I snuck into the Civic Theatre at half-time and watched *Toby Tyler* (Wikipedia will tell you all about it). That young man riding horses in the circus—what a perfect escape. I soooooo wanted to run away somewhere. And then the movie finished. I walked out and made my way back home. As I staggered into Otahuhu at 5 p.m. I was met by my darling mother, Von, who was, in essence, understanding, because my wanderlust comes from her side of the family. But it was more than that. She knew I hated going to that convent school. Both my parents did.

I heard Jerry once say to Von, 'The nuns are mistaking Michael's enthusiasm for mischief.' At the time I didn't really know the difference. Like 'silly' and 'stupid'. They seemed very different words, but I heard them all-a-tumble and ignored them. They were just words.

Back to my starving self on the side of the Great South Road, across from the freezing works and in the shadow of the water tower atop Mount Richmond. Von's voice was soft, consistent.

'Where have you been?'

'To the movies.'

'Why?'

I told her. She listened and, in casting her mind back to all the tawdry primary schools she'd been to, felt it unnecessary to say anything. She would have known that leaving home at 5 a.m., walking to the city, going to a movie at midday in the glorious Civic Theatre and arriving back home in a starved condition was something I would do only once.

The local police, however, were deeply irritated, having spent all day trying to find me. I was on the Radio 1ZB news. A lost child. I thought to myself, 'How can you lose anyone in New Zealand?' And the next day I was back at school.

Shortly after I tasted that heady mix of fame and trouble, my dad wrote another poem.

> *My name is Michael*
> *I'm a sort of vicious cycle*
> *In that normality*
> *Seems to occur to me*
> *Only as a possibility*
> *Before (inevitably)*
> *I recur to me*

The only respite from the relentless classroom was the occasional visit to the dental clinic. In the role of molar guinea pigs, we could be found tilted back in huge chairs, our teeth drilled by student nurses while talk show host Aunt Daisy or the soap opera *Portia Faces Life* burbled on the valve radio in the corner of the room. Daisy would cry out to us as if to alleviate the horror of the drill: 'Good morning, good morning, good morning, good morning. Good morning, good morning, good morning.'

Portia possessed a greater distraction. We imagined her as some dark, sultry Sophia Loren figure in a scarf and tight jumper. Her slacks were probably stirrup trousers, and they would surely have been satin. But what was satin? It shone.

With a life on the run looking decidedly dodgy, I entered a talent quest at the Otahuhu Borough Council hall, and reached the finals with a spirited rendition of 'The Longest Day' (from that tame, clean film about D-Day) to a crowd of about 400 kids. My fascination with war movies continued, so it was either that or 'Sink the *Bismarck*'. I balanced my war fetish with a total obsession with Hayley Mills movies. I had a scrapbook at home with photos, clippings and so on, and when *Whistle Down the Wind* came to town I was beside myself. Hayley BABY!!! I failed to win the talent quest, losing out to some twerp singing 'Peanuts' in a high soprano voice. I was sensible enough to realise why I lost—I couldn't sing. So I took up the piano.

Our next-door neighbours, the Lyons, harboured two teenage girls, Janet and Margaret, who took a shine to Geoffrey and me. They had a cousin, Harry, who ended up in Hello Sailor. We would walk through the orchard, clamber over the corrugated-iron fence and spend time with them, listening to records and being shown basic songs on the piano. 'Tammy' was one of them. It sank in. I had a go on their violin but it killed the goldfish, and Geoffrey was relegated to the ukulele . . . later a guitar. I would listen to Margaret play 'The Robin's Return' on the piano and vow, in no uncertain terms, that one day I too would play that majestic piece (I did, by the way).

We balanced the creation of music with listening to records on their three-in-one record player. It was a particularly banal period in popular music, but I was ignorant and became engrossed in the likes of 'Move Over Darling' by Debbie Reynolds and 'The Battle of New Orleans' by Johnny Horton. It wasn't long before the odd gem surfaced somehow, and I became obsessed with 'Fool # 1' by Brenda Lee and 'Tower of Strength' by Gene McDaniels. In fact, the latter spurred me to have proper piano lessons, and I found a wonderful, radical woman by the name of Mrs Beazley on the outskirts of Otahuhu who was an inspiration. Sidestepping (sideswiping more like it!) the whole exams palaver, she taught me the whole basis of what, in the end, would allow me a life in popular music—chords.

Instead of picking out and learning a Chopin ditty parrot-fashion, Mrs Beazley and I would tackle something like 'What Shall We Do with a Drunken Sailor?' or the 'Theme of *Exodus*'. It would take only a minute because the melody was simple, and I would make up my own left-hand part by reading the guitar chord, thumping it out. I liked the left-hand part. It had what we would much later call balls. 'Heart and Soul' was another simple number that succeeded by virtue of its driving left-hand chords. I spent more and more time on the piano as the improvisational possibilities opened up. Chords were the magic key to the lock of composition, and I dickered around on little home-made pieces. I also had a crash course in improvisation at the annual scout concert.

As a scout I was less than satisfactory, but when it came time for the annual parents' concert in the Otahuhu Church Hall, I was in. I chose the 'The Blue Danube' for some reason (despite my opposition to classical pieces), and in front of a hundred shuffling, shifting, fidgety adults, I launched into it with gusto. Rather typically, however, I started to daydream halfway through and suddenly had not a clue as to where I was on the page.

Instead of stopping and finding my place, I charged on, making it up as I went. I took a sideways glance at the audience and they were all laughing. I brought the proceedings to a grinding halt with a *dum-dum-dee-daa* C major then walked off. While the other scouts relegated me to the blew-it bin, I was happy inside. I was going to get more of this. I was going to fly by the seat of my shorts.

I found myself imagining what it must be like to be a pop star. Now and then I would use my hard-earned pocket money to buy a magazine like *Teen Stars*, and send off a coupon with a money order (kindly provided by my mother) for black-and-white photographs of teen idols. I would sit in my bedroom when they arrived and try to 'unearth' the fabric of their lives. Johnny Tillotson, Fabian, The Everly Brothers, Susan Maughan and so on. All Brylcreemed and hairsprayed. Nothing but a photograph and their hit singles floating in my head. A fairytale world at the age of ten.

I'm sure Von and Jerry saw this Hollywood pop-star

infatuation and quietly hoped it would vanish. If they themselves were ordering photographs from overseas they would have been of Frank Sinatra, Elizabeth Taylor, Marlon Brando and Marilyn Monroe.

Not long after the scout concert, I found myself in Wellington on a class trip. I was now at De La Salle College in nearby Mangere—an oppressive place. Compared with the nuns' wild and woolly mix of religion and discipline, the brothers were a vicious bunch. I was particularly in the firing line, owing to my class-clown persona. There was one lay teacher, however, who had human qualities, and it was he who chaperoned our sojourn south, the intention being to see the All Blacks play Australia. It was 29 August 1964 and they lost 20–5, as you rugby cognoscenti will know. However, it wasn't the football that charged me. As well as the All Blacks match, we were treated to one and a half hours of the most exciting, uplifting and fresh songs I had ever heard in my life. We went to see *A Hard Day's Night*. The Tammys, Terrys, Bobby's Girls and Sad Movies of the past few years dissolved in one quick rush as we sat goggle-eyed while all around us teenage girls screamed.

From then on The Beatles were a primary focus, a searing pinpoint for my pre-adolescent brain. Back in Auckland, Von saw the light and would bring home sheet music of Beatles' songs. 'From Me to You', 'Can't Buy Me Love' and 'I Want to Hold Your Hand'. Songs that were the toppermost of the poppermost. The piano was working overtime. Then the big moment—I went down to the local record store to buy a Beatles record.

On the way I stopped outside Hannahs shoe shop and saw my first real Beatle boots: zippered, Cuban-heeled, seamed-leather icons of fabness. Unfortunately never to be mine.

I skipped on to the record store only to find they had sold out of Beatles records! I spent my 2/6d on a single I'd never heard of called 'Hang On Sloopy' by The McCoys. I took it home, took Richard Burton reading *Under Milk Wood*, Frank Sinatra's *In the Wee Small Hours* and *Ella Fitzgerald Sings the Cole Porter Song Book* off my parent's stackable gramophone and played it. Oh boy . . . woweee . . . this was nothing less than splendiferous! They sang 'Yeah, Yeah, Yeah' too.

I started listening to the radio more and more, but there was only one half-hour show a week that played good music. It was hosted by Peter Sinclair, who said 'gear' and 'fab' and 'groovy', and I was drawn in. It was on Thursday nights, and I heard Dusty Springfield and The Hollies one week, The Kinks, Manfred Mann and Cilla Black the next . . . and so on. This music was free, hooky, edgy, vibrant, driving and, while a lesser animal than the likes of 'A Hard Day's Night', certainly of the same ilk. The same thread of invention.

As 1964 closed off, I was brimming with a sense of the new. I was aware that 'over there' in the northern hemisphere there were demi-gods in Beatle boots with stovepipe suits, Vox amplifiers and American guitars. Huge quantities of these beings, who presumably lived as fast as they played. One day I was going to be one. Maybe one day I would play a Höfner violin bass! ('But, Mike, Höfners are German, not American!' 'Yes, I know, dear reader.')

Twelve months later, I readied myself for departure from the De La Salle cage. My parents had scheduled my next five years as a boarder at Sacred Heart College in Glendowie, based on the premise that boarding school had seen my father right (I couldn't argue with that). In early December I sat the school's scholarship exam, but as January 1966 rolled around the news was bad. There were two scholarships awarded and I wasn't getting either. They had both gone to country boys. I whiled away the summer absorbing more pop music and readying myself for the mysterious lifestyle ahead. It could only be better than the two institutions I'd endured to date.

On 30 January 1966, Von and Jerry drove me to Sacred Heart College. I hopped out of the Morris Oxford, took my suitcase from the boot and walked over to the dormitory. I was assigned a bed. I draped the checked blanket that Von had given me over it, and put my stuff in the small bedside cupboard. Underpants, toothbrush, pyjamas, school clobber.

A man in a black dress with a white bib under his chin was walking around. He had a grim visage and didn't say anything. When evening came he spoke up, advising us to get into bed, and then the lights went out. There was no talking. Was it forbidden? Or were we all scared? There I was, surrounded by dozens and dozens of strangers. Who were they? They might as well have fallen from the sky. What did I have to be in this cavernous place? When could I be myself again?

We were able to leave the school grounds one Sunday a month. I would be home in four weeks. But I wouldn't be having dinner with my family. You had to be back at school by 6 p.m. for the Sunday dinner. And what might that be? Luncheon sausage? Stale bread?

Was anyone in my bed in Otahuhu? Was Jerry telling the

story of 'Slow Sammy' to Derek and Louise? What was Von going to buy tomorrow from the Hellaby meat store? Tripe? Surely not. Polonies and saveloys? Perfect. Would Von and Jerry sit in the L-shaped lounge, put Nat King Cole on the gramophone and drink gin and tonics? Would they miss me?

Here in the dorm, the grim brother, Rat, glided down the corridor, his silhouette moving across each of the steel-framed windows that looked out towards the Hauraki Gulf. A slow-motion movie of a dark ghost; a silhouette with no shape. No reference to real life. He walked slowly. Did he ever change his pace? Was he wearing roller skates? What was he looking at? What was he listening out for? Movements? Sounds? Crying? I'd heard they had canes in their pockets. The nuns used straps; so did the De La Salle brothers. I'd never been caned. What was it like? In less than twenty-four hours I would know.

Chapter Three
Hits and Myths

My first day of school up the stairs in Classroom 3A of Sacred Heart College was a virtual mirror image of De La Salle. Periods started and finished in silence. There were differences; one new subject was Latin. But really—all the same. The main activity was keeping quiet. Don't talk. Anywhere. Maths, French, English—all spinning in my head with no purpose. Lunchtime found us starting the social whirl where we might make friends, although on day one not much was achieved. Some of the kids already knew each other. Farmers' sons from the Waikato. No one was there from my Otahuhu streets. If they were, they probably got the bus in every day. And went home at night. As day-boys, they got to go home.

Our first foray into the dining room for dinner found us at our most social. The food was disgusting. We could talk about that. We worked out where we were from. We were all dressed the same. Some talked more than others; some said nothing. Zuke, the head of my table, looked like a very large version of me. Well . . . he had a big nose. But his eyes seemed bright and they skipped from side to side. It was his last year at school. He was soon to be free. I had only five years to go.

I imagined what it must be like to know that freedom was

just around the corner. It seemed like a simple thing. Walk down the corridor of some hostel for the last time. Your heart beating faster with each step. And then out through the gate, gone forever.

At 7 p.m. we returned to our classrooms for study. On the first day of school the homework was pretty meagre. I turned to the lad beside me; his surname was Schollum. 'What are we supposed to be doing?' I asked. As I spoke the door opened and another man in a black dress looked over at me. We all knew who he was because he paced around the school like a master of discipline should. His nickname was Butch.

'What's your name?'

'Michael Chunn, Brother.' I then proffered information that he might digest, saying that it was me who had been talking not Schollum, but he didn't let me finish. He had decided that I was telling him that Schollum was talking, not me. In his eyes I was a squeal. Yellow.

'Come out the front.' And I did. He walked towards me. His black dress and white bib looked very odd; he should have had a black military uniform on instead. As I stood with my back to the blackboard he thrust the rolled-up newspaper gripped in his hand into my stomach. His eyes never left mine. I was winded, coughing. 'Get outside,' he said.

Out on the landing above the quadrangle I could see out to the distant peak of North Head. Devonport. Miles away. They had Navy boats there. If I was in the Navy I could be on one and head out to sea and Butch would have to find someone else to cane.

'Don't try that again, you brat,' he said. 'Put your hand out.'

Ah. That was what the cane felt like. Four of the best.

I wanted to kill him. I wanted to throw him off the landing down onto the bitumen below. I would then descend the stairs and keep walking right out of the gate.

I went back into the classroom to find some homework to do. No one said a word.

And then we were all back in the dormitory. We cleaned our teeth. We didn't talk; talking wasn't allowed in the bathroom. We changed into our pyjamas. A valve radio up on a ledge was playing. I lay on my bed and listened to it. I was drawn into it. I judged every song they played. I dissected every song that was played. And then I was completely pinned down with a joyous sensation. All the boys in the dorm vanished. Rat, the brother over there by the steel-framed windows, turned into a mouse. The harsh fluorescent lights above us softened and seemed to drift in slow-motion circles, to and fro, like Catherine wheels. The Beatles' 'We Can Work It Out' was playing. I knew it. Geoffrey and I had listened to it only a few days earlier, in our Otahuhu bedroom. It was a number-one hit. It was unforgettable. We knew that one day we would learn how to play it. But that night it saved me. And one word kept spinning, entwining me in a dream. *Free*. One day I would be free. The lights went out. And I fell asleep.

When the weekend turned up, we finally got to coagulate and start the social discourse. It was on the banks of the 1st XV field that I met this lad from Te Awamutu. His name was Tim Finn. (His Christian name is actually Brian, but he is now known around the world as Tim—his middle name—so I'll stick with it.) I don't know why we were there by that perfectly manicured field. Its goal posts reached to the sky. And the painted sidelines were very straight, very narrow. We had probably chosen that place to sit and see what might happen; who might walk past and recognise in our demeanour a talent for rugby. After all, we fantasised, we little third-formers, that one day we might wear the 1st XV jersey and run out onto that very field and play for the school.

Tim's short hair looked like it would explode if he let it grow. His eyes were the strongest feature of his face, and he fixed me with a stare. He spoke with clarity—each word counted. And his legs were very thin.

He wasn't a complete stranger. At the end of the previous year, when I had gone to Sacred Heart to sit the scholarship exam to try for free boarding and education at the school, Tim had sat next to me. Not that we introduced ourselves, as talking wasn't allowed. He won the scholarship. A bright lad. And now here we were again, except this time we were inmates. And we were allowed to talk here on the side of the 1st XV field.

He told me that he was a tennis player and a decent swimmer. And would be signing up for the rugby. I told him I was a mean opening bowler in cricket and was going to run hurdles in the school athletic team. As well, I played left wing in rugby, as I was left-footed.

Tim and I joined a group of lads who quickly came to grips with the lie of the land, conforming to a satisfactory standard in all matters of mid-'60s academia and discipline. We sought escape as such. Escape that wouldn't find us maligned by the orders of the day.

I can't recall how we focused on it, but we supplemented our night-time study sessions with writing poetry steeped in morbid imagery and naïve adolescence.

Tim sent his home:

> *. . . Casting my thoughts upon life's spoken steed*
> *Emitting a train of flexible thoughts*
> *My voice does its best to portray my emotions*
> *But fails in a destitute condition of knowledge.*

I sent mine home too:

> *To give a sickening cry that sends*
> *a chill of fear to spine and nerves*
> *Fatigue that transmits to the brain a sin,*
> *but bliss will soon emerge.*

This failed to ignite much response from anywhere, so we set about the ritual of nicknames.

By virtue of my unusual surname having Oriental connotations, I became 'Chang'. Tim became 'Fang' on a sympathetic vibration, although he was generally called 'Hound-Dog' via the Huckleberry Finn/Huckleberry Hound connection. Among our peer group there were a host of others: Martian, Bounce, Buck, Chopper, Tank, Tub and so on.

And then there was Mass on Sundays. In the pews, we all put our heads on our folded arms and fantasised about being free. Whatever that was. What about sex? None of us had seen a naked woman, so there wasn't much to hold on to there. Sometimes we went to confession. 'Forgive me, Father, for I have sinned. It has been two days since my last confession and since then I have had seven hundred impure thoughts.'

Time dragged on. Tim and I played lower-grade rugby;

I also played cricket. I smashed the stumps with my out-swingers. Tim threw passing shots on the tennis court and powered down the swimming pool. And Free Sundays would eventually turn up, when Jerry or Von would drive in through the gates and I would dive into the car and get back to our house in Otahuhu. Geoffrey would be there and we would scroll through the hits of '66. Von had kept buying sheet music. 'Michelle' was one. It was anything but rock'n'roll. But then, a song like 'Hang On Sloopy' doesn't really work on the piano. Nor does 'A Hard Day's Night'. But The Beatles' 'Michelle' did!

Von would also have beautiful food waiting for me. And Louise, Derek and young Jeremy would hover or flit by, each emerging into age groups that found them changing, maturing. And then at 5.30 p.m. I would get back into the Morris Oxford, and in absolute silence Jerry would return me to Sacred Heart to an egregious Sunday dinner.

Towards the end of the year a huge change came over our lives. From living day-to-day in the often fruitless pursuit of catching the odd pop song on the radio, the first New Zealand pirate radio station arrived—Radio Hauraki—and from that day on we were immersed in a glut of outstanding music. From The Kinks to Unit 4 + 2, the Four Tops to Every Mother's Son, Small Faces to The Rolling Stones, Dusty Springfield to The Mamas and the Papas, Strawberry Alarm Clock to Crispian St Peters, The La De Das to Larry's Rebels and not forgetting Vanilla Fudge—all bowing in reverence to the extraordinary Beatles. It poured out of our tinny trannies and we were obsessed, lying awake at night with our heads under our pillows, one ear glued to the mono AM sound. The sound of the future. I found myself becoming more and more focused on New Zealand bands, and during the August holidays I bought my second record: 'On Top of the World' by The La De Das. I played it three or four hundred times and got inside it rather well. I was particularly impressed by the bass guitar dive bombs (perhaps google that—*dive bombs*).

At the end of the year, Tim's conscientious dedication to success took him to the top of the class. My conscientious dedication placed me only fifth, and I resolved to give the country boy more of a run for his money the next year. As well, Tim scored the more notable achievement of receiving the most canings in our particular dormitory. With a sense of satisfaction, he threw his smelly clothes into his suitcase and headed off to Mount Maunganui for a summer of surfing and family singing.

I scarpered back to Otahuhu as fast as I could, where Geoffrey and I spent an entire eight weeks listening to his new birthday present—The Beatles' album *Revolver*. Von and Jerry had displayed an acute sense of being 'with it' by buying this album. It blew our minds, and we dissected every note, word, drum beat and image that flowed from the songs, until they were coming out of our ears as opposed to going in. Never again in my life did I saturate myself with a record as I did that one. We ferreted around on the family piano trying to work the songs out. Not easy.

As far as other pursuits went, I was into surfing—but our family holiday place was on Auckland's west coast at Bethells Beach, where the waves thundered mercilessly. During the year Tim had come out and been appalled at the bad surf, which contrasted with the elegant waves at Mount Maunganui. As far as he was concerned, I was a 'West Coast sucker'.

The following February we all gathered back at college. It was the usual pattern, now repeated almost to a dull sheen.

I would hop into Jerry's car and, in silence, he would return me to Sacred Heart. This time, fourth form in 1967, the dormitory had fewer beds (fourth-formers were spread across two floors) but was still an array of disaffected youth. I would lie on the bed dreaming of Von's cooking and of listening to Jerry's home-made stories in the knowledge that the transistor radio under my pillow would be the equivalent signal for me to withdraw from the world.

Butch had yet to drift out of sight. One day Tim and I, with a couple of other lads, were passing a rugby ball around on the lawn in front of the dormitories. He walked over, drew us into his inner sanctum and asked why we were passing the ball around on the lawn when it was forbidden. None of us said anything, because it was a rhetorical question. He then said, 'You three stay off the lawn and find something useful to do. Chunn, you stay here. I'm going to cane you for having a supercilious look on your face.'

Talking about caning, this was the fourth form and first up was the caning record. Two years previously, a particularly enterprising 4A class had achieved a total of 644 canes from the form master Brother Stephen. It became our ambition to better this, and we quickly set about talking in class, arriving late, cutting up his cane, flicking ink, farting, clicking ball-point pens and failing to complete homework. Things started slowly, and by mid March we had amassed only 23 canes from the man. But there was time.

One day Brother Stephen asked us to write an essay titled

'My Dream'. We all wondered what *his* dreams were about. Caning boys? Maybe. I knew what my dream was. I dreamt I was in a band and we were playing the Auckland Town Hall to a full house. (Yes, Beatle reflections motivated this, but . . .) The best part was that I had a bass amplifier as tall as me. And when I plugged my bass in it was supremely loud. As I wrote each word of that essay I was shaking with excitement. If the Beatles could do it, why couldn't I?

So I handed my essay in and I was marked 'C'. Obviously Brother Stephen didn't have a rock'n'roll heart or take much notice of The Beatles. Speaking of which . . .

I had come to school in a state of extreme enthusiasm over *Revolver*, and quickly made it clear to Tim that there was something radical happening in the world of Beatles music. The mop-tops' 'yeah yeah yeah' songs about 'holding hands' and 'no reply' had been replaced by songs about death, the taxman and sleeping; there were backwards guitars and pumping rhythm sections.

By now, I was learning the piano from one Miss Curtis, an older woman in horn-rimmed spectacles who fell asleep as I plodded through sonatas and the odd polonaise, which I thought sounded like a spaghetti dish. I would wake her by breaking wind loudly, bringing her to consciousness in a shuddering torment. (Where was my Mrs Beazley!) The only reason I suffered this woman was because it gave me uninhibited access to the school music rooms, ostensibly for practising the current Mussorgsky piece. As the rest of the school grappled with trigonometry and Latin, I would grab Tim by the scruff of his neck and we would retreat to the music rooms, where we tackled the latest Top 40 hits and a stash of Beatles songs. Down below, in the concrete cloisters, the empty tuck shop and the brick toilets, our purposeful piano notes clanged around and around.

The *Sgt. Pepper's Lonely Hearts Club Band* album was now on the street; Geoffrey had poured colour on our home during the August holidays when he went up to the Otahuhu shopping centre one Friday night and bought a copy. As with *Revolver*, we couldn't turn it off. I was particularly excited by Paul McCartney's bass tracks. His melodic command was something I'd never heard before, and producer George Martin had mixed him VERY LOUD. Very soon everyone was talking about the bass guitar on *Sgt. Pepper's*.

On returning to school, I was standing outside the tuck shop when a kid with a trannie radio walked past; the *Sgt. Pepper's* title track was playing, and I stopped him. We stood there listening intently. As the song finished, the track segued into 'With a Little Help from My Friends' and all around us the crowd built up. By the time Ringo had sung his last note there were fifteen kids surrounding that transistor radio—stationary, silent and enthralled. The Beatles had us all by the nuts and we couldn't move!

Back in the music rooms we tackled new songs and things seemed to fall into place. I believed we should get up on a stage as soon as possible, so we approached our music teacher, Brother Ivan, for permission to hold a concert during music period.

Brother Ivan was enigmatic and influential. We called him Guff—no one knew why. Had we been aware of the term at the time, he would have been 'cool'. He never caned anyone. He had a gentle sense of detachment, and unlike brothers such as Rat and Boof he seemed to know that the world was changing, poised to become a more exciting place. Guff was a beatnik in disguise; we would hear him at nights, off in the distance, playing Dave Brubeck on the assembly hall piano. When he coached the school choir we could hear them singing through the coloured walls. He played guitar as well and would bring records to music class.

'Morning, boys,' he'd say. 'We're going to listen to Bob Dylan's *Blonde on Blonde* this morning.'

I'd pipe up. 'Brother, I've got the new Cream album, *Fresh Cream*—how about that?'

Guff: 'I'll give you three Cream tracks for three Bob Dylans.'

And we would sit and listen to records and it was beautiful.

But his crowning achievement came that year during school assembly. Brother Ivan led the school singing, and there had been signs of a willingness to stretch things a little by having the school sing Dylan's 'When the Ship Comes In' as opposed to 'The Lord is My Shepherd'. But this wintry day in 1967, as 650 teenage males of ascending sizes, assorted shapes and varying degrees of acne, skinniness and greasiness stood to attention in their navy-blue shorts and jerseys, Ivan presented them with his coup de grâce—The Beatles' 'Strawberry Fields Forever'. We sang it out. Tim was standing next to me. I watched him sing. It was all second nature to him. The psychedelic moment of a passing dream . . . steadfast. It wasn't lost on our hungry imaginations. We saw the eccentricity. The surreal situation. Brother Ivan was holding a torch for us all and a few of us took the opportunity to follow the beam.

Consequently, it was no surprise when Ivan okayed our

request for a class concert and allowed us to haul the pump organ over from the chapel into the assembly hall so that we could faithfully reproduce our Beatles and Procol Harum numbers. We roped in a couple of classmates, Buck and Tank (Philip Buckelton and Gene Paul), on bongos and guitar, and on 28 September 1967 Tim and I walked onto a stage together for the first time. In rapid and nervous succession we played spirited renditions of 'Homburg', 'Ticket to Ride', 'To Love Somebody', 'With a Little Help from My Friends' and 'Homeward Bound'. Tim hid behind my piano in fright, but did his duty at the microphone and stunned the class. He sang like a bird and froze the lot of them.

When Tim's voice filled the assembly hall, it was a peak moment. For a few seconds we dared to think that *it* might be possible. That there might be something there that could break through the rigid goals others had put in our heads and the restrictions surrounding us. But as we shuffled off to Maths, the spark of hope dulled. Brother Ivan in his wise way was careful to avoid inflating egos, and his reaction was more bemused than enthusiastic.

A few days later we dragged out the school tape-recorder and recorded seven songs in the school assembly hall. I was certain we had something extraordinary, and I was eager to do everything I possibly could to spread our music around.

After laying the songs to tape we played it back. It was this listening session that was *the moment* for Tim. The revelation. Here, for the first time in his life, he could hear himself as others did. He knew then that there was a chance. The tape was sent off to the Finn family in Te Awamutu, where all and sundry gathered around to marvel at Tim's vocal grace and ease. Tim's younger brother Neil in particular was most impressed. He recalls this moment as his realisation, also, of Tim's obvious vocal talents.

Meanwhile, back at Sacred Heart, there were two more tasks to be completed. In a moment of massed effort and sustained mischief, the entire 4A class, including the outcasts—the downtrodden, the rogue elephants and the isolationists, the gregarious and the plebs—pushed Brother Stephen to the limit. In a semi-delirious state of authoritative panic, he mass-caned the entire class and we took our yearly total to 825. The rest of the school cheered and applauded as we smashed the previous caning record with a figure that has never been beaten and never will be. Brother Stephen has now passed away.

The second task was to win the school's Walter Kirby junior music competition. For some reason, Tim and I had failed to think of forming a group and entering it. Odd.

As I was still learning the piano so that we could go to the music rooms during study period, I entered the solo piano division playing Mozart's 'Rondo Alla Turca'. The year before I had entered the same division and played a Mussorgsky polonaise.

The same thing happened both times. The judge said that I had failed to play the pieces in the way that the 'composer intended' and I was unplaced. My response to that was twofold.

How do you know what the dumb composer intended?
Who gives a fuck!

That was the end of my solo piano career. I'd already talked to Geoffrey, who'd just finished his first year at Sacred Heart, about forming a band for the group section for the next year's Walter Kirby. The year of 1968.

Chapter Four
Easy Rider and the Morphine Rush

A week after the Walter Kirby competition, we were on holiday. Both Von and Jerry turned up to collect me and Geoffrey, and we scooted back to Otahuhu to resume our musical pursuits. By now I had scored a guitar as a birthday present (which I still own and play) and thrashed the living daylights out of it, and Geoffrey got a snare drum for Christmas. We could be a band! Geoffrey had continued his foraging for radical records and brought home Jimi Hendrix's *Are You Experienced?* We marvelled at the gut-wrenching lead solos. Geoffrey furthered his reputation as a contemporary by introducing Iron Butterfly's *In-A-Gadda-Da-Vida* to the house.

With our return to school in 1968, there was a sense of purpose in our minds. We took up where we left off, working in the music rooms and periodically putting stuff down on tape. By now, we were dabbling in original songs with as many psychedelic notions as we could muster. *Sgt. Pepper's Lonely Hearts Club Band* had wiped the music-industry slate clean, obliterating all the rules and regulations of commercial pop music. Geoffrey was now in his second year at Sacred Heart so we utilised him on drums (or should that be drum?).

During the May holidays, Geoffrey and I borrowed a couple of tape-recorders and, using the most primitive tape-to-tape multi-track process imaginable, we recorded ten of our own songs. We called ourselves Astley Shrine. It was the only name we could think of; it had no significance whatsoever.

We took the tape to Stebbing Recording Studios, where they made an album out of it. The album was made of thick shellac and, of course, there is only one in existence—safe in my bottom drawer. The songs were all a natural extension of the morbid nonsense we had thrown up as poetry a couple of years earlier, although Geoffrey had a better way with words. I played all the dinky, naïve bass parts on the lower four strings of my nylon six-string guitar and realised something in the process—I loved playing bass.

Back at Sacred Heart, we put on various concerts throughout the year, all following the same pattern: drag the organ over from the church and put the word out that we were going to play. A crowd would turn up, happy to be missing study periods, and we would dish up a platter of recently rehearsed pop songs. Tim's soaring vocals always killed them in the aisles despite his ever-present stage fright; we would return to the dormitory and our shorty pyjamas charged with adrenaline, and clean our teeth.

By the end of the year we were ready for the real thing: the Walter Kirby music competition. There was a group section, which we entered with the help of Geoffrey on drums and a seventh-former, Stephen Streat, on piano. Stephen was younger than us even though we were only fifth-formers. An academic genius, he had scored a university scholarship in his sixth-form year at the age of fifteen. Aside from this, he had a strong creative, musical streak, and we would bash away in the music rooms with him. He adored The Beatles, of course! The competition rules did not permit the use of amplified equipment, which we felt hindered our chances of 'letting rip', but it was a moot point as we didn't own any.

We rehearsed one number solidly—'Yesterday' by The Beatles (naturally), and when the night came we gave it all we had. Which wasn't enough. We were beaten by a duo on guitar and piano accordion who played the theme from 'Man in a Suitcase'. We steeled ourselves and vowed that the next year, and the year after that, we would take the winners' prize. We also pondered another matter—who was Walter Kirby?

The year ended with a rash of School Certificate exams, which distracted us from music. Tim scored a creditable 335 marks out of 400, which wasn't good enough because I scored 342. After years of trying, I'd finally beaten the bastard!

The year 1969 found Tim and me in the sixth form tackling Scholarship exams, and the volume of calculus and T.S. Eliot was extraordinary. We balanced this academic overload with drinking as much beer as we could on the odd times we managed to get outside the school grounds, the occasional concert and many hours in the music rooms.

We Chunns also had a music room at home in Otahuhu. A shabby glasshouse with thick panes, shards of broken glass and dying plants stood about 20 metres from our house. Sitting on foundations of concrete blocks, it seemed to have been built for military resilience not just hot-house tomatoes. But those foundations were perfect. Von had the cool idea of turning it into a music room. 'We can call it The Pavilion,' she said. And that's what happened. The Hamburg German piano stayed inside (too heavy to move), but we purchased a pump organ and the bass, guitar, record player, et cetera all left the main house to settle in The Pavilion. How many hours did Geoffrey and I spend out there? Hundreds and hundreds. A paradise of musical adventure and discovery. Music, music, music. Songs, songs, songs.

As well as the enhanced musical life at home, a sublime, revelatory left-hand turn was soon to happen at school. We had an interesting English teacher, Brother Richard, whom we called Fingers. He seemed to have a focus on all things international, so we asked him about hippies. He said, 'They'll go inside come the winter.' We liked that. There was indeed something . . . *unsure* about the hippie thang.

Fingers' crowning glory, however, was when he took the entire class to see *Easy Rider*. Presumably he knew full well that, during that one-and-a-half-hour whirlwind of peace, love, sex, drugs and rock'n'roll, we were formulating our plans to have it all. We felt we were halfway there: there was plenty of peace and love in our lives, and we were forging ahead with the rock'n'roll. It was just the sex and drugs that were a problem. Aspirin and watching the kooks in the kitchen didn't add up to much.

As usual there was always Mass on Sunday mornings to savour. As Father Wood repeated himself over and over, we all put our heads on our folded arms and fantasised about scoring for the 1st XV, riding in the green room at Waimea Bay or playing through double Marshall stacks at the Auckland Town Hall. Me? I dreamed of being free. I made a quiet vow sitting there in my pew: I would forge a life where I could walk down a suburban street any day of the week and no one could stop me.

And then after Mass? Back to the music rooms.

The real excitement came mid-year when my particularly insightful Uncle John presented me with a birthday present of one hour's studio time at Stebbings. This was a real opportunity. We had been content to foster our musical life within the walls of the college; the concept of recording in a proper studio had seemed impossible, principally because of our naïvety. And no money of course. But here it was—a whole hour! So on a wet August night in 1969 we set off to Herne Bay with a carload of cheap gear.

By this time we had recruited another Sacred Heart lad, Paul Fitzgerald, on drums; as we had never managed to find a guitar player, we had yanked Geoffrey off the kit and thrust a six-string into his hands. He took to it rather well. I had recently purchased a Teisco bass for $35 from Sydney Eady's in Queen Street and I was ready to rip. That night, with Eldred Stebbing at the helm, we put down three songs: two originals—'Near Hosts' (an old melody of mine rejuvenated with a Tim lyric) and 'Take It Green'—and a weird version of The Beatles' 'Got To Get You Into My Life'.

We savoured the results: a good balance and loads of reverb from Eldred's deft fingers. The night was blissful. Tim and I both felt that our musical quest was progressing, albeit within the parameters of our own ignorance. Today we look back and realise that ignorance was bliss. We put the tape in a bag and went out into the rain. When I got home I put that tape in my bottom drawer.

A short while later, The Beatles' *Abbey Road* was released.

Instead of a crowd of fifteen hovering around a trannie, the arrival of the album into the school grounds found virtually every boy resident in Leonard House (the single-room dorm for seventh-formers and groovy sixth-formers) seated around the common-room record player. There would have been 30 of us waiting in anticipation that Friday afternoon. The needle was put on at the start of side one, removed at the end and the disc turned over in solemn silence, then taken off at the end of side two—and not one boy spoke for the entire duration of that record. Tell me something, dear reader: does that happen today?

As the end of the year drew near, so too did the Walter Kirby. We had received our first major knockback when we held a concert one Saturday night in the school assembly hall and foolishly invited the other school band to support us. They were led by Wally Wilkinson—he was a day-boy, which we held against him; we had short hair, which he held against us. When the big day came, Wally arrived with a wild array of professional equipment which he wouldn't share. He and his band blew us away, particularly when they played The Beatles' 'Come Together' from *Abbey Road*. We had planned to do 'She's So Heavy' from the same album but couldn't work it out, so we started with something else instead, probably something soppy. And our equipment was tacky.

Consequently, with this rough experience fresh in our minds, we entered the Walter Kirby intent on success. We rehearsed the Bee Gees song 'Words', which was a Tim Finn showpiece, providing him with ample opportunity to slide and glide over the romantic lyrics with tons of hefty vibrato. On the night we gave no mercy and it was a magic moment when we strode to the stage to take the first prize.

The next year, 1970, was our last at Sacred Heart, and we had seniority. The second term brought with it another rugby season. It was with a wild sense of achievement and an adrenaline rush that both Tim and I ran on to the field to take on St Paul's as members of the Sacred Heart 1st XV. We heard the roar from the banks.

Here they come! Here they come!
Blue red blue!

Tim had a great season, playing in all matches, and the team placed third in the competition. I had a unique experience in that first game, however. Two, actually.

In the first half I took a pass from our fullback, who had come into the backline. With that overlap and with the humungous speed of my skinny legs I hit open space, accelerated and dived into the corner. Every micro-second of my sailing across that try-line is embedded in my memory. The deep silence as I took off into the air. Not a sound. Maybe a sparrow who didn't know what was going on let out a quick chirp. But really—a profound human silence from years of waiting for this perfect moment. And when I hit the grass the hundreds of Sacred Heart supporters exploded, and I stood up feeling triumphant.

By half-time we were 8–nil up, and that was rather cool because their team was a moving mass of muscle, speed and danger. One of them was future All Black Bernie Fraser, but luckily he had the same position as me so he was way over the other side.

The second half started and it was tough. After about ten

minutes the ball went loose in front of me. I thought 'Mmm, I think it might be best to just kick ahead, chase, pick up on the bounce, accelerate away and score another glorious try.' So I did just that. Well, I began the sequence. As I went to kick it, so did the St Paul's centre. I missed the ball and so did he. He kicked my leg accidentally and both bones in my right lower leg shattered in two. I looked down. Half of my shin was swinging in the breeze. I looked up. A woman was standing on the sideline screaming, her face deeply contorted like a scene from *The Omen*.

'He's broken his leg!!!!!!!'

I looked down again. I thought, 'She's right.' But I had another thought. A question. A question I have asked myself in silence ever since I first saw that broken leg. It wasn't until late 2018 that someone actually asked me that same question out loud. Sir John Kirwan said to me: 'Why didn't you dive on the ball, Mike?'

To cut to the chase, the lost chase, there was an upside— the school doctor and my father (a doctor, as you know) ran on to the field and I was injected with a few grains of morphine. They were searching for my mainline. They found it all right. As they straightened my useless leg into a splint I felt nothing but a sweet, puffy exaltation, and I perused the crowd for a familiar face. The head brother, Stubbs, was standing on the field and I waved at him. His look was interesting. I sensed that he knew I had crossed the great divide and was lost to his Catholic world. My wave was a sincere gesture indeed, a quick moment to allay his fear that I might be wincing and squirming in pain. I was as happy as Larry. As the St John Ambulance attendant laid me to rest on my stretcher, I gazed into the heavens and saw God.

His deep, resonant voice came down through the clouds to my zinging eardrums.

'Chunn?'

'Yes?'

'Sins don't matter.'

I *knew* it!

The shattered leg also put paid to my athletic career. I would watch from the sidelines as the hordes whizzed around the track. There was one kid who had legs like large, thick stumps of kauri and he was a mean high-jumper. He was apparently a bit of a whizz piano player as well, but we were prevented from having anything to do with him because he was a day-boy. His name was Eddie Rayner.

Off the field, the focus was girls. While being a member of the 1st XV brought major social status, this failed to transpose to the female sex. In hopes of remedying matters, we put ourselves up for a slot at the Baradene College folk night.

The evening was a sedate affair, with nylon-string guitars twanging away and Joan Baez sound-alikes. Once we'd done our obligatory Simon & Garfunkel song, we decided to break the mould and did a blues version of 'God Save the Queen'. This allowed Tim the chance to do his glissando minor thirds, which had me in fits, and I tried a little Hendrix-like licking, which had Tim in fits. There was disapproving silence from the audience. Afterwards, shrouded in shyness, we failed to socialise and drove back to school, where we cleaned our teeth and went to bed.

By now we were in our Woodstock phase, when we

dreamed of having long hair, smoking weed and owning large amplifiers. We had to be content with Mass on Sundays followed by porridge for breakfast. The *Woodstock* movie had shown clearly the cohesiveness of the youth revolution and, much to our satisfaction, it seemed to revolve around songs. Words and music! The new American wave of youth fixation was following on from the British invasion, clearly inspired by The Beatles and their LSD admissions and exploratory musical directions—directions that never stayed still for a moment. From a distance, we were fascinated by the pure hedonism we saw. A world of invention and joy that was out of reach and outside the paths along which we found ourselves travelling. Somehow, however, we would cross that great divide.

There were still the music rooms. We saved up some money and returned to Stebbings, where we recorded another four originals. This time Geoffrey was on drums. He provided an original song that Tim breathed life into and Stephen Streat played piano on. After the session we listened back and deemed the results to be satisfactory. Geoffrey and I drove home to Otahuhu and I put that tape in my bottom drawer, where it still lies today.

Around this time, Von and Jerry made the decision to leave Otahuhu and head into the city. After fifteen years as a GP in Otahuhu, Jerry had woken up one morning in 1968 and said to himself, 'Time for a sharp left turn!' He had been troubled by allergic reactions, principally to dairy foods, and decided that the time had come to get to the bottom of it. And why not help cure the rest of humankind at the same time?

A positive, encouraging letter from the head of the Australian College of Allergy found Jerry in Sydney and then Melbourne, where he sat in on allergy clinics. He then returned, emboldened, to Auckland, where he sold his Otahuhu practice and leased rooms in the Dingwall Building on Queen Street. He farewelled a life of haemorrhoids, boils and common colds and became an allergist. On his first day no one turned up, so he took part-time work as the Union Steam Ship Company doctor just down the road.

A year later, Jerry's allergy focus found him realising that the cool scientific frontier of curing sneezing from eating eggs and headaches from drinking milk was in the United States of America. He wrote to various allergists there, and they all welcomed him to their clinics and homes. Those were the days. No immigrant paranoia then. With a seriously groovy education gleaned at clinics in cities like Mobile, Alabama, and San Francisco, Jerry returned to New Zealand and kicked his allergy clinic into serious gear. By the early '70s, he was getting busy. The only downside—was it a downside?—was the doctors around the place who thought that this new allergy science was nonsense. But in the manner of the Chunn, he thought 'Screw you' and charged on, even when he went on national television and was interviewed by some lass who asked him, 'So, Dr Chunn, there has been a fairly negative reaction from the medical fraternity to what you're doing. Would you say perhaps that you are a quack?'

In his quiet way, Jerry simply shook his head. Nothing was going to stop him. In a short while, all the doubters slipped away and Jerry rested his case.

While Jerry was building his allergy fortress, Von was building her own cool business: the Auckland Medical Bureau. This had come about when Jerry had been bed-ridden in the late '60s with hepatitis and had to find a locum to run his Otahuhu surgery while he lay sweating and hallucinating in bed. Von was assigned to the task. She bought the *Trade & Exchange*, but—lo and behold!—there was no 'Doctors Available for Locum Tenens Work' section. Having the requisite entrepreneurial spirit and the Williams get-up-and-go, she started the Auckland Medical Bureau, where she connected doctors looking for locum work and doctors looking for locums. By the mid '70s she had an office and two staff and doctors flying in and out like hummingbirds.

Both businesses needed a home, and Jerry wanted to set up his own clinic close to the city. He and Von decided on Parnell, and they went off looking for property. They came across a trio of town-houses on Parnell Road, and one was for rent. Jerry thought, 'We'll all squash in there while I look for more appropriate professional premises.' And that they did. The lease at 469 Parnell Road was signed and plans were made to move house.

With my leg still in plaster and Scholarship exams looming, my darling parents thought I needn't take part in the family shift. So one Free Sunday, I was picked up by Von and driven to the house in Otahuhu for the last time. (Where was Geoffrey? Academia had failed to spin his wheels and he had left Sacred Heart some months before, so he was already back at home.)

You never know what leaving somewhere is going to be like until you do it. You can imagine. But you may be wrong.

I walked into our bedroom where the future had been forged. Everything was the same as it always had been. The luminous crucifixion still above my bed. (I wasn't farewelling my bed; both mine and Geoffrey's beds were going to Parnell Road, where we would still be sharing a room.) I went out to The Pavilion with its harmonium, bass guitar, record player, acoustic guitar and snare drum and cymbal. A pile of singles still lay at the ready: 'Dead End Street', 'Ruby Tuesday', 'I Feel Good'. The new albums: *Blood, Sweat and Tears*, *Chicago Transit Authority*, *The United States of America*, *The White Album*, *John Barleycorn Must Die*.

What would happen to The Pavilion? Would it return to being a glasshouse? Would it be demolished? Who was buying this glorious house on its quarter-acre section with its towering phoenix palms? (On Sundays they were towering phoenix psalms; high-needled branches that watched us drive off to 8 a.m. Mass just in time to miss the Sunday morning children's request session on 1ZB.) We will never forget The Pavilion. It held all those notes and beats and cosmic rushes of anticipation as each new record arrived. As each original song got aired. The Pavilion. As I walked away from it and back into the house, I turned for one last look.

I had talked to the head brother, Stubbs, about staying home for dinner instead of being obliged to return by 6 p.m. He gave his permission. Perhaps he had once been in a cool home with rock'n'roll permeating the air, with a family that was larger than its parts, and had eaten a last supper there before going off to the celibate life of a brother. I suspect so.

Von's last Otahuhu meal was the magical concoction of sausages, mashed potato and peas with home-made gravy.

For once we talked around the table. As had been the case for the past eighteen years, there was no alcohol. We all decided that this house had served us well. The family had grown and flourished, and many paths of life lay ahead. For all of us.

Jerry and I descended the stairs and hopped into his car (now an Austin Maxi). And he drove me back to school.

By the end of the year, we were so full up of Simon & Garfunkel's *Bridge Over Troubled Water* album that we decided to tackle 'So Long, Frank Lloyd Wright' for the Walter Kirby. It also gave me the chance to play the new flute I'd bought. Those who know the song well will be aware that it is Paul Simon's farewell to Art Garfunkel (have a listen: at 2' 57" producer Roy Halee shouts out in the background 'So long, Artie'); and so too with us—this was our farewell to the brick buildings, quadrangles, locker rooms, common rooms, dining rooms and rugby fields that had locked in our bodies while we freed our minds. From the empty heads we had brought in to the packed, kaleidoscopic banks of information, memories, hopes, fears and ambition that we took away with us five years later, much had been achieved. Our constitutions were ready for the wild years ahead.

So with a flourish of concentration, superb vocals, competent guitar playing and passable flute, we took the first prize (we were first equal, actually) and the applause was rather good.

Von and Jerry were both there. I saw them watching, listening. They were always there. The scout concert in 1963. The Walter Kirby concerts when I played Mussorgsky and

Mozart (can you believe it?). And then the two Walter Kirbys with Tim and Geoffrey et al. And then this final foray.

As the audience drifted away, they both came up to me.

'You're getting better every year,' said Jerry.

'Well, we're just moving with the times,' I said.

'That you are,' said Von. And then they moved outside to their car and drove away to the new Chunn dwelling on Parnell Road. It would be the last time they ever came to Sacred Heart College.

In early December I sat my final Scholarship paper: Additional Mathematics. My class had sat ten Scholarship papers, totalling 30 hours. We were deeply bludgeoned. I returned (trudged) to the hostel and went to my room. Everything was ready for the Free Man Walking. I picked up my suitcase and tossed all the cloth paraphernalia of a past life into it. I went to the window and looked out at the vast green fields. The cricket pitches were there, waiting for next year's opening bowlers to start the run-up for the first ball of the first over. For the first time in five years, I wouldn't be one of them. I was going to miss cricket.

And then I went back out into the corridor and started down the exit path. I was on the carpet of freedom. I reached the door at the end that led to the stairs to the outside. I went through the doorway and never looked back.

Chapter Five
Tertiary Adventures

A few weeks before taking that last soft-shoe shuffle down the hostel corridor and out into the world, Brother Loyola called me into his room. He was hostel master or some such nomenclature, and his room was two doors away from mine. It didn't smell of anything in particular. I had been led to believe the brothers' quarters smelled of tuppenny-ha'penny whisky. We called Brother Loyola 'Chops', as he had large cheeks and as well—and unrelated—he was head of the Auckland Mathematical Society.

He looked up at me from his desk chair. A very plain chair. A few piles of neatly arranged notes were on his desk. A very plain desk; grey brushed metal. His black dress was brushed cotton. He had just brushed his hair. It was neat. There were mathematical symbols, Greek letters and that lone 'imaginary number'—i—scattered on the papers. This i was the square root of minus one and its existence was deeply mysterious and evocative. It is a lonely letter. (More on that later.)

'What are you taking at university, Chunn?'

I only half-listened to him. He had been the last brother to cane me. Two years earlier, I had been to a Friday night surf movie in Newmarket and snuck back into the fifth-form dormitory under shadow of night. In this vast room, all around me, schoolboy dreams and nightmares riddled the addled minds of those poor tossers who had probably had silvery-sheeny corned beef and yellow-eyed mashed spuds for dinner. Under their candlewick covers they gently shifted or stirred. I slipped beneath my own covers. A short while later a bright torch shone in my face.

'Come downstairs,' said Chops.

Being caned in the locker rooms has a dramatic resonance. First, it fucking hurts! Second, it's very loud, as the echo of each blow reverberates around the walls, along the tiled ceiling, up the stairs and into the dormitory. That night it might have even swept down the 'corridor of no return', where the brothers had their bedrooms. Some would have been asleep and been awoken by the slashing slap sound. Others might have smirked at another teenager, all too big for his boots and wallowing in arrogance and self-importance (surely!), being brought down. A few might have been drinking a Scotch on ice.

I suspect that Chops, being distraught and morbid owing to the tawdry life he led as a celibate, rotund male in a black dress, wished he was swift and lithe and could sneak off to surf movies too. By the time he left the brotherhood and got married—that's when we heard his real name was Frank Huckle—it was too late to step forward and take up surfing.

'What are you taking at university, Chunn?'

'I don't know,' I said.

'Ah. Well, people who don't know usually do engineering.'

There it was. An answer to the simple question of a future well planned.

'I'm going to do engineering then, brother.'

'Right you are.'

In mid February 1971, I went to enrol at the University of Auckland Engineering School. I had a plan. Enrol in the Intermediate course, which in essence was like doing school physics and maths all over again. It would be a doddle. And with a mixture of science students and arts students taking science (some do that, apparently!), I could meet and mingle with the horde.

I could see that horde. The golden horde. The population there on that enrolment day was a vast contrast to my first day at boarding school. Instead of lines of navy-clad, grim, short-haired, homesick adolescents, this crowd looked like a psychedelic cloud had blown in from the northern hemisphere and rained a kaleidoscopic array of multicoloured individuals all ready for whatever might come their way. I wanted to bury myself in the middle of them. I wanted life to flash into an *Easy Rider* playground. I would take Engineering Intermediate. The perfect introduction to this prescient stage of humanity, and I was to be a player.

I walked over to the man at the enrolment desk. The card in front of him said 'Professor Harris'.

'Good morning,' he said. 'I see you want to take Engineering Intermediate.'

'Yes, I do.'

'Well I have your Scholarship marks here and I can't see why you would want to do Intermediate, so I've enrolled you in First Professional and the Engineering Science stream, seeing as you have a penchant for mathematics.'

A *penchant*. Me? *First Professional?* Am I being paid? Will

I be a professor one day?

He sat there looking at me, presumably waiting for me to thank him profusely for saving me from easy science papers and large crowds of coolsters and lovely young women. I looked back at him. He had quite a lot of hair fluffed in his ears. I wondered if he had a wife. Perhaps she had never noticed his hairy ears. They weren't flattering. He should have snipped them; it would have made him look more intellectual. He could have trimmed his eyebrows, too.

And then there was his jacket: quite professorial, in keeping with his status. Light-brown, checked, single-breasted, reminiscent of what G.K. Chesterton probably wore when he sat down to write a Father Brown mystery. I bet Professor Harris knew all about i, the imaginary number. The square root of minus one. I had not one idea what was going to happen.

Geoffrey and I were rooming together at home. We had the piano in there, in our room. And a record player. Geoffrey maintained his role as the record purchaser. *Electric Ladyland* by Jimi Hendrix, that was there. Magna Carta's *Songs from Wasties Orchard* and a Chicken Shack LP. We'd stopped buying singles; that was the previous decade. It seemed a long time ago. And The Beatles had broken up. It felt logical to me that they would. Bordering on inevitable really, and besides they'd recorded so many tracks between '63 and '70 that we would be surrounded by Beatles songs for the rest of our lives. And we were all aware—yes, we were—that they didn't seem to get on with each other. That was Yoko Ono's fault, we reckoned.

As well as playing records, the piano and my guitar, I would buy the English music magazine *Melody Maker*, which ensured that the end of The Beatles was well documented. But that magazine had a far more enthralling aspect: the classified ads for guitars and equipment on the back pages. I would imagine buying a Gibson EB-3 short-scale bass or a Fender Mustang. One day.

Geoffrey and I were still trying to work out how to be a band and hit the road. He was working at a television production company in Greenlane, which had a large studio. We could rehearse in it in the weekends. Somehow.

Tim Finn was living in town over at O'Rorke Hall and had enrolled in political studies. He came around one day and we talked about finding some other musicians and, well, forming a band. The concept didn't seem too onerous. You just do it. We kept thinking about it. And with the thinking went the passage of time.

And so on: while learning about i, the imaginary number, I dropped into O'Rorke Hall. The O'Rorke hostel inmates had swerved into Auckland by train, motorbike, horse and bus. Every few minutes a transportation device would toss them out onto the footpath on Mount Street, and they would look up the wooden stairs and wonder if their plans for the year were foolish. There was no fresh paint to soothe their eyes, no fresh-faced walls of wood and enduring grain. The wallpaper slipped away and the lightbulbs hung like dead ideas that the previous year's tenants had failed to bring to fruition, and they had simply died (the ideas) over the summer holidays.

It was in this shambolic, egregious accommodation facility that Tim merged with others and they rose to the surface. One was standing on the roof of the hostel playing a flute. A curly-haired, thin lad with a warm-hearted grin and an infectious laugh. Rob Gillies was enrolled at the Elam School of Fine Arts, and was with (as in *with*) another O'Rorke inmate, Geraldene. (Most were quickly starting to be *with* somebody.) She was studying for a degree that had a geological focus, as far as I can recall. A Bachelor of Soil and Dirt? Such was the new playing field. Young men and women were going out by staying in. I was with Paula, who was seeing out a final year at Baradene College in Auckland. Next year, she would be enrolling in law.

More and more faces seeped into the social whirl. One in particular was Phil Judd, who was up from Napier Boys' High and enrolled at Elam too. Juddsy, as we called him, stood outside the circles and hubbub. His clothes were different. His hair didn't tumble and flay like everyone else's in their quick-to-the-mark banishment of anything that resembled a school haircut. His swept up and down, if you get my drift. It was Byronesque, I'm sure. He carried himself with surety, and his eyes fixed on you but you didn't know what he was thinking. But you knew he was thinking *something*—at some speed.

The fewer the people in the room, the more animated Juddsy became. He was at his most communicative when it was just you and him. He wasn't a team player, not that there was much team activity at play in O'Rorke. And he had a jack-of-all-trades aura about him, a feeling that anything might be possible. Give him a kazoo and he might play you 'Flight of the Bumblebee'. Down in Napier, he had reacted to his older brothers' love of The Beatles by listening to the Vienna Boys' Choir. It wasn't until he heard Led Zeppelin's 'Whole Lotta Love' that he felt he had heard anything sensational. He had arrived at O'Rorke Hall with an acoustic guitar and would jam with Rob and another Napier friend, John Hadwin, on stuff like the Bee Gees' 'Lonely Days'. Juddsy and Rob were in Room 129.

Another man on the scene was Noel Crombie, who buzzed into Auckland on a motorbike he'd ridden up from Wellington. He had been at Mana College with the artist Robin White, realising the artistic talents that had also steered him to Elam. He quickly forged relationships with Juddsy and Rob Gillies, and with a hammer, nails and planks of wood he built himself a bunk in Room 129. Noel's practical talents evolved in time to focus on cloth.

It was also at this time that dope, hoochie coo, reefers and joints, et cetera turned up. A lean, unhealthy, straggled and straggling man—he was about three years older than us—arrived with blocks of hash. He was nervy, like something awry was going to happen. I don't know who found him or how he found us. I thought back to the opening scene of *Easy Rider*, sitting there in the Odeon Cinema with Brother Richard, only two years before. I guess this person with the hash was a dealer not a pusher. The hash was wrapped in tinfoil and looked odd. Like a moist green marzipan lolly. We all bought one and I took mine home and hid it in my bottom drawer, as I didn't want to be seen with it in public and get twenty years in jail.

No one had really explained what you did with hash, so I reenacted what I'd seen in some movie the name of which escapes me now. Maybe it was *The Man with the Golden Arm*. I put a small crumbled bit on a piece of tinfoil and lit a match under it. As it heated up, a vapour (I wouldn't have called it smoke) drifted into the air, so I sniffed and it went up my nose. It had a sweet, engaging odour. The sort of smell that, if the brothers at Sacred Heart had been a cult of freaky moonagers, their Sunday evening benediction incense would have smelled just like it. I'm sure Von and Jerry were lying in their bed in the next room wondering what that delightfully exotic smell was. But of course how was I to know they weren't already eating hash cookies for dessert and grinning wildly, stoned out of their minds?

Anyways—I would sniff the ascendant vapour and then lie on my bed waiting for whatever record was playing to turn into cerebral insight, cosmic leanings and soft murmurings from outer space, slipping down to earth on the breath of the future. In the end nothing happened to me. I drifted off to sleep, thinking, 'How can *anything* be the square root of minus one?' And in the morning, after another moment of frowning at Jerry eating soggy Weet-Bix, and a rueful squizz from Von, I would walk out onto Parnell Road and drift down Parnell Rise, up Constitution Hill and mosey on through to the Engineering School.

The first year at that tertiary establishment of engineering prowess found all the streams—Civil, Mechanical, Electrical, Chemical and Engineering Science—attending the same stage-one lectures. On day one back in March 1971, I walked in to be confronted by 300 students all looking in my direction. I was standing under the blackboard. I perused the mob. All walks of life, I guess. Mind you—a lot of Swanndris. Their hair was growing, and moustaches and beards were on the move. There was only one true disappointment. Of the 300, two were female.

So we sat back and learned about many, many things that were interesting, abstract, convoluted, unyielding and freaky.

This extended world of the mathematics I had sat at Sacred Heart College had a purpose, I guess. But I couldn't see how solving the Cauchy-Riemann Theorem would get me into a famous band.

I knew that Von and Jerry believed in university degrees as a road to walk down, so that you can start something and finish—a purpose with an ethical ambition—and I shared that belief. Something that challenges you, so that instead of closing the book you turn the page. A world of the new that underpins a whole intricate and vibrant Venn diagram of life.

I worked hard at it. I almost always passed my papers. I never missed lectures. And I did it all for my ma and pa. But I still had thoughts of being in that rock band, and it was time to actually do something about it.

One night in a chance gathering, Tim, Juddsy, Robert and I decided to go to a music room in the hostel. Tim sang, I played bass, Rob blew a sax and Juddsy played drums. It was shambolic. But it was four people playing together and that's where seeds are sown. We didn't say much. But it seemed to me that we would be doing this again. And more so if you gave it a plan. If songs came from somewhere, something could happen. Someone could write songs. But how do you do that? It was also clear that Juddsy wasn't much good on the drums. But there was fire in his eyes and he was in. And we slopped away with heads tumbling thoughts aplenty, forsooth. I thought, 'Anyway, Geoffrey can play the drums.'

Not much later, as our end-of-year exams loomed, I was off to Western Springs Stadium with my brother Derek and his classmate, Neil Finn. Both had followed the paths of their older brothers and gone to Sacred Heart College, except that Neil was buried in there as he was boarding, while Derek was a day-boy. And Western Springs Stadium? It was a concert by Elton John.

In the naïve, early days of outdoor shows the promoters were polite. Hundreds of plastic chairs were nestled up to the front of the stage. And we shuffled into three of them and sat down.

The stage was huge and my eager eyes took in the large speaker stacks, the tent out front where the sound and lighting consoles were stationed, and the amplifiers and drum kit on the stage. This was the infrastructure of serious rock'n'roll. This was the pre-show tension, the murmuring anticipation, the 'When is it going to begin?' Expectation was the going word, and excitement the sparkle in everyone's eyes. What was going to happen? And why didn't we know? Because Auckland had never had a concert like this before in its tame, meagre history. This was going to be awesome. And?

Out came Elton and his two band members, Nigel Olsen and Dee Murray. Murray had a Fender Precision bass. It had flatwound strings; I could tell by the sound. I recall it being turquoise. His haircut was a bit boofy. As if they all had a stylist backstage and were coiffed and quiffed before assailing the heights. I was (we were) watching. And then a huge voice boomed out:

'Ladies and gentlemen. Would you please welcome to the stage the Madman from Across the Water—Elton John.'

Well, they started playing and it was OK. OK? Yes, well, there didn't seem to be a lot of energy. Power. Thrust.

Thunder and lightning. Songs came and went. We sat in our plastic chairs. And then Elton John stood up and kicked his chair away. Like, he *kicked* it!

Oh my God! What magical key did he turn? What powderkeg had been waiting, its fuse patient and dry? And oh my God—did we, the audience, the 20,000 patient believers, none of us knowing what totally unified combustion we were capable of, go crazy? We all leaped to our feet in unison and climbed onto our plastic chairs and screamed, called, shouted as if a sweeping wind of high-speed motion had flown in from a distant planet.

I looked over at Derek and Neil. Eyes riveted to the image on the stage, enthralled by what they were hearing. It was mesmerising. Yes, I'd seen *A Hard Day's Night* at the age of twelve and thought 'There go I', but that was a movie. That was a concoction, beautiful as it was. This was real and right in front of me. There was nothing impossible about it. It would be done. It could be done.

The three of us fell breathlessly out of the gates and shimmied off home. Neil stayed the night at 469 Parnell Road. I heard him playing the piano in the morning. I heard Derek talking to Von and Jerry about the concert. The three of us had just experienced Revelation 101. We now shared in the knowledge of what this new world of big rock shows was all about.

I had another lesson in revelation shortly after. At the chemist in Newmarket there was a very attractive lass behind the counter. I would see her there every time I walked past. Sometimes I would do a U-turn and have another look. Now, if I'd been a normal, socially aware and confident lad—in other words not a bludgeoned-into-silence fool from a boarding school—then I would have sauntered in and, well . . . made a proposition.

After the twenty-third journey past the chemist I finally went in, shaking with nerves. I went up to the counter. She was special. Up close. I could see her hands, her palms, on my face and her soft lips on mine. Her body edging closer. Steadily. All in the back row of the movies on a Saturday night with me.

I needed a reason to be in there. I had a brilliant idea. I was going to buy some pholcodine linctus.

'Hello. I'm Mike. I was wondering if you'd like to go to a movie with me on Saturday?'

'No,' she said. And I walked out.

Never again did I try that.

A nd then all of a sudden 1971 ended. Exams were over. A group of us slipped into the Globe Hotel to toast the end of our first university *annus adventurous*. The Globe (in the same street as O'Rorke) was owned by Paula's father. I'm not sure if that meant drinks were free. Maybe. Then we crossed the road, into O'Rorke Hall and straight into Tim's room.

I'm not sure where they came from, but someone held out their hand and on it rested four purple hearts—tabs of LSD.

Chapter Six
Tripping on Imaginary Numbers

O ne purple heart on each tongue, we swallowed and sat there. The hostel room was particularly nondescript. O'Rorke never had much embellishment in its décor. You would wander down the corridor and look into rooms that may as well have had exactly the same paraphernalia in them. Dirty socks, t-shirts draped over wooden chairs up against thin desks. A basin like something out of a prison movie. Alcatraz? No computers, televisions or any other screens to point your eyes at. After all, this was 1971.

The conversation in the room was light and frothy. What did you talk about as you waited for whatever was going to arrive? And then the door opened. In shot the familiar hash dealer, his eyes wide and moving in all directions. He sat down on the single bed and stared at each one of us. STARED. I was looking at the dealer's hands.

'What's happened, Wayne?'

Wayne put one hand on the other, staring at me. Then he held them out. They were—well, what were they?—torn.

Blood smeared across one of them. The other bruised and shivering slightly. Slightly?

'I was doing a pickup. The bastards were ripping me off. We had a fight.'

'How'd you get away?' I asked.

'I got away,' he said. His gaze took us all in, one by one. Both hands gripping each other now. What was he thinking? Was he safe? Was the enemy about to charge through the door?

'You'll be OK here,' I said. And the dealer softened and remained still, upright on the single bed.

A crackling sound came through the window. Soft, sorted, distorted explosions. Ones that don't cause damage. Explosions from the dusty remains of the recent Guy Fawkes Night. Tossed from the roof of the hostel by invaders of the peaceful realm. Each gunpowder missile floated downwards, shifting sweetly into terminal velocity until the fuse bit the gunpowder and flashes lit the small space outside the window. We looked at them. They looked at us. One of them was the square root of minus one.

'Did you know that the square root of minus one is i?' I asked them all.

'Yes,' said one of them. He was a stranger, but his voice was all-knowing. He looked like someone who had an intellectual patience, waiting for all facts and bizarre knowledge to seep through his face and into his skull. The square root of minus one. I stared at him. He had a guitar leaning against his chair. He picked it up; I could tell he wanted to play it. And I knew that because it was me.

We all stood up as if a planetary magnet had pulled us to our feet, and we walked out through the door of the room and onto the stairs that led down to Mount Street. No one said anything. I put the guitar under my arm and plucked a note with the pick I had in my pocket. The note spun out from the guitar and shot off towards the northern hemisphere. We all stood there waiting. The note skimmed over the Arctic Circle and traversed Europe and Africa until it flew under the Harbour Bridge and back, safely, into its home. The hollow body of the wooden grain of this musical fountain. And then we descended the stairs and left our real world for an unreal Symonds Street.

We emerged from the pale fluorescents of O'Rorke into the gently bright dusk. We were meerkats, all agog and gregarious, coming from the House of Chatter and Myths, Blythe Ghosts and Spurious Charm. The streetlights flickered in their chocolate, orange and turquoise hues. The buildings along each side of this wide road, ever widening, were like security guards keeping the grey and shadowed crowds of people who were poised to take on this day—this Tuesday morning about to happen a few hours away—all at bay, beyond the pale, beyond our circle of joyous minds. Those buildings in their leaning parade, edging to collapse in their dying purpose, had been there forever; sentries at the sturdy, monolithic wall beyond which was our keen future with its shock of the new.

We walked slowly down Symonds Street as we weren't going anywhere. We walked beside derelict humans with shabby faces who had edged through the cracks in the strange gates in the walls of the buildings. Humans who looked at us as if we might engage their searching, pathetic eyes and draw them into our fold. But we couldn't, as we were fixed to the sidelines of the footpath. The summer flowers were blooming and each of us had our favourite biological specimen. I kept looking for gorse bushes but they didn't materialise. One of us wanted a fairy-light gully weed, but that never turned up. And nothing mattered. So we sat on the brick border of a student hostel and watched the slow-motion mobs in their post-exam meanderings and their safari searches across deserts of facts and figures, all of them searching for the square root of minus one. And the hours slid along the arc of time, carrying us with them. Each was a guardian angel mothering us in their biblical protection. It didn't seem right to tell everyone that angels didn't exist. It didn't seem right to challenge anything that could be, one day would be, something real . . . As we shuffled towards dawn, Father Time wrapped us in his loin cloth and by 10 a.m. the next morning we were all asleep. Somewhere.

As 1972 broke and the usual, almost childlike parapher-nalia of beaches and beer, sunburn and growing hair had set up the vague, foggy plans for the coming year, we all returned to Auckland uni. I felt that 1971, in its introduction to higher learning, drugs, new faces and an urge to expand our social circle, had set us up for a new year with new adventures, where things might actually happen. I wanted to be in a band! I wanted to make records! But matters were going in different directions.

Geoffrey, in '71, had mastered the acoustic guitar and ended up playing in the three-piece band Rosewood, with Graeme Gash and Kevin Wildman. My master plan from a few years before, where Geoffrey and I were a hot rhythm section, a singular tumbling match of bass and drums—

well, that would have to wait. So without him, in mid '71, I answered an advertisement in the *Herald* from the 'Acts, Bands and Halls' classifieds. 'Bass player wanted for three-piece covers band.' Why not? If I joined a band I wouldn't have to work out how to form one. I rang.

'Wally speaking.'

Holy shit. I knew that voice.

And so it came to be that I joined a three-piece covers band with Sacred Heart College lads I had been at school with: Wally Wilkinson and Alan Maher. Their band was called Moses.

I bought a cheap bass and a cheap amplifier and I was *in a band*! We played church halls, community centres and the odd school dance. We were enthusiastic and not much else, but the understanding, the rhythm of life in a band, came to reality. And I got it.

There is something special about being in a band. It brings forces to play that you can't anticipate. I watched Wally and Alan at rehearsal. Their individual roles; all of ours so different and yet so united. There you are: three lads with a guitar, a bass and a drum kit and an audience out front—how many? Who cares? Even if there's only one person, as there was at the Mangere Community Centre one dank, lonely Saturday night. It doesn't matter—you have to obey the rules. You start a song. And you're off. If you stop after a few bars and announce to the audience that you made a mistake and would like to start again, then you may as well put your bass in a rubbish bin and go home. When you start a song, you're underway on some luminous trail across and through the sweat and space that fills that hall! You keep going no matter what. You don't talk to each other. You don't look at each other. You don't look at the floor or your guitar neck. You make eye contact with the crowd.

Between songs you don't come out with a mechanical 'Thank you' every time. You talk to them. You're a weapon and you have the means to thrill. Listening to songs is engaging with an essential truth. A world of proclamation and faith; or nightmares once hidden and now revealed. Or love. No melodrama there. The mundane day-to-day of life is translated for the audience into fragile decisions, a recoil, a cavernous descent or a towering uplift. Whatever you need to say when you write a song, it can be said. And we, the boys in Moses, we carried those concoctions of words and music out to the public arena and painted the room. It was joyful.

Moses gave this list of directives a good shot but really, we were particularly average. But I understood what it was all about. And I knew that on a stage with a bass strap around my shoulders was where I wanted to be. The turning, swerving bodies in the audience; their faces, eyes, arms . . . all held high with proffered responses to what we did. We, the band. Moses. And on we went. The crowds never grew in size.

But we were a covers band; we weren't songwriters. We did try. It was profoundly difficult. I think we managed two or three, which in hindsight wallowed in the audience's pool of neglect. Such is life.

In parallel with this rock'n'roll adventure I went to lectures at the Engineering School. Nothing could be more different. Wrangling sparkling lines of numbers, Greek letters and i continued to map out my morning waking hours. (Very few lectures were in the afternoon, which suited me right down to the ground. I'm a morning person. Show me a café that opens at 5 a.m., I'll be in there drinking coffee.) In this, my second year at uni, I found the labyrinthine mathematics, algorithms, computational techniques, et cetera devoid of relevance. I just couldn't see how a pile of calculations could build a skyscraper or dredge a harbour. So I zeroed in on the maths and saw it as a jigsaw-puzzle world. A playground of abstract shenanigans.

At least I wasn't alone. In my Engineering Science sector of this worldly-wise Engineering School, there were nine of us, as I recall. From all places, shuffling out of suburban streets, from nondescript towns and cities. But we were tight, although I don't think any of us ended up working together after uni. Did one of them build a skyscraper? A submarine? Did Paddy O'Brien over there invent the MP3?

Perhaps the most legitimate and interesting outcome of this fabulous, nutty class came many years later when John de Pont, who sat across from me, found out—at the same time as me—that his son was going to marry my daughter Georgia. His son, Antony, is also an Engineering Science graduate and knows all about *i*. Aside from that looky-look into the future, Engineering School was a cool, kaleidoscopic insight into a wacko world and one that gave a balance to the high volume and urgency of the Moses pursuit.

As these two rails of ambitious meandering rolled on, I kept in touch with Juddsy. He was flatting now, in Mission Bay, and keeping his imagination fiery and spectacular. The arrival of LSD had led to a series of occasional trips, and now and then I would be in there. The experience continued to provide adventures that were out on the horizon. There was no tension, danger, freakshows. Just long, detailed adventures where interpretation took on wildly evocative possibilities. In the comic I was reading, I needed to know: was Ivanhoe really wearing lipstick? It took me about two or three hours of Sherlock Holmesian analysis to come to the conclusion that he was.

Juddsy's focus on all things musical was no secret. Listening, listening, listening. Juddsy lying on his back under a concave sky while listening to Led Zeppelin. What was he planning? What would he bend, turn, straighten, twist, contort or mould to his plans and designs? Those were no ordinary observations surrounding his head.

Running alongside the LSD ethos that was becoming more and more the wheel of life, there was the new breed of pot—Thai Sticks. They were easily identifiable: tinfoil wrapped around a grotty portion of dope rolled around a thin bamboo stick. Got that? I first came across them on a bright summer afternoon on Arney Road in Remuera. Beside a swimming pool. Salubrious. Upper middle class. A group of eight—seven lads, one lass. Joints were rolled and smoked.

In a matter of seconds I found myself walking round and round the pool. A mantle of silence—well, soft voices in occasional query, unsure in their enunciation. And me? All akimbo. Whoever owned those voices let them worm out into the sunlight with nothing eventual to say. Across the pool two lads were sitting in safari chairs looking at me. I hated them. Their eyes like deep gun barrels aimed at me. Who were these people? Why had we done this? I went inside, into the kitchen and opened the fridge. I shut the fridge. I looked out of the window. I opened the window. I shut the window. Expensive cars drenched in shining silver and navy paint rolled up and over the hill road. I needed to get in one of them. Ask them nicely in my soft musical voice to take me home. But I wasn't moving. I kept watching the cars go by. Once I put my thumb out of the window, my upright thumb, my hitching-a-ride-home thumb, but I was frightened. If a car stopped and they looked up at me, what would I do? And then some guy walked into the kitchen.

'Hey, Mike, I'm heading home. You want a lift?'

Four, maybe five minutes after sliding through this suburb of bright trees and nasty thorns, in a speeding extrication from our self-induced entrapment, I put my key in the front door of 469 Parnell Road. My parents weren't home, but I felt their presence. Their looming arrival. I was safe.

I went upstairs to my bedroom and sat in the chair that held my bass guitar safe from falling to the floor and gazed out at the trees of the Auckland Domain. They loved me.

In August 1972 the Students' Arts Festival loomed, and Tim and I thought we should perform. He and Juddsy had been increasing their shared musical interests, although to say they had a 'plan' would be incorrect. Tim had patches of original songs and was playing piano. Juddsy was keen on playing drums. And Rob Gillies was at the ready with his trumpet. I put my hand up for bass.

I was doing double duty, playing with Moses as well. Mind you, I have to admit that the whole Moses thing was starting to fade. Playing Joe Cocker and Led Zep songs to a crowd of ten in the Pakuranga RSA hall was starting to pall.

There was one night when it all seemed too dangerous. Wally had booked a community hall in Glen Innes and we dutifully turned up. The week before we had stapled small posters on lamp posts advertising this event. This rock'n'roll night, Wally also hired a security guy with an Alsatian.

About fifteen punters turned up, and then a number of Head Hunters gang members. Everyone took off, including the security guard. I had the door-take money, which was about $45, and I stuffed it into a teapot just as an HH wearing a Nazi helmet walked into the room. It was the tea-room, as you can imagine.

He looked at me.

Did I look too pathetic to bother with? Had he heard us play 'Locomotive Breath' and been impressed? Did he long to be a hot bass player? I'm sure that was it. He just walked away.

They paused outside to throw beer bottles through the hall windows and were gone. The money was safe! Holy shit. And as I cruised the dark, dark Saturday night streets home I started thinking that maybe Moses wasn't going to get me to a full house at the Auckland Town Hall. What would?

Back to the 1972 Students' Arts Festival. I had already booked in Moses for a thrashy set, and Graham Nesbitt, the festival coordinator, was happy to include Tim and Juddsy's combo, which was going by the name Mellodrone. They pieced together a twenty-minute epic: a montage of pieces written individually and on the night; the theatrical stance was supreme. Tim sat at the piano in his long greatcoat, Juddsy was on drums with blue checks painted on his face, and Rob stood to attention, his trumpet at the ready. I cradled my bass and, well, I realised I looked like an engineering student who had wandered onto the stage. In some ways that was true. The stage was littered with a gruesome assembly to boot: Noel Crombie stood expressionless the entire performance while his partner, Raewyn Turner, sat in a chair knitting; another friend, Roger Brookfield, wandered around, his face painted blue (Blue-Boy); and other friends Paul Pattie and Jenny Harland completed the line-up of non-performing performers. I think Jenny wore gumboots.

Tim shut his eyes, clothed his stage fright in steely reserve (for twenty minutes) and sang loud and clear. I sensed the crowd watching him. Crowds watch singers—that's how it is. But this was new to him, and I felt he wasn't running the Mellodrone flag up high enough and marching out into the future with a hi ho and a silver lining. This band, this ensemble, had a point of difference visually. Musically we knew what was meant to happen but we couldn't bring it to the surface.

Tim sat on his piano stool and dragged out his post-Beatles twists and turns, but failed to crash everyone else's party out there on the Peter Pan Cabaret dancefloor. It seemed to me that Tim needed to charge on through this minuscule moment in time to get to the greater thing, the higher platform that was out there. What was it? Where was it? None of us knew. But I was the eternal optimist, and I knew that those on that stage at this arts festival were undergraduates of musical greatness. Young life-blood proponents of adventure who had it in them to rise to great heights. I stared at them. 'They're all freaky masters of change coming in from the cold. They aren't like the Cook Street Market mob or the campus lunchtime campaigners. They are poised to take melodies and words, and with that union—songs—stop everyone in their tracks.' I knew I had to keep holding on to their coat-tails. I couldn't let go.

It was a night to remember.

In the post-Mellodrone rush, Juddsy was motivated, and would spend hours at the piano concocting chord sequences and accompanying lyrics, with Tim fleshing out melodies and contributing the odd line at their place in Mission Bay. In late October, Tim rang me and told me that he and Juddsy were working on some songs and were going to form a band. He'd thought of a name, which he'd culled from a page of scribbles in a book—it was to be 'Split Ends'. He then jokingly said that their first performance would be at the Great Ngaruawahia Music Festival, scheduled for the third week of the new year 1973 and a big deal at the time. We both laughed. A three-day festival with Tim and Juddsy? Right on.

He rang again three weeks later. He and Juddsy had met a brilliant violinist by the name of Miles Golding, and their material was really coming together. Juddsy and Tim had written two songs in one night: 'Split Ends' and another called 'For You'. But they needed a place to practise.

'Can we come and rehearse in your bedroom? You've got your old piano there, yes?'

'Sure. And yes.'

So they came round. By now they'd written three songs. The third was called 'Wise Men'.

Miles looked like a boy, with a swathe of curls all over his head. There was something innocent about him. Had he never crashed a car? He didn't direct proceedings or even say much. I guess that's what violinists in orchestras do: wait for the conductor to bring his (her?) baton down on them.

And then he put his string to his bow and we all stood still. We stared at him when he played.

Tim sat at the piano, Juddsy set up his drum kit and they proceeded to bash away. As an ensemble it was a mess. I didn't say anything. Geoffrey and his bandmate Graeme Gash were there, watching curiously. (Their group Rosewood was still in action playing at folk clubs, blues nights, et cetera.)

Then Juddsy hopped off the drums and picked up an acoustic guitar; Tim picked up a tambourine. Tim explained that their intention was to break up their rock set with an acoustic bracket, and they had written the three songs I've mentioned for that purpose. Juddsy and Tim proceeded to sing them. Juddsy strummed out these weird-shaped chords and the two of them sang in a strong, spirited fashion. The songs were unlike anything I'd heard before in a live setting, and we all listened intently. How the hell did Juddsy learn the guitar so quickly? And, more to the point, how had he forged all those strange chords?

At the end there was silence in the room.

I was stunned, floundering in this discovery. I walked over to Tim while trying to look non-committal.

'Tim,' I said, 'if you're looking for a bass player, I'd be keen to play.'

He looked at me. 'Well, actually . . . that's why we're here.'

Chapter Seven
The Arrival

Tim, Juddsy and Miles slipped away. They'd got the response they were hoping for. What was I thinking? It was like waking up on a strange planet where a new breed of imagination was at hand and you could reach out and hold it. I fell into a world of intense creativity that said, 'You can come in and be part of this. Play bass. Write your own lines. Don't play cover songs any more. Get out of bed and come outside. No more dreaming. You've woken up. We have songs. You've just heard them.'

And I had. And I knew that I had lived an experience I would never forget.

I was enthralled by what I had heard from Juddsy's guitar, his lyrics and the song structures. What had brought this reality about? Was Juddsy going through a rebirth forged from his tripping adventures, where people and their whys and wherefores and the tribulations of the day-to-day made him create what we had heard? Some chemistry of change, some resurrection, had taken him to a new, free world; one that gave him and his imagination room to move.

And Tim? He was already shaping a persona that I'd never seen before. At school he'd stood stationary on the stage and his voice was correct and his expression close to lifeless. Now he was away. His future ringmaster-meets-the-clown character was yet to be realised, but as we all know the clown is a wise man who is wiser than the wise men. I watched him singing 'Wise Men' to us in my bedroom. He had found the paramount point to project his real self and we were the lucky ones to witness it.

Now what? Well, I rang Tim and said that we needed to have rehearsals, and the next thing Juddsy, Tim, Miles and I were in my bedroom playing those three songs. They seemed to have fallen out of the sky into our heads, our hands, and I added my bass lines in seconds as the truth of what they had presented to me became real. I had a huge, open playground on which I could do what I liked. I looked down at my Fender Mustang bass with its flatwound strings. Every note was there waiting for me to play it. Not for a second did I feel lost, confused, wayward, searching. There was this energy in the room, the invisible, deep energy that turns songs from ideas into a fierce reality. Magical.

We played them all about five times and then I thought, 'What the hell.' I said to them, 'Let's book a gig and play these songs at it. Sure, we've only got three, but so what? Let's book a gig. Forget the drums and all that. Forget the piano. Let's do them like we are right now.'

A quiet mysterious agreement emanated from them, with touches of fear—stage fright? But I was ready. I'd played the same bass lines every time we rehearsed each song and that was because I believed in those songs that had just landed on Planet Earth. My passion for the bass players Dennis Dunaway (Alice Cooper) and Glenn Cornick (Jethro Tull) rushed to the surface. I was deeply into their craft. I 'knew' them. It was like they were standing there. They spoke in unison:

'Come on, Mike. Fuck's sake, man, these are very cool songs. That Finn geezer. Fuck he can sing. You know what to do. Rip off our best tricks; take our tossing, tumbling hooks and make them your own. We won't sue you. Time is right, Mike. Now.'

I thanked them, and to this day Dennis Dunaway and Glenn Cornick still creep into my bass lines.

'If we're going to do a gig, where will we play?' asked Tim.

I had already asked Geoffrey where Rosewood played. He suggested we book an early spot at the folk and blues night at the Wynyard Tavern in Symonds Street, then go down the road and play our three songs again at the Levi's Saloon folk night. Easy. All on a Sunday. Our own version of Sunday Mass. Juddsy and Tim agreed to this instant decision-making process and the bookings were made.

The Wynyard Tavern. 7.30 p.m., Sunday, 10 December 1972. By now, we had increased our membership to five. A flute-playing compatriot of Miles's, one Mike Howard, had attended rehearsals, so we had acoustic guitar, tambourine, flute, violin and bass ready to go. The combination of those five instruments—dreamlike! A tambourine is a superlative instrument—it gave us a range of musical colour that was perfect for the three songs. And off we went.

We played them at Wynyard, but as I looked out at the audience I sensed their bemusement at the shortage of 'blues' in the songs—like, where were the Buddy Guy-type lead solos, man? Mmm. I could see we were in the wrong place. The eyes of those punters were shifting. They shuffled their feet and twiddled their fingers. The clapping? The audience response? It wasn't like I'd witnessed at the Elton John concert. The three songs came and went, and we dutifully loaded our gear out the door and fell down Anzac Avenue to Levi's Saloon. And we went in and did it all over again.

The audience here was transfixed. They didn't take their eyes off us. It was a joy to behold. To have songs that created so much attention. And performances that triumphed. Tim's vocals. Juddsy's inventive guitar playing. Miles and Mike— breaking down the orchestral barrier. And lil ole me. The Engineering Science student who was finding the letter *i* to have minimal relevance in his kaleidoscopic new life.

I had a vision of the year looming—the 1973 possibility. If we could get up here on this stage and play out these cool songs, all in a few short weeks—what did 1973 hold? Would this riveting short story turn into a novel? Except all the characters, plot lines, reversals, et cetera would be the truth— so *not* a novel? Aw, damn . . . call it what you will. Could Juddsy and Tim's grip on their unchanging past now be a mighty future with new profound secrets set free, and vibrant visions falling into a worldwide frame? Perhaps? Why not?!

And so there we were at Levi's Saloon on Customs Street. And we played our three songs and left the stage.

As we walked to the corner of the room this geezer with a cowboy shirt and a funny beard came up to us.

'You only played three songs.'

'True,' I said. 'We did.'

One of the other musicians in the room, a member of the band Tolepuddle, came over and said, 'That was really good. Do some more.'

I thought, 'Mmm, this is a conspiracy. They know we only know three songs and now there's pressure, and if they lay it on thick enough we'll end up running home to our mothers.'

We turned around and went back to the stage and played the same three songs again. We played them like they'd never been played. Well . . . they'd been played once already. But we weren't ones to split hairs. We played them again. We were magnificent. And we left the stage and went back to where we came from. A nondescript corner of the room.

The geezer with the cowboy shirt came up to us again.

'I'm Barry Coburn,' he said. 'You guys have a manager?'

A manager? I looked at Tim, who had a flummoxed brow. I looked at Juddsy, who was thinking, 'Why don't we play our three songs a third time?' Miles and Mike were floating in the ether of this folk night here on Customs Street in the not-too-flash city of Auckland. (It was December 1972, after all.)

'No, we don't,' I said.

'I'd like to manage you guys. And, by the way, I'm putting on the Great Ngaruawahia Music Festival in a few weeks and I'd like you to play at it. Can you write some more songs?'

I thought about this question. It rang bells. It took me back to school, when Brother Chops had asked the class if we thought it was a good idea that man (should that be Man?) had landed on the moon. And Simon, sitting in the row behind me, asked in response, 'Does the Pope have a cock?'

I looked at Tim. We hadn't done much in the phantasmagorical world of rock'n'roll . . . but tonight we'd charged in and kicked up some dust.

Tim said, 'Yes, we can write more songs.'

'Excellent,' said Barry. And we were booked to play the

Saturday night, before The La De Das, on the main stage.

This was freakishly exciting. Juddsy and Tim went home and wrote songs like only true songwriters can: very well.

One of them was called '129', the room at O'Rorke Hostel where only a year ago Juddsy, Rob and Noel Crombie had lived, along with Ray McVinnie (yes, that Ray McVinnie). Another one was called 'Spellbound'. We were spellbound. Simply so.

There were more. 'Time for a Change' was one of them, and the first time I heard it I was stunned.

We were doing another night at Levi's Saloon in early January when Juddsy said he was going to play a new song with Miles, and asked the rest of us to leave the stage. You might think that odd, but it seemed perfectly normal at the time, and we went and sat down. Juddsy started playing finger-picked arpeggio chords that bore no resemblance to any chord I knew. Where had he worked all this out? How could he do it? And then he half-sang, half-spoke 'Time for a Change', which was followed in the second half by a violin solo written and played by Miles. It was shockingly good. The lyrics were evocative. Riveting. And to this day all of us hold that song as a truly triumphant slice of imagination from Juddsy and Miles. It is always on the Split Enz playlist, no matter whether it's a concert today or in ten years' time. It is always there. But we must return to the past.

Barry Coburn became our manager and started thinking about more than just the Great Ngaruawahia Festival. He started talking about a university orientation-week tour. He mentioned his upcoming John Mayall tour of New Zealand. Did we want to open for him throughout New Zealand? Holy shit! How do these things happen? But first—the festival.

We set up a tent near backstage on the Saturday morning and waited nervously. There were 18,000 people on the site, and 17,896 had never heard of us. All around, young men poured beer down their throats as a precursor to their big moment: the return of Kevin Borich and The La De Das.

We walked onstage at 8 p.m. to a restless crowd who failed to acknowledge our arrival. Tim was spinning out, and started talking to the crowd in an Irish accent. Committed to this strange pretence, he was obliged to stick with it. I glanced at him. He looked different. But he was the same. His presence had 'command' written all over it. He stepped up to the plate. Every week in the past months had seen him advancing. One foot forward. Two toes back.

I felt confident. No matter what was about to happen, we were up there and our childhood dreams were out and about. Ready to spread our conjuring tricks.

We kicked off with 'Split Ends', which sounded weedy by virtue of me having plugged my bass guitar into the wrong amplifier. It was a yellow amplifier. A Wasp. Trippy and cool. For half the song I was playing away in silence. We followed this with 'Under the Wheel', which we had just learned that week. It was delivered rapid-fire and fuelled by intense adrenaline, each of us incapable of any rational control. The crowd failed to respond.

We played 'For You', followed by 'Lovey Dovey'.

In the vast expanse of the night sky, our acoustic display was drifting away in the breeze and we started to feel alone.

After 'Spellbound', halfway through the set, the stage MC, Adrian Rawlins, came up to Tim and said that we had to get off. They had the Maori Concert Party ready to go on as a ruse to quieten the restless mob. Ruse is right.

Tim reacted instinctively by going up to the microphone and asking a question: 'We've just been told we have to get off. Do *you* want us to finish?'

We all looked at each other, which breaks Rule No 3(b) of the onstage code: *Don't look at each other!*

There was little need for the crowd to discuss this among themselves. In a roar of unanimous approval they screamed, 'YES!'

Shocked and confused, we charged off into '129', our last chance to prove ourselves. Tim sang as if he was staring into the eyes of every drunk who wanted him out of there. He filled his lungs and made an extraordinary effort.

We walked off as the Maori Concert Party walked on, and went back to the tent. We shuffled inside. Not much was said. Was anything said? I was thinking . . . What did I think?

I thought, 'Never again will we ever be booed off a stage.'

And we never were.

Chapter Eight
Three Songs and the Starter's Gun

Despite that wayward rejection by the festival populace, Coburn booked us in to Stebbings in Auckland to record our debut single. Two tracks were chosen, the first two that Juddsy and Tim had written—'For You' and 'Split Ends'.

On the day, all five of us crammed into my father's Morris 1800, and with my father's cassette of Richard Burton reading Dylan Thomas's *Under Milk Wood* playing extremely loudly we rolled in merry abandonment to the studio that awaited us like a launch-pad for souls that are heaven-bound. We literally ran inside, with St Peter the holy usher whisking us through.

We played our hearts out. The Great Ngaruawahia Festival shrunk away into the past and it all came together. Dennis Dunaway and Glenn Cornick were watching me from the control room. They were happy. My bass had flatwound strings on it. Their basses had flatwounds too. (Bassists in the in-crowd played flatwound strings in 1973. Dig it.)

With our two tracks under his arm, Coburn secured a single release through Phonogram's Vertigo label. They released it and it was completely ignored by the whole of humankind. I have only ever seen one copy and it has initials written on it: 'Y.C.' Yes, Yvonne Chunn. My darling mother went and bought one. I can't be sure but perhaps that was the only copy sold.

And so we sat and looked around my bedroom at the next rehearsal and wondered. And then Miles told us the news. He was leaving for London to play in the Royal Philharmonic Orchestra. We knew he was that good. And he was leaving.

A few days later we again gathered in my bedroom and had a final Split Ends bash. 'Spellbound' had become a glorious, evocative roller-coaster ride with Miles at his freewheeling best. We played it out a last time. Then Miles put his violin in its case and shuffled out the door onto the footpath that took him down Parnell Road.

Juddsy and Tim saw that moment as the end of Split Ends. How could our band charge on without Miles, who had brought so many facets of colour and harmony to what came off our stage? I looked at them both. I was thinking. Barry Coburn had us pinned to his noticeboard as the opening act for the John Mayall tour. Tim and Juddsy saw this as something we couldn't do without Miles on the stage. But why not?

The two of them started their final shuffle down Parnell Road, making their way to their new flat on St Georges Bay Road. I walked outside. They were exactly side by side. They were talking. What were they saying? They must have done a lot of talking in the past six months; those months that had taken five lads from disparate corners of this odd country to stages small and large. To audiences resplendent and tawdry. All showered in the most amazing songs. Songs that came from some magical kitchen of life where the ingredients fed the mind, and the soul was blessed.

I ran after them. They turned as my footsteps drew me close to them.

'Hey, guys, we're mad to just stop what we started. We have the John Mayall tour booked. Let's put together an electric band and do the tour.'

They looked at me. I'd thrown a curve ball . . . well, an out-swinger . . . and they listened and thought about it.

'Let's ask Geoffrey to play drums and Wally Wilkinson to play electric guitar and rework the songs we have. Let's do the tour,' I said.

'OK,' they said. 'When does the tour start?'

'In twelve days,' I said.

A few moments of silence.

'OK,' they said.

And after I'd asked Geoffrey and Wally, who both jumped at the chance, we all gathered in my bedroom (Geoffrey was no longer sharing it with me; I was twenty, after all) and starting rearranging those glorious songs.

Mike Howard turned up too, but sadly his cool flute-playing got hammered by the electric onslaught and he found it opportune to leave our ranks. I can still see him walking out onto Parnell Road. He was angry. And he had every right to be. We had forced him out. Why couldn't we have talked about Mike, his role in the band and how it probably wouldn't fit in the new regime? And one of us—all of us?—could have met him and explained this to him. But we didn't have the bottle. In the end, all the 'firings' of Split Ends (and Enz) members were done heartlessly. You'll find that out as we traverse the unruly, rugged landscape of this unique band.

From the second we walked onstage at the YMCA Stadium in Auckland to open for John Mayall, I knew—we all knew—we were about to present a repertoire of cool songs with a great line-up, and a naïvety that gave us a purity of performance. Our belief in this new era was convincing.

Backstage, Coburn was thrilled with the results. And so we flew off with John Mayall and his very cool American jazzo dudes and walked onto big stages all over New Zealand. Press reviews were great.

And then Coburn made his next move. (He was good at that.) He had entered us in a national television talent quest called *New Faces*. This was screened on prime-time television and original songs were encouraged. And for the second time we ran into Stebbings and set up to record a song for the show. Juddsy and Tim went for '129' as the track to record. (You might know the song by the title it was given when it was released in Britain, 'Matinee Idyll'.) It was a session where a vast array of musical instruments and vocal arrangements poured out and onto the recording tape.

The song started with a recording of people drinking and talking at the Gluepot pub just down the road. Then Juddsy on a mandolin, Tim on piano, Wally on electric guitar, my flatwound strings. Our dear friend Bob guesting on brass. Wally on wind chimes. A hippy moment? A patchwork quilt of coolness and light? It was us.

And Coburn sent it off to the *New Faces* crew, who flew us down to Wellington, put us up in the Waterloo Hotel and filmed us miming it the next day. The NZBC aired it as part of the competition's heats in August, and we were chosen by the judges to be in the finals. *Yes!* That meant going back to Stebbings to record another song.

We met with Coburn in Von and Jerry's lounge (we did meet in some odd places), and Tim said he and Juddsy had a new song called 'Sweet Talkin' Spoon Song'. None of us had heard it, but we all said 'Cool!', and Coburn went and booked the session.

It followed the '129' ethos. We threw a lot of stuff into it. Mandolin again, tuba, Bob on trumpet, my flatwound strings, Geoffrey on drums. He and I nailed it. I stood close to the studio wall and watched him play out his part. I cast my mind back to when he and I recorded on the home tape-recorder. The Otahuhu festival of sound. We were out of time. We were shambolic. Our innocence was spectacular.

But perhaps that's how it must be. The yearning to be in a band that does things like make records and play concerts probably has to be forged in naïve exploration, with an uncorrupted pair of minds sharing the mysterious path ahead. We knew that day how we must sound. What we must play.

And that day at Stebbings we did too. On 'Sweet Talkin' Spoon Song', I felt Geoffrey and I had reached that place. We had realised what we had to do in the context of a group of young men forging something very distinctive. A time of joy.

The song was mixed, sent off to Wellington and once again we were put up in the Waterloo Hotel and the television people filmed us miming it the next day. The judges didn't like it, however, and we were placed second to last. I thought, 'What the hell, I don't care.' The whole *New Faces* affair had us broadcast on national television twice. That must have counted for something. The thing during the year that hadn't counted for much were the live shows we did sporadically after the John Mayall tour.

To put it nicely, there was no demand for Split Ends to play live. Coburn put together one or two shows here and there, and while a fair few punters turned up, they often didn't stay. We were short on live experience, and while the thrill of supporting John Mayall had served us well, doing a headline show in a small Hamilton hall to about twenty people was too much of a contrast. It became clear to us that headlining a show was very different from playing five songs as a support act to a major draw. There wasn't a lot to prove. And Juddsy in particular wasn't taking to it.

Tim rang me. He said that Juddsy didn't want to perform live any more so we shouldn't look for any work. Tim adopted Juddsy's plans of existing as a recording act only, and 1973 ended in limbo.

While at the time this development seemed sudden, it now appears almost logical. The 'rejection' of our performance in the *New Faces* final was an enormous let-down for Juddsy and Tim, who had imagined the show would send the band soaring into the stratosphere. When the reality struck, their natural reaction was to retreat—and that meant avoiding live work.

This state of affairs was mirrored in the release of 'Sweet Talkin' Spoon Song', backed with '129'. It followed the path of 'For You' to nowhere in particular, while The Carpenters sat on top of the charts.

And it wasn't just the talent quest. Miles had gone, and the live shows were fraught with technical problems as well as the small crowds. The only real achievements, in Juddsy's view, had been the records we'd made, in that they had reached his expectations and he found the recording studio to be the ideal canvas. And Tim followed suit. They virtually disappeared into the shadows of their flat on St Georges Bay Road. Wally, Geoffrey and I ended the year not knowing if we would ever meet as Split Ends on a stage again.

On Christmas Day 1973 I was sitting opposite Geoffrey for the family ham and turkey lunch. (There may not have been a turkey, but that didn't matter.) We'd been sitting round that table since we were seven and eight. From Otahuhu to Parnell and all those moments of musical exploration. The imaginings and the searching for answers. Well, we had the questions but answers were elusive. What did it really take to be in a band that kicked up dust and drew excitement and reaction from an audience? Well, we were learning fast.

I started to think about this band we were in, now called Split Enz after Juddsy came up with that cool idea. We had to play live. Yes, The Beatles stopped playing live. But they could do whatever they liked. They could have bought Belgium and got change. We knew why—they were from another planet. Juddsy wanted to record. He didn't want to face the crowd. Be stared down. Tim respected Juddsy's move and talked of recording only, never live shows. But, the thing was, he was so good out there at the front. And, man, could he sing.

In late January, we were all back in Auckland from our various holiday distractions, assuming that nothing was happening, which it was. Then Barry Coburn rang me to say that we had a 30-minute television special, courtesy of the New Zealand Broadcasting Corporation, as a result of being one of the *New Faces* finalists. The show would be entitled 'Six of the Best'. We needed to record four more songs to add to '129' and 'Sweet Talkin' Spoon Song'.

And there was the possibility of concerts ahead, as Radio Hauraki was planning a series of 'buck-a-head' shows of original artists at His Majesty's Theatre on Queen Street.

'Buck-a-head, Barry?'

'Yes, Mike. A dollar to get in.'

Aha! Recording sessions—that would get Juddsy fired up. And a cool concert in one of Auckland's major theatres. I rang Tim and explained this to him.

He immediately saw the worth of the TV show, so we got Coburn to book time at Stebbings to record the tracks. And the concerts sounded ideal—radio advertising support and the magnificent His Majesty's Theatre to play in. We talked more and decided that, even though Juddsy wasn't interested in playing live, we would expand the group and Juddsy could be involved from the sideline—contributing ideas, concepts and songs.

In early February '74, we asked old buddy Rob Gillies to come in on sax and trumpet. We had a few rehearsals, and after the hiatus were breathing new life into the songs. Tim had just purchased a Mellotron keyboard, courtesy of a loan from his folks, Dick and Mary, which used strips of magnetic tape to reproduce the authentic sounds of violins, cellos and flutes. This was going to help re-create the string sections that had featured so prominently on the records.

Consequently, we needed a second keyboard player to play it, and he had to be brilliant. There was only one choice: Eddie Rayner.

Eddie was known to us by name, but that was all. He had gone to Pakuranga College and spent the sixth form mucking around at Sacred Heart College. I've already told you that. Even when he was at school, he was already a professional musician playing nightclubs in the city. A pro! Still at school! We had lost sight of him; then, like a meerkat, he popped up out of the ground into the band scene. There he was onstage at the Students' Arts Festival in 1972, playing with a band called Orb, led by Alastair Riddell. (Mr Riddell will return to the story later.) They played what we now call British progressive rock: songs by artists like Yes, Genesis, Jethro Tull, et cetera. Orb may have had original songs. Maybe not. I was in the crowd about six metres from Eddie when he was playing keyboard and I was mesmerised. His skill, his total control, was like nothing I'd ever seen before. He never played a wrong note, never skipped a beat and never looked down at his knobs, keys, whistles and paraphernalia. He was a magician.

So of course we asked him to come along to a rehearsal to see if he was interested in joining us. Eddie turned up with his innocent face and long blond hair, and took a seat next to Tim at the piano. He had a knowing eye, a swirling demeanour and an odd pair of trousers, like a Russian politician. When he played a couple of chords on the piano his hands moved like he'd played that piano a thousand times before. Hands that weren't skinny or delicate. Quite fulsome fingers they were. Like his legs.

Very little was said, because very little was ever said in our wacky world. We just plugged in our guitars and hit young Eddie right between the eyes with a thumping, desperate version of 'Lovey Dovey'. I looked at this young musician as he sat watching carefully.

We finished. We played it again and Eddie played it with us. How the hell did he do that? He was in. And we became a six-piece band with a concert looming and a bunch of recording sessions. Goodbye, 1973. Hello, 1974. Coolness and light.

Chapter Nine
Welcome to the Terrordome

I n February we checked in to Stebbings. The six of us had rehearsed like madmen and were ready to go. We put down four songs (all of which are ensconced on the album *The Beginning of The Enz*) and it all fell into place. Eddie fitted in like a glove. Juddsy had become master of acoustic guitar arrangements. His melodic backdrop in 'No Bother To Me' is extraordinary. Again I found myself asking the question: 'How did he gather this talent in such a short space of time?!' And Geoffrey and me—it was yet another champion moment of advancing along the lifeline of a rhythm section; the drums and bass (with flatwound strings) working as a single instrument. Dennis Dunaway and Glenn Cornick hovering in the control room. Smiling. What a day; what a time.

Rehearsals for the buck-a-head concert were buoyant and dedicated. We had Juddsy in the room, and he and Tim had new songs. We dusted off those from the Miles era that needed beefing up in the new environment with the new line-up. We gathered our forces.

At virtually every rehearsal in that double-brick town-house on Parnell Road I would occasionally look up the stairs and more often than not our father would be sitting on the top stair, listening. Watching and listening. He'd taken a shine to Juddsy's lyrics and would ask me about them. 'How does he come up with them?' I wish I knew. He especially liked—loved—'Time For A Change'. And that made sense to me. I spoke to him one day in the kitchen.

'Jerry, what do you actually think while you're listening to the rehearsals?'

'Well, it seems a mystery, really. How you don't say much but you all seem to know what you're doing. How do you know what you're doing, what you should be doing?'

Mmm. Good question.

'Haven't thought about it, old man. But you know, it's probably because we've spent our lives listening to recordings of songs and just picked it up. And in that process just made sure we made it all "ours". Make sense?'

He looked at me and nodded his head. He had learned the piano as a kid, but his teacher was a nun and she would whack him on the knuckles if he made a mistake. As well, he was made to learn pieces of music that he would never want to listen to. Madness. It was in his eyes. And I imagined him saying to me: 'I envy you, Michael. If I had been born in 1952 I could have been in your band. I would have wanted to write lyrics. I can write verse. Is it so different?'

'No, it's not, Jerry,' I said in silence. 'But you're fifty-one now, dear man. So keep writing your verse and your poems. One day, I'll put them all in a book.'

And I did.

Days rolled by in fervour and feverish preparation. A week out from the concert, which Radio Hauraki had promoted to the hilt and was looking like a sell-out, Tim was standing beside me after a rehearsal at a church hall in Parnell. He looked at me. 'If I could, I would break my leg so I don't have to do this show.'

What? He doesn't want to do the show?

I think back to that moment, which stands so clear, word-perfect, in my memory. He was grappling with the responsibility of being the 'man out front'. The ringmaster. But he must have known he could do it. All he had to do was get to the finish line after sprinting through these glorious rehearsals on Parnell Road, and with outstretched hands cross it, his head held high.

I thought after he said that to me: 'You may not be able to see it, Tim, but you will kill them in the aisles.'

On 12 May 1974 we waited backstage for Coburn to tell us 'Get onstage!' We had a full house of 1200 people. Radio Hauraki DJ Fred Botica announced us and the curtain lifted. None of this running onstage shit. We were already there, all motionless in our beautiful positions.

I looked across at Geoffrey. He was going to start this thing, this first song called 'True Colours'. Nothing would happen until he hit his hi-hat four times. A few micro-seconds went by. I looked out. The crowd weren't doing that shouting, whistling, cat-calling array of provocative shenanigans. How could they? Ninety-nine per cent of them had no idea what they were about to see. They were politely waiting.

I looked back at Geoffrey. He had his sticks poised. Two more nano-seconds went by. Tim was standing out front with his microphone stand draped in plastic flowers and aimed like a benevolent howitzer at the crowd. What was he about to do? My knees were knocking. True! Please . . . believe me. My knees were knocking. *Knock, knock, knock, knock.* And then Geoffrey lifted his right hand and brought it down.

Oh, man. All those years that had passed, all those Pavilion moments in Otahuhu, the Sacred Heart music room hideaways and urgent hurry-alongs that didn't seem to go anywhere. Think of them now! For the last time. We are about to banish them!

Geoffrey hit the hi-hat. Four times. And Tim leaned forward, closed in on the mic and sang 'Let's rock!' We were away!

It was during 'Stranger Than Fiction' in the second half that the truth was laid out for us to savour. That unique song started by Miles Golding, with Wally's riffs, Juddsy's lyrics and Tim's melodic adventures all segueing into the mesmeric 'Time For A Change'—it was written on the faces in the crowd. What visions did they have? All these New Zealanders drawn in by curiosity. What were they thinking? Did they share our journey here? A journey that catapulted lyrics and melodies at them line by line? Did they think they were hearing something they would recall in a few decades' time? I think so. It was in their eyes.

Juddsy had a role during the show, with his head swathed in bandages. I'm not sure whose idea that was. His? I guess you could say he was Mr Anonymous. But there you go. A random thing, let's call it, with Noel Crombie standing in a theatre box acting out a role as an explorer. Possibly some in the crowd would have thought—correctly—that the guy in the theatre box was an explorer looking for the guy with his head in bandages. They worked in unison, as such. And then as the final moments of the concert closed, Juddsy tore off his bandages and revealed himself as he ran across the stage, his eyes bright. They had stars in them. There were enough punters in the crowd to know who he was and cheers rang out. Tim had earlier in the show acknowledged his (Juddsy's) songwriting prowess. And how could he not?

So what was Juddsy thinking? That look in his eyes. The stage, the concert, the audience, the musical performance—it had all woven a seductive lure for him.

Juddsy's dash across the stage with his disguise abandoned was an indication of what lay ahead. It was the last piece of the jigsaw puzzle that this mysterious journey was all about. But I didn't want him back on the stage. The six-piece band that had just triumphed was a glorious Venn diagram of the right musicians, the best singer in the land and a truly unified, kaleidoscopic vision. Juddsy and Tim could write songs and hand them over to us, and we would turn them into musical conjuring tricks that no one else in New Zealand was capable of. We'd shown we could do that. And I thought, as I watched him:

'Please, Juddsy, stay in the wings. We killed it tonight. Why can't it be like that forever?'

But I knew it wouldn't be.

A few days after this watershed concert, still revelling in the sense of achievement, Tim came to rehearsal and told us that Juddsy wanted back in the group. Tim was adamant that it should happen, and talked of the opportunities it gave with songs like 'Under the Wheel', previously discarded, being brought back to life. Tim was laying himself bare.

I looked at him as he said these words. It wasn't dictatorial. But it was non-negotiable. Juddsy was back in the group, having witnessed the extraordinary musical triumph of the buck-a-head. It was an easy thing to do. He'd been there before.

The reaction from the rest of us was, on the surface, 'We'll give it a try'—but it was couched in pessimism.

At the next rehearsal Juddsy came along with his electric guitar and the period of readjustment commenced. Tim was relieved to have Juddsy back . . . It was Split Enz as it should be, although the reunification of Tim and Juddsy was soon to shift in Tim's eyes. Julie (Juddsy's partner) was pregnant and Juddsy's attention was, naturally, on his forthcoming fatherhood. Tim sensed this, and on the night Julie went into labour, Tim, although sharing in the excitement, realised it was the end of the incredible bond that the two of them had shared. From the moment Juddsy's daughter Amy arrived, the dynamic between Juddsy and Tim would never be the same. And they would never discuss it, because nothing was ever discussed. The two of them, and for that matter all of us, moved in silence to the point of least confrontation.

There were problems at rehearsals. In my opinion, Juddsy's electric guitar capabilities fell short of his talents on an acoustic guitar and his vocals were an obvious contrast to Tim's efforts. It seemed Juddsy was uncomfortable with his prodigal son status and felt he had lost some of the presence he had in the previous year's line-up, which in his eyes had been a smaller, more manageable unit.

It wasn't long before Rob Gillies and brother Geoffrey decided for themselves that the new line-up was not on a par with the previous one, and they both left the group in July.

In keeping with our lack of internal communication, their departure was accepted without discussion and a replacement drummer was sought. It wasn't felt necessary to replace Rob. Two guitarists would have shared parts. That was Rob's lines covered. But a new drummer? That meant Geoffrey was gone. *Geoffrey was gone.*

Radio Hauraki and Coburn booked another Buck-A-Head concert for 18 August 1974, this time at the Mercury Theatre. They were buoyed by the first one. We were, too. It had been a hit. But the magical line-up had changed. What was going to happen when the curtain went up the next time?

The ripple of peer-to-peer gossip and conversation around Auckland had been fairly buoyant after the first buck-a-head show. It had even reached Von and Jerry, although they had no time for it. A fair few of their inner-city professional friends thought my storming the stage with a bunch of likely lads in weird clothes and playing freaky songs was nothing less than irresponsible. How could they allow their son with his university education in engineering to forsake a successful career building skyscrapers and dredging harbours to chase the impossible dream of being a pop star? Fortunately they both categorised these flimsy, opinionated friends as twits.

On the Mercury stage we had another full house in front of us. At the sound check in the afternoon I looked across at the drum kit. Paul Crowther was sitting on the drum stool. He'd come from Alastair Riddell's band Orb, in which Eddie Rayner had been playing prior to our nabbing him. Everything was connected. People who knew people took stages with people, and moved around as people sought people to populate these things called bands. People as currency. A not overly thought-out process. But this wasn't about working for the man. This was about shaping futures with our own work ethic. The quick, surefooted fix. The time-is-running-short-let's-act! logistics.

And while we stood on the Mercury stage Geoffrey was in the audience, with a full house around him. He wasn't on the drum stool.

I don't recall talking to him about why he left the band. I didn't discuss it with him. All those teenage years of being told to 'keep quiet!' by men and women of the cloth. The ambling, shuffling mob of the past. They had been successful in keeping me mum. Making me nervous about communicating. That first line. What do you say to someone? It would be many years before I found my voice.

We started playing, and the new Split Enz faltered and surged, twisted and flayed. We weren't ready. We weren't sure about this new world we were living in. We drove the theatrics as hard as we could. Probably to the distraction of the music. Tim was on fire. Juddsy's return was a true impetus for him, and he thought—had always thought—that Split Enz had to have Juddsy in it. Up there on the Mercury stage I watched the two of them. There was a potent contrast in their stage presence, their voices. It looked right. It just needed to sound better.

Who was I in this mix? I felt a small sense of alienation with my other half, my drummer foil, gone. Assembling this new rhythm section (drum and bass) ethos with Paul Crowther (let's call him Croth from now on) wasn't easy for me. He and I had come from different places. I would have to remould my approach in seeking out a true unity with this new man on the drum stool. After all, underpinning our future were these songs from Juddsy and Tim. Old ones like 'Under the Wheel' that had been dusted off. And brand-new ones like 'The Woman Who Loves You' and 'Amy (Darling)' expanded the genre of our adventurous band with its almost vaudevillian camp (yet extremely clever) style. And so we lifted the curtain and on we played.

The audience was uncertain. When I saw Geoffrey after the show I said, 'What was it like?'

'An abortion,' he said. And he drifted away to pick up his acoustic guitar and think of another road to walk down.

A week or two later, I was spending a night at my partner Paula's family home. They were away in Australia, and I and a few others just, well, thought we'd stay there. One of those random moves you make when you're 22.

Sitting in their lounge in front of the TV, someone produced LSD blotting-paper pieces and we swallowed them. About an hour later we slipped into the happy analysis of life; that softly slow-motion receiving of colour and sound. The wallpaper in the room with its streaking redness and opulent nothing-in-particularity kept us warm on this cold August night. The corridor leading away from the lounge door was a yellow-brick road. Ah, how serendipitous. Should we all walk down it singing about whistling happy tunes? Why? I don't know. Why care when nothing matters? A Janet Frame corridor stanza of floor, wall and ceiling all forging, contracting into a shiny basin against a shiny wall. Then someone knocked on the door, walked in and produced a joint.

'What's this?' I asked.

'A little taste of Thai Sticks for this cold winter's night,' she said.

I looked back at the television as my turn to smoke this narrow paper tube came to be. Did I not listen to what she said? Thai Sticks.

'A joint for friendly sharing,' I said. I inhaled. Say that again?

I inhaled and a new little adventure got underway with be mixed like some happy-go-lucky chemical reaction with what was going on already. What was going on already? There was an Isaac Hayes special on the television. This was 1974 and New Zealand television was now in colour. I looked at Mr Hayes on the screen. His velvet suit was funky red. Or was it blood red? He looked at me from the screen. He suddenly scared me. Why was he looking at me?

I stood up. He was still looking at me, his blood-soaked suit and his white dagger teeth laughing at me, calling to me 'Go! Go!' So I did. I looked down the corridor that led from the lounge. The yellow-brick corridor was melting. I looked over at the front door. I should walk out that door and go home. But I didn't have a car. And if I walked home stray dogs would devour me. Passers-by with their knife-like fingers would lash at me. Scream at me: 'Go away!'

I quickly climbed the stairs to the upper rooms where there was no light. Thin, sharp beams from street lights lined up on the walls. A maimed bannister looked back at me from the stairwell. 'Stay away!' My heart just kept beating faster and faster. What was around me in this black shadowed labyrinth of wallpapered cells? Cages? Open a door. Close the door. Go to a window. Look out at the gnarled, cracked rooftops and witness the acrid, cloudy skyline above Auckland.

I had to move on. Back down the stairs. A crippled corridor leading back to the TV room. How could they watch this demonic blood-soaked man, his voice deceased and his black-forest stare carving, carving out into my eyes? I quickly left the room.

No one could see me. They were watching the TV. I didn't want them to see me. I ran down another ugly corridor to a bathroom and vomited into the sink. I watched my sordid vomit fly into the sink. I was terrified. What would happen to me? Where could I go? I didn't have a car.

I wanted to run into my father's bedroom over on Parnell Road, wake him up and cry to him, 'Jerry! You're a doctor. Do you have an anaesthetic injection? A sleeping drug? Ether? What have you got, Jerry? Help me. And please don't ask me what I've done.' But I couldn't walk home. I just couldn't. Clouds would drench me in acid hail. I could feel my heart racing, racing. How fast before it collapsed into a deathly stillness? Please, do it now. Stop beating so fast! Just stop. Stop. Stop. Let me die. I am terrified. And I can't get home.

I woke up. It was 7 a.m. Lying on a bed! And all terror and panic had ceased. How? Was it a dream? A supreme nightmare? How lucky was I to be breathing? My heart beating at 75 bpm instead of—what? 150 bpm? It must have been. Why? I don't care why. If I avoid all drugs for the rest of my life I will be free. I will never fall into that black furnace again.

And as I made my way along Broadway and onto Parnell Road, I reached 469, took my key out of my pocket and unlocked the door—clickety latchety. In I went and climbed the stairs—those stairs that have cradled me—and walked into my bedroom and cried.

Chapter Ten
Costumes and Disorder

W hile our obsession with Split Enz was all-encompassing, we weren't the only band on the scene. Alastair Riddell, formerly of Orb, had a new band, Space Waltz, and they had entered the *New Faces* competition in 1974, as had we the year before. His band included Greg Clark (guitar), Brent Eccles (drums), Peter Cuddihy (bass, roundwound strings) and himself on vocals and electric guitar. He also had our Eddie Rayner in as guest keyboard player. They played their song 'Out on the Street' in the heats.

The song was so well received that EMI rushed it out as a single, and before long it reached number one in the singles charts. We were extremely envious but held it back. Our turn must surely come! How soon?

On the back of this chart success, Space Waltz was booked to play The Founders Theatre in Hamilton, and it sold out prior to the show date. That was cool. (Envy again!) We were asked to play support. Space Waltz didn't have their usual bass player, so Alastair asked if I could play for them.

'Of course,' I said. All a bit odd; Eddie and I playing in

both bands. We shouldn't have done it. Split Enz was starting to gel. How would the others feel standing side-stage watching Eddie and me cavort around? Would it all be wrong? Well . . .

Backstage, in readiness for the show, Noel Crombie, who had merged into our world and become a full-time member of the Enz as a character, walked into the dressing room with a bulky suit-carrier and pulled from it a selection of brightly coloured suits. For the first time we looked upon a set of Crombie original costumes designed and sewn by the man himself. In crazy pastel colours, with distorted shapes and angles, the suits stood before us as a symbol of the new era. They were quickly titled (at times) 'the Zoots' or (at other times) 'the Twits'. Mine was yellow, and I loved it. That night we had everything right and we shook off the Mercury concert in a wild, tight show.

The costumes we were wearing had transformed us into a unified force. Each of us was of the other. We had a collective spirit in that wacky cloth, which whirled like something from a bazaar for excitable children. That we were. It was on our faces. Juddsy, who had been somewhat inert after his re-entry, was safe in the suit of dark red, the still but truly powerful pin-point. And Tim on fire—out there scooping up the Waikato masses and spinning them above his head. Cracking his main-man whip. We had reached a new level of presentation and conviction and it was delightful.

After the show was over Alastair asked Eddie and me if we would fly down to Wellington to record and film a clip for their 'finals' song—'Beautiful Boy'—because yes, they, like we had been, were in the *New Faces* finals. Once again Eddie and I would be put up in the Waterloo Hotel after recording and filming the song and then, the next day, attend the judging of the finals in front of the expertly judged and judging judges.

The recording and filming went well. I had slick-backed hair and flared trousers (the '70s!). Not sure how that happened. But all was good and we were cheerful and light-headed and went back to the Waterloo Hotel after the filming. We had our chicken dinner there and all stood to leave and, well, socialise in the house bar.

Not me.

As I was walking away from the dining room it hit me. The exact same sensations—racing heart, spinning thoughts and that sense, that reality of true, unadulterated terror. At Paula's house, not long before, I knew what had been to blame: Thai Sticks. Coming down on a tripping mind. A mind that denied stress as only a fool like me would or could. Geoffrey had left my band. He wasn't my drummer any more. I was loosened, strained. Lost. The perfect storm of terror was in my head. But here? Just a chicken dinner. Why was this happening?

I raced to the hotel room I was sharing with Brent Eccles. Luckily, he had gone off somewhere else. Riddell's hotel room, I'm guessing. I rushed into the bathroom and emptied my bowels. Water. I glanced at my face in the mirror. Stripped of life, haggard, shattered eyes. I stood up, leaned over and vomited into the handbasin. Terror. My heart going at 150 bpm and my head unable to hold a thought for more than a nano-second. The trio of terror, panic and fear. The wave of despair was so . . . profound. All caused by . . . what? Nothing? Why had this happened again?

It was 8 p.m. and I climbed into my single bed and lay there. I felt my heart beating. Insane. I could die from this rapid, thrusting strain. I tried to hold a thought. Impossible. One thought. Come on! A thought!! I couldn't do it.

Eccles came in. Did he wonder why I'd gone to bed so early? I pretended to be asleep. He went out again. I got up and vomited again. I made sure I avoided the mirror.

Around 2 a.m., with Eccles now sound asleep in the next bed, I got up and went down to reception. Every step I walked on, walked down, felt like it was covered in large spiders. The exact same feeling of terror. But there were no spiders. There was nothing but stairs. I reached reception to find a woman vacuuming. I stammered out a query.

'Is there someone here who might have sleeping tablets?'

'Are you unwell?' she said.

Unwell? I'm mad. I'm freaking out. I'm in a panic. Is that unwell?

'Not really,' I said.

'I think you're going to have to wait till the chemist opens in the morning. It's only a hundred yards down the road.'

'Thank you,' and I climbed up the stairs, keeping out of the way of the black, haunting spiders that covered each of them. They were invisible. At least if they had been real I would have known where to run to.

I crept back into that Waterloo Hotel room and slid into bed. My mind kept racing. My heart kept up its maniacal beating. I drove my head deep into the pillow to try to avert the side-to-side flashing behind my eyelids. If only I could get back to Jerry on a mystery jet, maybe this time he could put me to sleep. For how long? I didn't care how long. I didn't care if it was forever. If this was going to happen again, I'd want to die first. My mind kept flickering that thought in its pathetic rush: will this ever happen again? And in a while—some time, at some non-specific but God-given hour—I collapsed into an unconscious state.

The next day I started to go into the studio for the judges' judging session. Suddenly I turned back: scared, scared, scared. I couldn't go in. I must have made up an excuse to the others. Or maybe Space Waltz didn't notice. I watched the filming on a remote TV in the green room. I was shamed by my inability to go into that room. I was cut down. And then the judges judged.

All I recall is one of the judges describing the Space Waltz song as 'obnoxious rock'. I thought, 'I want to go home.' And a few hours later we all did.

Split Enz. Space Waltz. Both crucified on the altar of the temple of the damned. The impaling spires of *New Faces*. The judges in their black hoods. So what?

Our plane landed and I drove back to Parnell Road as fast as I could. Safe.

In the first week of November 1973 I had walked out of the University of Auckland School of Engineering for the last time. Exam results came a few weeks later and I had a Bachelor of Engineering degree. That was a bit of all right. But I was completely uninterested in utilising its glorious mathematical matrices, statistics and computations. I thought I could park all that permanently in my wacko past. However, by mid 1974 I was poor, so my wonderful father rang a man he knew at Fisher & Paykel, Bassett McClurg, and I was hired into their management services division.

It was in essence a career move. Well, I had a job. But my job description had not yet been mapped out in the corridors of the human resources machine. And it never was. I guess I was kind of a spy. A bass player with a Bachelor of Engineering degree majoring in Operations Research. A lad who was put on the Hoovermatic assembly line to write a report on parts wastage by the layabouts who populated it. You don't believe me? It's true. I still have it.

The best part of this corporate roller-coaster ride happened at 10 a.m. every day when the tea trolley came around, and I would get a strong instant coffee and three twenty-cent sultana buns. My real life lay somewhere else entirely.

Radio Hauraki and Coburn had booked His Majesty's Theatre for another buck-a-head, on 1 December 1974. Christmas was looming, you see, so we concocted a nautical-meets-North-Pole scene. While the mythical wellspring of songs was not offering many up to Juddsy and Tim, we still had a cool repertoire to choose from. In fact, when I was looking at our list and thinking of what order the 'Pantemonium' set-list should be, I thought, 'I am one of the luckiest people—no, musicians—no, bass players—that's what I am, a bass player. With flatwound strings. And I get to write what I play from my own imagination. All those creative bass parts that I weave into these very cool songs.' The concert at Founders Theatre with Space Waltz had cemented our true selves.

Crombie turned up with a new set of costumes. Wally and I were dressed as sailors. We looked . . . well . . . weird. Weirdness is good. And with Tim, Juddsy, Crombie, Croth— we pulled together a spectacular show. And the rock magazine *Hot Licks* reviewed it.

How can one describe their concert? The Oxford University debating team on acid? Peter Rabbit as seen/played by Syd Barrett? Monty Python visits the Queen Mother under the direction of Pasolini, Marcel Marceau and Ray Davies? Split Enz are the cream of the crop. The finest band New Zealand has ever seen.

A few days later we met a beaming Coburn.

'I have two things to tell you,' he said.

'Tell us both of them,' we cheered.

'You've been booked for a New Zealand tour for university orientation week in February. All the unis. And after that you have been booked to play three weeks in Australia on a group exchange with a hot Oz band called Hush. Sound good?'

'Of course,' we chimed. A New Zealand tour! Excellent. Australia? Holy shit!

What about England? England was The Beatles. Australia? What was happening in Australia? We didn't know. We all knew 'Sadie (the Cleaning Lady)'. And we knew about Rolf Harris. But this band Hush—who were they?

The sum was now much bigger than the parts. Joy was in the air. But I was thinking about what lay ahead, and a layer of tension covered my brain. Would those attacks of terror ever come back? If so, why? Surely I was simply mad. Like my grandad Bunny. Too many unknowns. Too many what-ifs, why-nots, wherefores and forthwiths. Humbug! So I went outside, put my new bass—a Gibson Les Paul Triumph—on the back seat of my tinny Simca 1000 (a twenty-first birthday present from Von and Jerry) and sloped on back to Parnell Road to report in on the new wave of activity looming.

I took out my key, opened the door and went in. Von and Jerry were at the kitchen table. I watched them carefully. Could they see in me the new, fragile, watered-down man who was different from the exuberant child? I could go and ask them about me. Michael, their eldest boy.

'Von. Jerry. If you promise not to ask any questions, can you answer mine?'

'Of course, Michael.'

'Do I come across, here, now, as a fragile man? A flickering silent movie? Of sorts?'

'No. But you're an actor, son. You can pull the wool over our eyes. It may be best to just tell us what's going on. Can we ask one question?'

'Sure, I guess.'

'Why isn't Geoffrey still your drummer?'

I didn't want to talk to them. I didn't want questions. Questions. Falling birds. Light rain. Sleeping inordinate dreams. I didn't think they would understand what it was like to be in a band. So I walked back outside and hopped into the car.

I sat there for a while. We were going to Australia.

I resigned from Fisher & Paykel.

We rushed into the New Zealand university tour feeling ready to make the big splash. Crombie had made, stitched, needle-pointedly concocted and fashioned a set of costumes called The Clowns. Wally and I (we were often dressed the same, like classic examples of Sacred Heart College flotsam and jetsam) had gargantuan bow ties in red-and-white polka dots. Every show was sold out. We had reached a pinnacle. We were getting great press reviews. We had a beautiful repertoire of songs.

On 13 March 1975 we all flew out to Sydney. I sat in the Auckland airport lounge staring at my departure card. It was about 60 minutes away from that sprint down the runway. Where was I going? I closed my eyes and heard the noises all around me, like I was lying in a river that thundered and roared but didn't move. Slivers of light forced their way through my eyelids like slow-motion lightning bolts. I was excited to be going to Australia. But, if I opened my eyes on the plane, would thousands of black spiders be walking, shuffling, sprinting towards me? Real in their invisibility? Or invisible rats with long legs and gold-green eyes? Smiling, sadistic rats? Would that happen? What wilderness world would be there in Sydney? How could I get to Jerry if I fell into some molten reality and couldn't take it? Would I burn to death, deep swathes of darkness spitting fire at me as I cringed and coiled? Curled up tight like a dying baby?

I boarded the plane. While my head was poised for mania and devastation, my heart knew that this was a move I had been dreaming of and planning and waiting for.

And we flew. The terror stayed away. And there was Sydney at our feet. We had walked into the cryptic foreign land.

Chapter Eleven
Across the Ditch

The plane carrying our line-up of eager, twitty New Zealanders landed and got processed, and we checked into two rooms at the Squire Inn, Bondi Junction, which was over the road from the Bondi Lifesaver nightclub; a convenient position because this was to be the venue we would be playing at that night. Tim, Crombie, Eddie, Croth and I all crammed into Room 416. Two beds, three stretchers. Salubrious rock'n'roll accommodation. The others—Dave Russell (our tour manager), Murray Ward (soundman), Wally and Juddsy—were a floor above. I can't recall ever going to their room. Why didn't I ever catch the lift up and drop in on them? I don't know the answer. Maybe they all slept in a double bed and we just weren't prepared for that confrontation.

When we went to the suburbs to pick up the Hush sound system for our debut gig, it wasn't there. The Hush dudes knew nothing about our using it. They'd never heard of us. I looked at Tim, who looked at Juddsy, who looked at Dave. We had to flag the Lifesaver show. On the way back to the hotel, weaving through the miles and miles of Sydney streets, we read a small press mention in a music rag. It heralded our arrival as 'New Zealand's raunchiest rock'n'roll band'. Tim looked at Juddsy and Juddsy looked at me and I looked at Dave. On our return to the Squire Inn, Dave went mad trying to find a sound system.

While he was distracted, we took in Sydney and found it to be loose, fast, bent and full of semi-derelict and submerged life-forms; an extraordinary contrast to the staid, plain and protected social structure back in Auckland. Pornography had flooded in, and newspapers bulging with hard-core sex were lined up at corner shops beside the *Sydney Morning Herald* and the *Women's Weekly*.

Prostitutes lined Kings Cross; it was at its sleazy height. Teenagers in hot-pants and fishnets lolled around, their eyelids filled with lead; a few metres away, the squinting eyes of a pimp with slicked-back hair and a wide collar. Light brown loafers shining out from under his shimmering turquoise flared slacks. You didn't want to catch his eye. There was a song on all the radios called 'Girls on the Avenue' about these pathetic lasses. To this day, and on to tomorrow, I'm sure, if I hear it I am back at the Cross aged 22. What an age to be filled with wonder.

None of us seemed to talk about our female partners left on the rocks of New Zealand. Maybe the whole social strata of pop music bandhood and partners was too much to be real. To be manageable. It was easy for Tim. He didn't leave anyone behind. Juddsy had left a wife and child. For me there was Paula, and there were other names for other band members. They were out there somewhere, on the other side of the ditch.

Right here on the wide perimeters of interstate highways and hippy footpaths with meandering groups eking out a living, well . . . there was a neat, balanced contrast. Metal-flake, V8, pot-bellied bizzaro clowns and gangsters scoured the inner-city borders with mile after mile of flag-waving second-hand car yards and that wasn't all. The cars were advertised on television as well, phones were push-button and the hi-fi shops stocked exotic, slick machinery. Music instrument stores displayed the world's best guitars, amps, drums, et cetera. It would be some years before New Zealand joined the party. Back at the Squire Inn, we lived on cereal and Vegemite sandwiches washed down with continuous cups of instant coffee and non-dairy whitener stolen from the maids' trolleys.

I had some decisions to make. Each time I had fallen into the mode of fear and terror, the panic attack, I vomited. Surely there was a reason. Did I have a physiological dysfunction? I must have. Let's start somewhere. So I stopped eating when day turned to night. No dinners. None. 'That may well ward off this horrendous illness of the head,' I thought. I'm a scientist. I'm an Engineering Science graduate. I must *know* something! I decided to try it. I started losing weight (well, of course). I also stopped drinking alcohol, in case that set off the terror. I mustn't be triggered.

After about two weeks we got our shit together and had a gig booked at the Bondi Lifesaver. We planned to wear the zoot suits. Cool. My special yellow suit. And after the wait we would be ready.

As the Squire Inn was so close to the venue, we changed into our costumes in the hotel rooms and ran across the road looking like madcap freak children, smiling, whooping and hooping, through the door of the Lifesaver to wait that short time for show time. Well, I didn't. I hurried back to the hotel room, turned the key and ran to my camp stretcher. I lay on it staring at the ceiling. The invisible spiders moved across the floor, pouring over my body. I screamed. There was no one there to query it. The fear and terror did their usual sadistic bitch. Heart racing, racing, racing. How many bpm? Maybe 160? The fastest yet? Thoughts in my head speeding round and round. Could I hold one for an infinitely short duration? I couldn't. I had to get back to the show. What will I say? How can I not go back to the show? I had to get back to the show. My heart was screaming. *Get back to the show!*

I ran back out the door, down the stairs and out into the street, my yellow zoot suit shuffling in the Sydney breeze. I went into the changing room just as they were all walking onto the stage. As I joined them and walked between them, over to pick up my bass (flatwound strings), I was suddenly free. Whoosh! I felt perfectly normal. It was as if nothing untoward had happened. There was nothing the guys could see in me that told them what I'd just been through. To repeat myself—I was free. And we started the show and we were very, very good. We had arrived.

The crowd got off on it. On us. Split Enz over from New Zealand. I looked at the others in the band, those beautiful boys from across the sea. The intense, circling lead singer Tim, the slow-swaying master Juddsy, the Eddie man with his lightning fingers, the Crombie flaying the crowd with tricks and mysteries, Croth flying across the drum kit, his hands electric, and me. My Gibson Les Paul bass, my saviour. I wasn't holding it; it was holding me. Embracing me. Keeping me from harm. Here on this Sydney stage. All of us: from a world that was not the place to be. New Zealand. I thought, 'I just need to stay onstage and I will survive.'

One thing quickly became clear to us. We had to stay in Australia by whatever means possible and just go for it. We had to relocate to this Australian environment. Hence a number were sent back to New Zealand to sell cars, gather or not gather female partners, close rent on flats, et cetera. I became more and more screwed into whether or not I would actually live long enough to be the bass player this band needed when the big time hit. The niggling fear seemed to be ever-present except onstage. Not eating at night seemed to confirm my self-diagnosis and most nights I could relax, despite being in the hunger zone. But I just couldn't deal with matters of real life like girlfriends and cars, so I left it all hanging and refused to let it toy with my head.

Crombie, Tim and I wallowed in the Squire Hotel waiting for the rest of the band to return so we could start doing more shows. We sat up in the restaurant when it was closed, as they had a piano there. It was up there that Tim took an old piece he'd written from 1972 and stretched it out. It ended up becoming 'Maybe' once Juddsy returned. We also dealt with boredom in a cool, productive fashion by deciding that everyone should use their middle names. (I've been using their middle names already in this book, so you'll just have to go with me on this.) As a means to grapple with the dull throb of another day and a seamless garment of tawdry nothingness, changing to our middle names seemed—well—OK. And it happened. When he returned Juddsy didn't change his from Philip to Raymond, though, and I don't blame him. I took on Jonathan but wasn't enamoured of it. It went back to Mike in due course!

Otherwise we swam in the Squire Inn pool like some

English pop band who has had a global hit and is killing time in the sun. We did find the Sydney climate to be very appealing. And Tim came up with the title for our hopefully-one-day-to-be-recorded album: *Mental Notes*. I thought that was very cool.

And then, lo and behold—one day they all returned. Dave, our guy on the spot, had a date booked, so we clambered into this vehicle or that vehicle and the next thing you know we're onstage at the Coogee Bay Hotel and Michael Gudinski, the main man of Mushroom Records (the main man of the whole Australian industry), is in the audience. This was outta sight.

And how did we play? It may best be summed up with this loving little tale. After we had finished, a lad by the name of Ted Mulry came backstage. He had had a few Aussie hits. He's worth googling. He looked at us all, sweating and breathless, and said, 'Holy shit. There are only two bands I've ever seen where I couldn't take my eyes off them. One was The Beatles. You're the other one.' *Aha!* We all talked in silence (our speciality) about how this might be the moment when Gudinski walks in the door. And he did.

Well, it wasn't actually that night. It was a few days later. But he offered us a recording contract and we took it. We didn't think about it. I don't recall having a lawyer advise us. We just said, 'Yes!'

The month of May was set aside to record this album that we had been dreaming of recording for what seemed like an eternity. We had barely been in Australia for 30 days.

And then Gudinski rang again. Roxy Music were flying in from the UK and doing a show at the 5500-seater Hordern Pavilion in Sydney and we were booked to open the show.

This got us thinking. Roxy were top-class. Big hits. High-level stuff. Of course we wanted to support them. They might stand side-stage and watch us. Which was exactly what they did.

The more we felt their eyes on us, the better we played. We pulled out all the stops. Back in the dressing room, prior to Roxy taking the stage, their manager and their guitar player Phil Manzanera came in. This time we had voices, we had language. And Gudinski was poised and hearing it all.

Manzanera expressed an interest in recording us, but after details were put on the table it turned out he wouldn't be able to be a part of the *Mental Notes* sessions. A scheduling issue. This was a real pity. The recording of a debut album here in Australia with a Roxy Music man at the helm would have really woken up the Australian industry and we would have had a head of steam when the album came out. But it wasn't going to happen.

The next best thing came to pass. Manzanera and his manager set aside time in 1976 for Manzanera to produce our follow-up album to *Mental Notes*. That would be in London.

We didn't really analyse this suggestion. We put our faith in fate that the commitment would, well, just work out. And it was to be in *London*. The centre of the universe. We were in! Everyone shook on it, and Roxy Music flew away.

In a week we found ourselves down in Melbourne, where Gudinski had booked us into a concert called the Reefer Cabaret. This was the left field. The avant-garde. The stoners. We were ready for them.

We felt at home, and were able to muster the old buck-a-head sense of presentation. Crombie had turned playing the spoons into a concert highlight. Tim was the Harlequin and he sped from side to side. Juddsy was projecting his almost rigid stage persona and many eyes never stopped staring at him. Wally and I in our matching costumes played our parts, side by side. We'd been together on stages for three years, from an empty RSA hall in Pakuranga to the Hordern Pavilion in Sydney. We'd been on stages together for what seemed a long time now. How long is three years? Croth tumbled and flammed. Eddie shocked them with his gargantuan talent. It was us. Split Enz performing at its height. To the right audience, down there in Melbourne town.

The press reviews spoke volumes. The following from *Juke Magazine*:

Kerrist, they're madder 'n us. Leaping about the stage, pink suits, blue shirts, red suits, long legs, short legs. Doll faces, human faces, new faces. Cackling, screaming, leering, bounding, jerking, lurking, always prepared to pounce on my poor nut. Pictures of the giggle palace thrashed through my scone.

In Split Enz you will find classical and neo-classical; music hall honky tonk and sleazy vaudeville; acoustic and electronic, good ole rock 'n roll, a piano full of cool jazz and some Gregorian chants or Calypso shouts for good measure.

We had a resurrected James Dean, [Judd] white-faced and hollow eyed in a teddy boy suit of bright red . . . the lead singer [Finn] moves like a sped-up movie of Charlie Chaplin doing an imitation of Harpo Marx—or is it vice versa? He comes on with a patter that sounds like *Waiting For Godot* done by a music hall M.C.

In that show, we transcended the 'curiosity' status formerly bestowed upon us. It was a turning point. We were still adamant about holding an inimitable position in this very active, commercially driven market, but we realised that it would be impossible to spend weeks planning one-off extravagant and theatrical concerts. We were going to have to play hotels, cafés and clubs because we had to eat. So we developed, very quickly, an extreme presentation in which each of us hid behind a fanciful disguise, cloaked in one of Noel's extraordinary costumes.

In New Zealand we worked outside of any system if only because, when it came down to it, there wasn't one. But in Australia we were confronted by managers with quick tongues, record company people (we had never met any in New Zealand), agents, flared jeans, roadies, Mandrax, coke, trucks, overnight drives, schedules, Polaroids, Mogadon, t-shirts, Quaaludes, blotting paper and abuse. The only aspect we rarely came up against was groupies. We were plain and sexually impossible to categorise, so best *left alone*. So we rebounded into ourselves, seeking out a collective sense of purpose to avoid being part of this menagerie. And New Zealand slipped into the past.

The *Mental Notes* recording sessions started not long after the Reefer Cabaret show. It was 8 May 1975. We were at Festival Recording Studios in Pyrmont. Richard Clapton had recorded 'Girls On The Avenue' in that studio not long before. We all knew what a hit that had been. Maybe it was hit time for us.

It was all systems go. We were brimming with expectation and a fair quotient of paranoia, which had leaked into the band's psyche over that time. We had limited recording experience but wanted to create a masterpiece. We were all worried about how it was going to turn out.

The rhythm tracks kicked off reasonably well. Within three days, my Gibson Les Paul Recording bass, Croth's drums and Eddie's basic keyboards were down. Then started the overdubs. By now it was clear that the engineer was uninterested in the whole exercise; it would not be unusual to find that he had literally gone fishing. Damn. Why didn't we insist on another one? No one knows the answer to that question.

Juddsy, in a stroke of opportunism, rushed in after the rhythm tracks, recorded his vocals and was done. He then followed that with a colourful array of guitar parts that he had concocted, and was able to clock out of the studio and into the control room. Smart move.

The follow-up sessions were fraught with problems. The guitar overdubs found Wally sweating in a tiny room with a huge Marshall amp screaming out, while in the control room it sounded more like a twanging rubber band. Over and over he would play, and a sense of jinx set in.

It got no better when Tim came to do his vocals. After one session he wrote home: 'Well, it's been a tortuous week. The tension and nervous strain have been unbelievable. Because we have waited so long for this album we've been striving for perfection and any imperfections that have arisen due to musical fumbles or emotional traumas have appeared worse than they actually are . . . I feel very drained of energy.'

I watched all this evolve. Everything turning into slow steps. Slow steps forward. I had finished my parts. I sat in the control room watching the repeating spools of tape recording the same thing over and over again. The more someone recorded themselves, the more they seemed to get it wrong.

And then—I knew it was going to happen. Maybe I made it happen somehow. One day, I had to get out. I was suddenly trapped in there. I avoided everyone and went and sat in the reception area. For a while. Then I took off and started walking down the street; a street with no hedgerows. It was under a motorway bridge and heading east. I walked and walked and walked. I didn't look at anybody. I sidled past department stores where you could buy one-kilo blocks of Rocky Road. I passed a shop selling Ferraris and Maseratis. They looked alive in there with their spotless paint. I sped up. I went through the Cross. More hookers. Pimps. Deep-fried food that could kill you. Junkies lying on the grass in the feeble, small parks dotted here and there. I went as far as I could. Through the Eastern Suburbs. And I kept on walking into the surf at Bondi Beach. I fell under the waves.

I had escaped . . . but from what? Was my subconscious (my head) telling me to keep going? 'Keep swimming, Michael.' Across the Tasman Sea. Back home. But my heart kept me stationary. Still. Lifting me up on each wave and falling down with it and driving me back to the beach. Returning. Returning. The dim glaze of the sun filtering through the surface. Like hundreds of small underwater lamps cradling me.

I stayed in that surf for over an hour. Then I got out and bought a towel, dried off in the sun and caught the bus back to Bondi Junction, where I lay on my camp stretcher and wondered. That's all I could do. I'd already done my wandering. Now I wondered. Why? What was driving me? How could I know?

I could go and see a psychiatrist. But I didn't. I didn't tell anyone what was going on. I must have thought, 'How can they understand?' But really, I didn't talk to anyone because I was so embarrassed to have brought this deeply foolish life upon myself. I was a buffoon. A wretched, slowly wasting, wasted bass player in a really good band. Let's leave it at that.

The *Mental Notes* sessions reached their conclusion with a vague sense of security about what was 'in the can'. They were our songs. We'd played them. From the songwriting flow of Juddsy and Tim and the moulding and orderly business of our not-so-orderly imaginations, *Mental Notes* existed. And then we all packed our wobbly suitcases for a flight back to New Zealand.

Chapter Twelve
Mental Notes

B arry Coburn had booked a New Zealand tour of town halls and major venues and it was looking like they would all sell out. Von and Jerry were very taken with those 'House Full' signs. The 'Mental Notes' tour would have a mid-June launch, and the album would be in the stores all a-ready to be purchased. Except that this wasn't to be. The record company couldn't get the album out until after the tour finished, so you could come and see us play but not buy our record. Ah yes—the bumble-footed world of the Split Enz fruity machine.

I awaited the first show with peace and quiet in the beautiful Aucklandness of life. And I caught up with Paula, as did some of the others with their others. Men and women— the infrastructure that hovers just out of reach for a band that runs through nations like hyenas. And then we left town to take our songs to the public.

It was a gas. The halls were full. We wore Crombie's new black-and-white costumes. Mine had big black circles on it. Maybe Crombie knew something. Were they reflections of my black eyes? I don't know. I was just glad that as the tour evolved I seemed able to ward off the attacks of terror when I was out there night after night in the protective cradle of the stage. Maybe not eating was the answer. Better to starve to death than die in a lunatic asylum.

But the looming threat of the terrors was always there. I had to talk to Jerry. Even if it just came down to anaesthetic capsules every night! There he was in his study. I walked in. I thought, 'It's now or never. I need to do something.'

'Jerry?'

He looked up from the album's lyric sheet. 'Yes, Michael?'

'I've been having problems lately onstage. It's stage fright, I guess. I'm up there and I get nervous and it's starting to interfere with my bass playing. Do you have any suggestions?'

It was far from the truth, but it was the best I could do. How could I explain to him that I was filled with terror at odd times? That I feared I had fried my brain with acid and these attacks were the result? That, in fact, the time when I was onstage was the only time I was guaranteed to feel calm?

'Well, I do,' Jerry replied. 'I could prescribe you a drug called Serepax, which is a calming drug, really. A tranquilliser. That should help. Shall I do that?'

'Good thinking, Jerry. And how often do I take them?'

'When you feel you need them. Can you tell when you're going to get nervous?'

'Generally,' I lied. 'It's probably something that will go away the more often I take the stage.'

And the next afternoon I had a bottle of yellow pills in my pocket. I took one straight away. And waited.

I fell into a weightless dream. All around me lay the dead spiders who in their prior lives had cased my joint. The hawks and vultures were gone. The rats had been lured away into a cave. In the side of a mountain.

I thought about the trip back to Australia and decided it was going to be a groovy and cool thing to do. Yes, I would stride onto that plane.

And I thought about food. I was hungry. I was always hungry. If I had eaten in recent times I would have been at war, my head and my heart tearing at each other. My head telling me to stop this deeply stressful Split Enz caper and just lie low. The heart reminding me in no uncertain terms that my life was dedicated to this roller-coaster ride, this spinning merry-go-round. A commitment had been made in stone to a life in rock'n'roll; it was that life I was riding.

I went out and bought a hamburger from Al and Pete's, the local burger joint. It was delicious.

In July we packed our bags again and headed back to Australia to play some more dates and promote the album. I made the very clever and scientifically self-proven decision to take a pill each morning with breakfast and each evening, about two hours before sunset, to defeat any potential night-time attacks. And how did that go for me? I was the dreamiest, most laid-back and soporific band member in the whole of the world. (Well, that's a lie. A whole screed of Mandrax addicts were waiting for us in Australia, but that's another story.) I felt my resistance to the attacks strengthening.

I looked out the plane window as we flew into Melbourne and smiled. I did still wonder what illness I had. Was it a simple case of brain damage from drugs with classic madness to boot, and would I be like that till my last breath? The Serepax kept it at bay. But it was there. Waiting.

We had decided to set up base in Melbourne because we felt that city suited us better than Sydney—it was a much more happening place for a band like ours. The music scene was more trippy and we had genuine fans there. Also, both Mushroom Records and its booking agency arm, Premier Artists, were based there. Soon after our arrival, Premier turned up the heat and some shows in pubs (mainly) materialised. Night after night. Show after show. And I never had an attack. I smiled the internal smile of a gently stoned bass player, sliding along through life on a tranquillised travelator. I found myself sensing things in slow motion. Watching Tim's now brilliant role as the ringmaster. Sometimes his rush across the stage appeared to be such that his feet failed to meet the ground. His beautiful high notes slowly spirited themselves to the four corners of sweaty, grimy rooms like the Sundowner pub in Geelong, and I could watch them travel. Watch them fall into the punter's ears. Lucky punters. Lucky us. Lucky me. I was drifting in a pleasant world.

Eddie, Croth and I lived in a house in Elwood, Melbourne. We had secured the tenancy by saying we were post-office workers—inane really, but maybe the landlords had seen us at the Sundowner pub and thought we were fabulous (which we were) and they liked the idea of having a pop band in their house. No matter. In between gigs, which was about two days off a week, I would sit on my bed and look out the window. Sometimes I would play a cassette of Richard Clapton's album *Girls on the Avenue* and dream of the beach he sang about on one the tracks. Byron Bay. It sounded perfect. The song was 'Blue Bay Blues'. It held me.

When it finished, I would go back to looking out the

window. It was a window with opaque stripes on it. Lightly coloured. Not frosted glass. Some other glassy thing. I would often fall asleep. Serepax was good for that.

Once I tried to write a song, as I felt that somewhere in my life an attempt at songwriting should be brought to fruition. I recall very clearly the day I did it. I was playing an acoustic guitar, which I do in a fairly amateurish fashion. I thought of a chord sequence. Maybe that's what successful songwriters do. They must. I'd never talked to Juddsy and Tim about *how* they wrote songs. Why not?

My chord sequence went G Bm Bb Am7 D7. I thought that sounded very flash. Well it does, because it's the opening chord sequence of Paul McCartney's 'Here, There and Everywhere'. So what? He'd never know. Then I thought if I wrote some lyrics they would fall into some appropriate melodic place. So I did. Here they are:

Yes, you're right. There aren't any. I couldn't think of any.

And then the postie came. There was a letter from New Zealand from Paula saying that she was pregnant. I looked at my page of lyrics. The blank sheet. The guitar was resting on my knee. Eddie was tinkering on a keyboard out there somewhere down the hall. My eyelids felt heavy in the tranquilliser zone. It was around 5 p.m. Heavy eyelid time.

Paula was pregnant with my baby. This meant respon-
sibilities. Nappies. Feeding. Stories like Jerry used to make up.
'Slow Sammy'. And records like the ones on the Children's
Request Session. 'The Enchanted Trumpet'. 'The Laughing
Policeman'. 'The Noisy Eater'. And so on. I could do all that
stuff. And I presumed a wedding went with the array.

I got a blank aerogramme and wrote a reply to her
suggesting we get married. She should fly over and move in.
We should get that family wheel turning.

And that's what happened. A date was set in September
and I became a husband. Tim was best man. We had a
one-night honeymoon in a Melbourne hotel, and the next
night I was back onstage playing my bass at a University of
Melbourne gig. And then, the next night, another gig. Gig
after gig. And no panic attacks; I was sure-footed, in my sleepy
fashion. I knew what note to play next. Luckily for me, being
a bass player, I only had to play one note at a time.

Time passed. And it all became a grind.

Mental Notes failed to ignite the populace. We had our core
fans, but that ensemble never really expanded in numbers.
And the source of new songs dried up. Where were they? The
purity and excitement of the Roxy Music show and the first
buck-a-head were fading. And I could see Juddsy struggling to
find his role on an electric rather than an acoustic guitar, with
Wally over there beside me spinning out his own lines. They
didn't merge their parts. It became a random blur. It didn't
work. Something had to give. Someone had to go.

So what did we do? Did we call a group meeting to discuss
this, with the agenda: 'Where is Split Enz at right now? Are
we satisfied? If not, why not? And what moves do we need

to make to get the mojo back? Should we work hard on re-arranging the songs so that the two electric guitars work along a carefully constructed, melodic, rhythmic and chordal pathway? A highway where the songs shine through, not a dirt road where the instruments all tumble over each other?'

Did we call that meeting?

No.

John Hopkins, our tour manager and general fix-it chap, was asked to go round to Wally's flat and fire him. And he did. And Wally was gone. And to this day, this minute, I am saddened by our pitiful role in that. So we then became a five-piece band? No. Someone rang Rob Gillies and he flew over and he was back in the band. Rob blew trumpets and saxophones. They wouldn't clash with Juddsy's electric guitar.

Rob's first show with us was at a Christmas Reefer Cabaret. The fans: the connected stoners and night-time trippers. We triumphed. We slayed them in the aisles. There was only one electric guitar. Juddsy's.

I should have been confused and troubled and maddened and distraught by all this. But I was drifting in my haze and thinking of going to England to record with Phil Manzanera and wondering how you folded flannel nappies and realising that hit singles are the key to the lock but we had never had one and would we have to go to a Catholic church for our wedding and so on . . . but it was all couched in a tranquil afternoon snooze, a nodding head in the van driving down to the Lorne pub or sifting fragments of dreams from the refugee light that made its way in through windows from a blazing Australian afternoon. I couldn't find the headspace to be concerned about anything. Numb.

J uddsy wasn't convinced about the band, in parallel with what I guess was probably a whole band confusing themselves. As 1975 turned into 1976, he announced that he was leaving. That was 3 January. On 5 January he said he wasn't. And we flew off to Perth for three weeks of pub gigs.

The temperature was nudging 40 degrees the whole time. We took to the stage in the cool, air-conditioned comfort of crowded bars and lounges. I ate alone every day in some bistro at our hotel, having king prawns while porn played on a television screen. Kind of weird, really—they should have had a big sign outside: *The Porn and Prawn Bar!*

Word had spread across the outback—we were an OK band. There was rushing here and there to get to places, and it all seemed frantic. All in all, we were really just wanting to get to London town and record this second album with Phil Manzanera. The sessions would be in April. And what till then? As long as Jerry sent the pills so that I never missed my daily fix—well, I'd be OK. I could snooze on the big plane as it flew back to New Zealand for another national tour.

This one was called 'The Enz of the Earth'. We had a brand-new set of costumes. Mine was principally orange. I loved it. From the minute I put it on I became another person. A bass player cocooned without and within.

I knew my notes. We started with '129' and I played a deep D. D is a key I love to play. I started 'Walking Down a Road' with a C sharp. A chromatic climb up to D sharp. That wasn't difficult. But no one else was doing it. Just me. On my new bass. A Madill. Standing on these big stages across New Zealand, we were able to expand. To widen our stance and stride the stage because we owned it. The small pub venues across Australia had shrunk our reach. Sure, at some west Sydney dive, Tim still filled the room with his singing and rapport, but the rest of us were squashed, if you get my drift. We didn't spring, sway and slide like we knew we could.

But now we could. Here in Aotearoa. We felt we knew these New Zealand people: all enthusiastic and poised in front of us. Often (always) before shows I would peek out from the curtains and eyeball them. Who were they? What were they expecting? I wanted them to be taken aback with a joyous impact, a cannon (canon) of sight and sound aiming directly at them. Every individual Split Enz fan, each curious wanderer, each golden member of this collective multitude sensing they were somewhere special.

The tour rolled out across New Zealand. How did it go? Here's the review from *Hot Licks* magazine of our show at His Majesty's Theatre in Auckland. It had been less than two years since we first played there.

I can only comment that my dimmed hopes of July 1975 turned to absolute jubilation when Split Enz gave the finest rock concert I have witnessed in Auckland since Roxy Music last year . . . Split Enz are certainly the most conceptually evolved and sophisticated group to come [*sic*] this portion of green world . . . I'm sure the world is their private oyster and I wish, hope and know they'll do it all the way. Thanks for the vision, thanks for the trouble and thanks for the time!

TOP The Chunn family, artfully posed around the dinner table in 1974. Seated (from left) are Jeremy, Jerry, Von, Derek and Geoffrey. My sister Louise and I are standing.

ABOVE In the Pavilion at 9 Hutton Street, Otahuhu: (from left) Geoffrey, me and Paul Fitzgerald.

TOP Winners of the group section of the Walter Kirby Music Competition, 1969, in the Sacred Heart College assembly hall. (From left) me, Tim Finn, Geoffrey, Paul Fitzgerald and Paddy O'Brien. SACRED HEART COLLEGE

ABOVE The first Split Enz publicity shot, December 1972. (From left) Mike Howard, me, Miles Golding, Phil Judd and Tim Finn. JULIE JUDD

TOP Split Enz in November 1974, photographed at 473 Parnell Road. (Back row from left) me, Wally Wilkinson, Paul Crowther, Phil Judd and Eddie Rayner; (front) Noel Crombie and Tim Finn.

ABOVE Split Enz plays the Auckland Town Hall in June 1975. (From left) Tim Finn, me, Noel Crombie and Phil Judd. TERRY FONG

OPPOSITE TOP Tim Finn onstage at His Majesty's
Theatre, Auckland, December 1974.

OPPOSITE LEFT Me in my full stage makeup,
England, 1976. GIJSBERT HANEKROOT VIA GETTY IMAGES

OPPOSITE RIGHT Phil Judd onstage at Auckland
Town Hall, June 1975.

ABOVE Split Enz on tour in New Zealand, June
1975. (From left) Tim Finn, Paul Crowther, me, Noel
Crombie, Wally Wilkinson, Eddie Rayner and Phil
Judd. ALEXANDER TURNBULL LIBRARY, *EVENING POST*
COLLECTION, 1/4-022755-F

OPPOSITE TOP The launch of the Mental Notes album at the Albion Hotel, Auckland, June 1975. (From left) Barry Coburn, Eddie Rayner, Noel Crombie, Tim Finn, Phil Judd, Paul Crowther, me and Wally Wilkinson. MURRAY CAMMICK

OPPOSITE CENTRE Rehearsals at 473 Parnell Road for the first buck-a-head concert at His Majesty's Theatre. (From left) Geoffrey Chunn, Tim Finn, me, Rob Gillies, Eddie Rayner, Wally Wilkinson.

OPPOSITE BELOW (From left) Eddie, Geoffrey, me, Rob, Tim and Wally.

ABOVE Phil Judd on tour in Australia, 1975.

LEFT Somewhere in England, 1976. (From left) Noel Crombie, Tim Finn and Eddie Rayner.

TOP Paula Sheahan, circa 1974. We were married in 1975.

ABOVE Playing video games with Nikko, circa 1982.

And then we flew back across to Australia for the 'Enz of the Earth' tour there, but it was a mere shadow of the victorious New Zealand series. The agency had too many tours running. There were major inefficiencies, and on arrival from Auckland there was no one to meet us. We cancelled shows in Newcastle and Canberra that were looking shonky, but we forgave all when our old home, Melbourne, turned on a full house at the Dallas Brooks Hall. The tour finished on a high note. This concert epitomised the standing we had in Melbourne, and it focused how supportive that city had been of our development. From our first visit there—when punters took the time to absorb our music and tolerate our bolshy stance—right through to the full houses, there had been a tangible endorsement. Without that initial support, we might well have perished.

Chapter Thirteen
Prams and Second Thoughts

I was focused on something else besides my busy band. On 31 March 1976, a son arrived to Paula and me. We called him Nicholas. (He is now called Nikko.) He looked like Mr Magoo, but they all do. Even Grace Kelly did. His eyes staring at the ceiling, his arms akimbo, his legs kicking up and down. A baby.

How do you be a bass player in a band flying around the world *and* a father of a child who doesn't? I needed to get my soft brain to gather its thoughts somehow. Mind you, there was virtually no time. Five days after his arrival I boarded a plane to London. Paula and Nikko would follow two or three months later, and they would find in London whatever I could find first, which was an unknown quantity of nothing in particular. We all imagined soaring into the air of professional grandeur as the new album took hold out there in the marketplace. Touring: Europe, Australia. Hey— even South Africa and Canada! The USA? So would Paula and Nikko wait patiently in London as we all disappeared? Why not stay in Auckland? In essence, though, it was all simple. In the short term. None of us had any idea what was waiting for us except the gentle, amiable frame of one Phil Manzanera.

But I did know what we were taking with us. A seven-piece line-up of musicians, singers, songwriters and characters that knew what they were capable of. A group who knew the tricks and dynamics of the stage. Individuals who had laboured in the Australian sun, dug trenches through miles of rocky countryside with our spades. A seven-piece army of intent. Ready to walk into Basing Street Studios in London and make that glorious album. The studio used to be a church. Jimi Hendrix recorded there. This was going to be our real Mass on Sunday.

And there we were at Heathrow. There was no one to meet us. We waited around for three hours for John Hopkins to turn up. He didn't, so we climbed into iconic London black cabs and started rolling.

I was settled and dreamy. This was a cool symbiosis. And I sat still, gazing out the cab window.

London was the City of Dreams, literally. We were uplifted. The streets, like Snakes and Ladders, perpetrated the easy rise, easy fall of this city of allure. The city of hit songs, Waterloo Sunsets and Harold the Barrel. People were selling England by the pound. The city of *Melody Maker* and *New Musical Express*. Wimpy burger bars with bright red awnings to ward off the autumnal rain. And coolster Londoners with pearl-handled gossip. Archways, lanes, church towers and columns. The bells of St Martins. Long lines of brick terrace houses with eager faces behind the front doors and cups of tea on windowsills being lightly sipped as they, the hovering mob, all waited patiently for the Split Enz emergence. The footpaths waited patiently for a warming sun, not far away, so that they could shine in cleanliness and draw the public out of their two-up two-downs and into the parks. And the squirrels would watch them all. Everyone smiling. I was smiling.

We arrived at Basing Street Studios and met up with Phil Manzanera. He was on his home turf. He was relaxed. I knew that feeling.

Recording was to start on 19 April. In the interim we found accommodation. I was in a house in Streatham with Croth and Peter, our roadie. He'd come over with us from Australia, and used to stir the sugar in his tea for so long, with its incumbent *clink-clonk-clinking*, that Croth and I would run outside and dive under ten-ton buses to escape it. (Not really.) I did go outside and wonder where we were, though.

We were in SW16 and there wasn't a tube station close by. But there were buses sliding around. I could hop on one of those.

My bedroom was on the first floor, the biggest in the house, and some time in June three people would be in it. I had received letters with photos of Nikko. He was still pretty much a Mr Magoo.

I was a father. I felt that fatherhood, motherhood, parenthood, childhood—these things should be planned. How was I going to fit this into the compressed life of a bass player in a busy band? A band that was a spinning wheel in a stagnant pond; a thrashing, strait-jacketed amphibian in a viscous atmosphere of questions and confusion. A world where grown-up men seemed to be the ones who controlled our lives and much of that through indecision. We weren't those men. We were boys. But we knew how to play. So I picked up my bass and plugged it into a little Vox amplifier and played some Dennis Dunaway lines from 'Halo of Flies'.

My window looked out onto the street, but more interestingly it also looked out onto a park of trees in which squirrels played out their skippy, jaunty lives. I envied them. Tranquillisers don't make you skippy and jaunty. They keep you just numb enough to avoid a panic attack. I missed being skippy and jaunty. My enthusiastic nature was becoming mellow, blunted. Maybe I could balance the Serepax with tiny doses of amphetamines? Then I could die like Judy Garland. And I could have the rush of spiders coming at me.

Silly thoughts. I hadn't had an attack for some time. But the drugs certainly slowed me down. That's what they were meant to do. How long would I need to take them for? Presumably forever. How long *should* you take them for? But as I trundled along on the double-decker bus to Basing Street Studios all I could think was, 'I better play some good bass today. We can't have Manzy [as we came to call him] thinking, "He's a B-grader!"'

I have great memories of laying down the tracks. 'The Woman Who Loves You'—that was a challenge. But I got it. I could have written an easier bass part—one note every two minutes—but I wanted to show off. Isn't that what got this whole thing started in the first place? Buy an instrument, learn it, play it and then show off!

Dunaway and Cornick popped up. 'Too fucking right! You tell 'em, Chunny. We been watching you spank the plank. You've cottoned on to how this works. No one else does 'cos bass playing is a mystery. You have to be some kind of magician. One note at a time? No fucking way.'

Michael Gudinski, who had come over to try to do us a deal, was busy with all this. After some interest from Island Records fell over, he started chasing Chrysalis Records, who had a cool history with the likes of Jethro Tull. They liked the recordings but wanted to see us live. *Yes!* They put us on as support for their act Gentle Giant in a theatre in Southampton. As we drove in I could see the grey, greasy docks and the docksiders. The seagulls. The cranes. Over there in mid 1953, Von (pregnant with Geoffrey) and I had boarded the *Dominion Monarch* to sail to New Zealand. It took six weeks. Luvverly. But now I was here for a different purpose. And we walked into the Gaumont Theatre.

Up on the stage I stood on my spot and thought about who had stood there before me. Certainly The Beatles. There was a photo in the green room. But everyone else too, it seemed. The Who. The Rolling Stones. Genesis. Jimi Hendrix. Maybe even Engelbert Humperdinck. Val Doonican? No matter. We were joining the long list of the dedicated, and we had better be good, as record-company people were putting us under the microscope.

We obliged with a fabulous show, our costumes keeping us moulded into that unified force. And so it came to be that Chrysalis Records signed Split Enz.

In keeping with what was usual, they took us out to lunch. The Chrysalis lads outlined the path ahead and projected a release date for the album of the second week of August 1976. The first step, they said, was for us to secure the services of an agent as, without one, we would be stationary. No agent; no live work. So we all put that thought in our heads: agent!

We found the Chrysalis guys to all be enthusiastic chaps

with public-school airs and gentlemanly graces. No ties, but cool pink shirts with button-down collars. The atmosphere seemed potent. The tone of the soirée was lowered rather when I ordered steak tartare. (Any of you done that?) In my extreme ignorance I was expecting an agreeable rare slab of hot roast beef with dollops of tartare sauce in the vicinity. On being presented with what looked remarkably like a high-quality uncooked hamburger patty, I wrapped it in a napkin, put it in my coat pocket and fried it up when I got home. It was a haute-cuisine hamburger right there over the road from the squirrels. I imagine they scurried over, having never savoured such a high-class odour in their bushy-tailed lives. And they almost certainly stood on the window ledges watching me. Fruitlessly.

And then the recording sessions began. Oops-a-daisy. There was something missing. We played methodically, correctly. Quite a number of the songs we'd recorded before, and as any true aficionado of life in a pop band will tell you, once you record a song it sheds its outer layer of fizz and freedom. It almost says to you, 'Don't record me again.' But we weren't listening. And we charged on.

At least there were a couple of events to buzz us. One day the studio door opened and Brian Eno (who by this time had left Roxy Music and had become a bit of guru record producer) walked in. He addressed Manzanera.

'Phil, guess who just rang me? He wants me to work with him in Berlin. Record a new album.'

'Who?'

'David Bowie.'

Sheesh. That got us thinking. If I could have looked into

the future I would have seen myself in three years' time at Western Springs stadium in Auckland watching David Bowie singing 'Heroes'.

The other cool moment was when we somehow secured a gig at the Nashville Rooms on Fulham Palace Road. Sitting at the front table were Manzanera, Eno and Kevin Godley from 10cc. That spun our wheels. I stood up there thinking that we were now masters of the stage. And that it was a pity we weren't masters of the studio. But there you go . . .

When the album (which Tim had titled *Second Thoughts*) came out in the UK we received a fair splash of media in the rock press. That was pretty much it. Sales of the album were meagre. In the end, it seemed that the emphasis was more on how we looked. We had reached the pinnacle of made-up faces, bizarre haircuts, Crombie's costumes and so on. It seemed to me that the media thought we'd gone overboard. *I* thought we'd gone overboard.

I looked at our photo in the *Melody Maker* rock magazine. Who were we? Why were we? What were we? When the punters listened to 'Sweet Dreams' or 'Time for a Change', did they see us as we were portraying ourselves? Or some skew-whiff parade? I wasn't sure about it all, but I decided to let time go by and leave fate to intervene. I was drifting on my own private stream of cool, clear water, much like the Lady of Shalott except I was yet to be dead. As long as the terror attacks stayed away I could enjoy, or feign, a comfortable happiness. I knew the pills were a shield, a damp blanket thrown over my true self. Maybe it was only a matter of time until the weight of that protection became too much.

Chapter Fourteen
The Mother Country

There were two things that happened next to our band, there in the iconic climate of global pop-music triumph. Both equated to a turgid nothingness.

First, the heatwave of 1976. It was incredible. Rolling around the 40-degree mark, we slept with damp towels draped over us. We tried to find coolness. We failed. I received a telegram from New Zealand; a postie knocked on the door in Streatham and handed it to me. It was from Jerry. It said: 'But screw your courage to the sticking post and you'll not fail.' I loved that man.

Second, as the Chrysalis mob had told us, 'You have to have a live booking agent to get you gigs, otherwise you won't get any.' Chrysalis told John Hopkins that he *had* to secure the Cowbell Agency. They had listened to the album and said 'No!' Stalled.

There was a third matter. My son Nikko turned up, aged two months, with Paula and moved into our Streatham flat. I had bought him a cot. He seemed happy in that. We walked on the common. It suddenly occurred to me that this was England. England England England. I was in a band on a global search trying to be one thing and a father trying to be something else. Not to mention the matter of retrieving a semblance of sanity in the swirling insides of my head.

Might I board an underground train on the Happiness Line and go round and round and round until a smile as wide as the English Channel saw me alight and alert on a station like Charing Luminous Cross? Or could I catch the 137 or the 419 bus heading southwest, and might the oak trees of Clapham Common march on over and sweep me in their branches and make everything come true? And what truth might that be? I could lie asleep under Westminster Bridge and dream of a future that wasn't planning to destroy me.

Chrysalis Records wanted to promote our album. No, we weren't performing anywhere. We didn't have an agent. So they hired the Marquee Club in Wardour Street for 19 August 1976 and on that day, during the afternoon, we went in with our guitars and sticks and costumes and all that palaver and stood on that stage. It was mesmerising. The Marquee was where Jimi Hendrix destroyed the puffed-up, egocentric English brigade of guitarists in one night nine years before. It was 1967: the summer of love. Jeff Beck, Jimmy Page, Paul McCartney et al. were there. They witnessed the coming of the most unique guitar player in the history of humankind.

I stood on my spot, just beside Croth's kit (as always) and stared at the scuffed, ragged floor. Which of those footprints were Jimi's? All of them, I suspect. And with that legacy, with that sense of holding on to something that truly surrounded us, we played to the Chrysalis invitees; the media layabouts and laggards who stayed out in the foyer with their free drinks; the European snoopsters and nosey ones desperate for a scoop; the UK trade mags . . . The big wheel of publicity—no, of trying to get publicity—was the primary focus of the Chrysalis machine. And, well, they did fairly well. Around a dozen interviews were held after the show. All with Tim, in essence. A touch of Juddsy. A smattering of Noel. And the audience. The Chrysalis team let us know who had come to see us. Which members of which bands, like Kevin Godley from 10cc. That was cool. If you're going to strut your stuff, you want the competition out there checking you out. That's par for the course.

Those musicians who stared at us, knowing full well that we had brought them something special, all seemed to be happy with what they got. Unfortunately it appeared that our performance wasn't enough to make them all resign from their esteemed positions in the game of rock'n'roll.

How best to sum up that night? Here from a Croatian music magazine: '*Split Enz su potpuno čudno i tako čudno da mi je skočio gore i dolje i pio previše.*'

Got that? Here's the translation: 'Split Enz is totally weird and so strange that I jumped up and down and drank too much.'

And then the album was released. We got reviews. Here's one from *New Musical Express (NME)*.

Split Enz are preserved from aesthetic obscurity by their compulsively droll humour and exacting musicianship. The band's two writers, Tim Finn and Philip Judd, have chosen as theatre of operations a curious environment: the baroque and the berserk, alternately reminiscent of early King Crimson, Genesis with Gabriel and Roxy Music.

I read that sitting in a greasy spoon in Crystal Palace. I was having fried eggs, liver and fried toast. (I had recently had a pill, so eating was on the agenda.) I thought to myself, 'That review is cool. They got it right.'

In the end, all the toing and froing and probing and sublimating of the public relations world of the country that had won the Battle of Britain and all that led to our album bubbling away in a simple broth of neglect. Ah well. Shall we record another one? Then it was just a matter of looking out over Streatham at the squirrels and wondering, 'What next?'

I'll tell you what next. We fired Croth.

We *what*?

We fired Croth.

OK, so our motley crew had no live work. There had been a gently humming, inconsequential response to our album (an album none of us thought had anything extra special about it), and there was the grappling with life as parents that Juddsy and I were trying to cope with. Well, what do you do? Normally in life you all get together and talk about the stagnation, the dragging to a halt, the foggy future. (I've alluded to this concept before.) But not us. The decision was made to fire Croth. And the job of doing that was given to me. Why? Because they (we) were all pathetic and I guess, if you have to look at this practically, Croth was flatting in the same house as me so . . . give it to Chunn.

I will never forget that event. Every fraction of every second stays with me.

Croth was sitting in the lounge working on some electronic thingamajig, which presumably was connected to something Split Enzish like a synthesiser. Croth was (and is) an electronics genius. I sat down across the table from him. He looked at me. I told him the band wanted another drummer and, well, you know, er, um, the time was right for another drummer and, you see, er, um, ah.

The look in his eyes. He was being fired. And his face told me that he knew that there wasn't a good reason. He knew that someone had to be a scapegoat for our tawdry, fuckwitted existence and it was to be him. I felt like one of Stalin's henchmen advising some simple member of the proletariat that they were about to be shot.

Then Croth was gone. Not too long after that he flew home. What were we thinking? For Christ's sake!

The next day a small bottle of Serepax arrived in the mail from Jerry. I could continue my restful and ordinary journey through life.

But then we got the news. We had an agent. And no drummer. The Cowbell Agency decided to contract us and live dates came pouring in. Like flies on raw meat. In they came. And what about this missing drummer? Too bad. Cowbell booked us on a national tour supporting the Geordie band Jack The Lad. We were going all over the place. We had eleven days to find a drummer. And we did. We fashioned an audition process of the most amateur nature and ended up with one English lad called Malcolm Green.

I thought back to the first buck-a-head and my time onstage with Geoffrey. He should have been here on that kit, here in London town. But he wasn't.

Then the tour began. My small bottle of 'keep Michael calm' pills were close at hand. So far, so good.

The Jack The Lad tour gave us an escape from all things mundane. Jack The Lad had fans and they all turned up to the shows. Sure, none of them knew anything about us. We were used to that. So we charged out and turned up the gas and truly impressed them all.

There was no indication or sense, however, that this would lead to anything. Fans of a Geordie band weren't going to suddenly become fans of a band from way over yonder. A band that rattled their day-to-day. Their complacency. And, while we never talked about this or anything else, we did seek solace—nay, release!—when it came to the last show of the tour, which was in front of 3000 punters at the Manchester Free Trade Hall. That was a cool place to walk out onto, by the way. The Beatles had played there in 1964! But it got better. Some of us took our clothes off.

During our encore Jack The Lad ran onto our stage in their black-and-white Newcastle football jerseys and all played the spoons. Why? Because we were wearing our black-and-white costumes and all playing the spoons. They had invaded our turf because they were larrikins. It was very funny. Hold that thought.

During their set we devised a complex routine whereby various Enz members walked across the stage during the final Jack The Lad number, in progressive stages of undress. The climax featured Juddsy, Mal, Eddie and me running naked through the lot of them, clutching underwear in case we were tackled by the lithe Geordies. They didn't get us.

After the show we drank Guinness and sparkled in the

glow of a successful tour. It was with a hint of sadness that we farewelled our hosts. And we awaited the release of our second album, the reworking of *Mental Notes* for the UK market that would be known as *Second Thoughts* in our part of the world.

I sat sleepily dreaming on the drive back to London. Why can't we just tour the world for ever as the support act for Jack The Lad? They knew what it was all about. They enjoyed life . . . as long as Newcastle won their footy games!

On arrival in London we were advised that the Cowbell Agency had put together a vast array of university gigs for us. We had recently recorded the only new song that had come through in 1976, titled 'Another Great Divide'. Not exactly a positive title. And it was scheduled as a single release. Once again, ye olde Split Enz had come up with a song that was anything but a single. Not that we talked about it or planned it or discussed 'what exactly *are* the components of a hit single?' The madness of this was that we all knew what a hit single was. We'd been listening to them forever. They are like all the thousands of hit singles that have gone before. Therein lies the answer. Surely. So? So what!

'Another Great Divide' slipped away without a trace. We were in a hole. The punk era had arrived, and the likes of The Damned, Sex Pistols and so on were sweeping bands like ours over a cliff.

We could have made quick, subtle shifts in our whole ethos. Maybe Juddsy and Tim sat in their town-house working out some plan. If so, I didn't hear about it. No one was to blame. Maybe everyone, including Chrysalis Records, the Cowbell Agency, the music industry and the Queen, thought punk would just slip away once the winter snow came. Maybe. We could always wait and see.

On 24 November, we kicked off the thirteen-date headline tour of universities that Cowbell had put together. Because of the high cost of hotel accommodation, we would more often than not return to London after each show. Consequently, we were in a van, wrapped in coats and scarves against the cold, driving up to twelve hours a day. I was usually falling asleep as lamp posts flew by.

I don't believe any of the other band members knew I was surreptitiously taking tranquillisers, most often on a couch in a green room that had no one else in it. A corner of a theatre. And the attacks? I could hide them very well. I could pretend to be asleep. The inert image of a bass player. 'Is he asleep?' The stable covering. Tousled hair over a teeming, terrified mind. And the more it happened, the better a phantom I came to be. A ghost.

Occasionally, wobbling on another van journey, I would lift my head and look through the windscreen at some approaching city. The first sign would be a grey, insipid haze on the horizon and then the sharp, defined edges of the factories, smoke stacks, wire fences, brick walls, funnels, pipes and gushing steam of some county metropolis emerging, advancing like a frame from a medieval Marvel comic. It might be Sheffield or it might be Hull. Preston, perhaps. We came upon Bury St Edmonds. Was the next town going to be Destroy St Albans . . . followed by Smash St Farthings? Did anyone know where we were? Who was driving?

I never offered to drive, as I would have drifted off into a tranquil sleep, sending them all slicing through trees and barbed-wire fences on the outskirts of English castles. Was this the M1, the M4, the M3, or the M64? Was there an M666? Were the doughnuts in the next service centre going to be stale? Was the coffee real? Were the toilets locked? Football hooligans loaded with darts ready and waiting?

There was an inherent humour in the proceedings, but Juddsy and I had a subdued though growing concern. As parents, we weren't overly enamoured of the time we were spending away from our families. We just didn't have any plans. For a band member standing squarely on the ground floor of one of the world's most gigantic music industries, a family can seem invisible. Where are they? They're over there. They can't take to the road in the vans, jostling up and down and spinning round and round. They just—stayed in London. But really, as I've said, they should have stayed in Auckland. Home. Juddsy must have been thinking these things too. But . . . well, I don't know. He and I never talked about it. (I could ring him now and ask him. Maybe.) These thoughts flew around the van and then sailed out the window. And the British nation rolled by.

We went to one city that met us with a sweep of sheer beauty. On the Welsh coast we savoured the history and timelessness of Aberystwyth. As if to emphasise our sense of satisfaction, the local university students gave us a resounding reception in a setting that was pure Dylan Thomas. I can't remember now if they clapped for ten minutes and we played three encores, or if they clapped for three minutes and we played ten encores. Whatever; it was a moonless winter night in a 'small town, starless and bible-black'.

I should have left the band and started a three-piece Welsh folk band in Aberystwyth. I could have got a deal in a cool ancient bar where I got free board and meals in return for playing five songs on Sunday nights. Ah, bliss. A thought. But it faded as we rolled onto the M4 back to Blighty.

The tour ended on 11 December with plenty of ovations echoing in our heads but no money in our back pockets. Oh well. And then Chrysalis advised us they wanted us in the United States in early 1977 to promote the new *Mental Notes* by playing a raft of showcase concerts in clubs and the odd theatre. A chill went through me. The United States? OK, the United States.

But first Michael Gudinski had booked us on an Australasian tour, all over New Zealand and Australia. We had to earn some money, as we had been scrounging off Chrysalis Records for some time. (They call this advance royalties. They can slowly strangle you.) Let's get home! Juddsy and I saw our wives and children off on the big silver bird back to New Zealand on a freezing day in late November.

We ourselves closed up flats, packed suitcases and boarded a plane to Melbourne on 14 December. I was sweetly numb as I walked onto the flight. I don't remember who I sat next to. (I remember who I sat next to on the flight *to* London: it was Eddie. We listened to Debussy's 'La Mer' on the idiotically antique plastic-pipe headphones.) I had received a postcard from Von and Jerry a few days before wishing me all the best for the journey.

As the plane lifted off the ground I watched the drops of rain scream along the window beside me. London vanished under a sheet of icy water. Would I miss it? Would I look back on 1976 as the breakthrough? No. What had it been, then?

It was the year when the fifteen-minute epics that fell under the English progressive rock banner vanished and, in a sympathetic vibration, we looked likely to follow. In my mind (and in my life), the progressive rock era had enveloped me, had enveloped us all. We had come up with musical works that were bloody inventive. 'Stranger Than Fiction'. 'Under The Wheel'. But always at the back of my brain was the three-minute pop song. Lurking. Poised. Waiting for its moment. The towering achievement of three-note hooks and quick-flick stories of life and love that drew us in. 'We Can Work It Out'. But we didn't work it out. It had become too much.

Once upon a time, in January 1973, Juddsy and Tim had brought new songs to every single rehearsal. Here in 1976 we (was it 'we'? Was it Juddsy? Tim? Who was it?) came up with one song and it was as much a hit single as the first single by every unknown band we've ever not known. (God bless them all.) And now we had the United States waiting for us, after the Australasian tour. California, Texas, Georgia, D.C., New York, Massachusetts, Illinois. Unless some of us couldn't take it and fell to the ground. And then—after America?

The twisting streams of rain were still on the 747 window but slowly heading into slow motion. I was going to be safe on this flight. Two pills down. Dreams to follow. Dreams about our band. We were a band out of time now, but we were going to play the game. That was enough for me to drift off to sleep. Surely.

The Australian and New Zealand tours that went under the title 'Courting The Act' were a gas. There's nothing like leaving a freezing nation such as England where a modicum has been achieved but, really, a record company is left with a bunch of bills and little confidence in the act they signed. They can't have thought they were onto a winner. We hopped off the plane in Melbourne and thought of the present and walked onto stages all over the place.

One thing that worked in our favour was the presumption that the UK media coverage we had achieved meant we were on a roll, and the Australasian media lapped it up. They wanted a good-time, this-band-is-making-moves story and they wrote that. And people read it. So they bought tickets to the shows.

It was thrilling to witness. The halls were full. We were crossing the finishing line and breaking the tape. The Australian tour was a triumph. And then to New Zealand and two full-house Auckland Town Hall shows.

The first show found us in our Medieval suits. I became another person again (mine was like a dress, but I liked it). We all did. And as was always the case, Von and Jerry were two or three rows from the front, taking it all in. A cool sight. What were they thinking? Envious? I think so. They'd never walked onto the Town Hall stage. They never thought they could. It was a magic place and somehow or other their son and a bunch of other likely lads had not only made it up there but also put a bum on every seat. They were smiling.

At the Auckland Town Hall the next night, I have one spectacular image of two guys aged about twenty going completely berserk during the ending, the tail, the coda of

'Another Great Divide'. Yes, that single had stiffed all over the world, including the Antipodes, but somehow enough people got to know it so that when we played it the crowd was energised. Frantic. Those two lads reminded me of Neil Finn and brother Derek at the Elton John concert. The looks on their faces. The motion that was triggered. It was a crowning moment for me up there on that stage which I'd dreamed of playing on, way back at boarding school. Simple images of old that had formed in my imagination over and over, most often when bored out of my mind at Sunday Mass. Kneeling there, imagining. And now those images were real.

I also thought back to the days when audiences walked out on us. The struggle of 1973, yet here we were three years later killing them in the aisles! In New Zealand. In Australia too. Maybe it really was a matter of time. Keep doing shows year after year and the force builds.

But Tim and Juddsy's minimal songwriting was now a focus for us. Only one new song was written, recorded and performed in England in 1976. And here on the cusp of the next year we were looking at a virgin territory where the pop music machine was huge. How huge? What did we need to do to make an impact? Play just like we were doing on the New Zealand tour? Was that enough?

Chapter Fifteen
The Land of the Free

On 30 January 1977, the seven of us farewelled family, wives, partners and children (except for Robert, who had his wife, Geraldene, with him, and Noel, whose partner, Raewyn Turner, was now the Enz lighting operator) and flew to Los Angeles. I hated leaving Auckland. Why? I didn't know. But it was real. A simple, thoughtless fear just lodged itself in my brain. A tension. A sustained echo of terrible things. All out of focus. I was increasingly tired of trying to analyse it. I was mad and, fuck it all, I was to blame. So there.

I took two Serepax from the large bottle of pills that Jerry had given me while I was visiting them at Parnell Road, and off I flew. I farewelled Von and Jerry at the front door. Why were these departures so superficial? They must have thought, 'What the hell is all this about? Why is our son a skinny, dour shadow of the jumping and skipping kid of days gone by? Is it worth it?' But I never thought too much about what they believed, as I didn't want to know if they thought it was slowly killing me. I had a bass to pick up and a stage to walk onto. Up on the stage my attacks never happened. Up on a stage I could live forever. (If only.)

But I always had to walk off the stage, and go somewhere. Like the United States of America, the Land of the Free.

As we walked off the plane in LA I glanced at our shuffling team—our group on an adventure. None of us had any expectations. We must have appeared like a tribe of lost young men looking for something called 'success'—in whatever form that might present itself.

We had a Chrysalis Records reception party and a fleet of stretch limousines waiting for us. Is that 'success'? And we drove off down the freeway with FM stations blaring, televisions clicking off and on, cocktail cabinets opening and shutting, electric seats swishing to and fro, electric windows zooming up and down, electric sunroofs sliding back and forth, heads popping out to scan the wide vista of palm trees, and rows upon rows of enormous, clunky American cars driving beside us as if in a silent pilgrimage to nowhere. Karl Malden from the television show *The Streets of San Francisco* was in the next lane, his gaze blank and fixated, his spongy nose a dead giveaway. A small whirlwind of cigar smoke was spinning out the top of his electric window. I watched it spiral into the sky, where it was lost in the brown muck hovering over our heads. The ceiling of this polluted town. We couldn't see the Hollywood sign.

We checked into the Hyatt on Sunset Boulevard. Jerry used to talk about the movie of that name, and I thought of him as I caught the lift up, up, up. Once suitcases had been tossed onto beds, we, in mercurial fashion, all ended up on the roof sitting in the lazy sunlight, under the pale blue sky, around the swimming pool. The water in it was faded blue too. On the other side of the pool were the members of Electric Light Orchestra. They were 'in town' as well.

I looked at them. They ignored us. But then they probably thought we were ignoring them too. Rooftop politics. They had hit records around the globe. We had none. That swimming pool was the Great Divide.

I dived in, and as was (is) always the case I drifted to the very bottom and lay there. A bottom-dweller. The perfect place to not be human any more. To disappear. Mind you, I ran out of air and surfaced soon enough, and then we all went back downstairs.

On our beds were media/promotion itineraries. Upon reading, we knew this was going to be one organised six-week trip. Screeds of radio and TV interviews, record-store appearances and so on. And then the list of shows we would be doing. We were to start in San Francisco and finish six weeks later in Chicago.

Tim was always at the front line of being interviewed. I would often tag along because there would be free coffee and food. Sorry, but yes, it was a plan in action. One of the first interviews was at the Magic Mountain syndicated radio station that went across multiple states. We were walking along the cool, air-conditioned, purple-carpeted, posters-on-the-wall corridor when we were introduced to two kids who were being interviewed after us. The little one had a handshake like warm plasticine. His name was Michael. His older brother was Jermaine. The Jacksons.

At night, I'd put on clothes that fitted our 'point of difference' dictum. Stovepipe trousers (Jerry's in fact), black leather shoes, a white shirt and a thin black tie. (Yes, I was being a Beatle circa 1964.) The rest of the band looked equally away-with-the-fairies, each in their own we-don't-give-a-damn parade of colour and shape.

Radio-station people would sit down and join us. They all looked like they bought their clothes from the same shop as Farrah Fawcett-Majors. This was the era of heightened '70s kitsch, of loud mouths and relentless hyperactivity.

LA was a society languishing in sex and coke. Aids was what you did when you helped somebody cross the road. *Charlie's Angels* was the hit TV show. The West Coast ethos was overdrive. You could feel it all around you. Our Chrysalis tour chap would take us driving now and then to get a break. We slipped past 10050 Cielo Drive, Benedict Canyon. A sign at the front said 'Entry will be met with armed resistance'. That sign wasn't there when Sadie Mae Glutz and her Charlie Manson friends crept in back in 1969. The end of the golden era.

We also dropped in on enchilada joints and maple syrup diners and one-stop Doo-Drops and a Dickey's Barbecue Pit. The Twisted Root was one that caught the Kiwi eye. There was a definite feeling that these Los Angeles people thought of us as simpletons. We thought they were lunatics.

Sitting in the ground-floor coffee bar of the Hyatt one smoggy afternoon I was gazing out the window while Tim coped with a journalist from *Teen Date* magazine who wanted to know why we were so zany, spoony, daffy, flipped-out, doltish and Corybantian. Malcolm McLaren, the manager of the Sex Pistols, walked past in zippers and safety pins and winked at me through the window, one short, fragmented piece of body language that said many things. Presumably one of them was, 'Get ye out of this place, Kiwi ignorami. Regroup, refocus, shake off that wrinkled façade and return to conquer!'

It was him all right. He knew, I guess, what we were in for.

We had our first taste of the Chrysalis promotional thrust when we were presented with a gimmick that they were sending to all media. It was a clay model of Noel's head, with holes on the moulded hair for planting grass seeds. You were then supposed to water it and watch Noel's freaky hairdo materialise.

This gauche marketing ploy was presented to us at a Chrysalis restaurant dinner to which they had invited some major radio honchos. The blonde, large-breasted, wide-cleavaged thing escorted in by one particular ham picked up Noel's clay head and exclaimed, while eyeing one of Noel's pointy clay-hair prominences, 'Am I supposed to suck it?' I forget what the food was like.

The first show was in San Francisco, so we drove up the Ventura Highway and onwards. Juddsy was driving the Chevy I was in. As always I was in the back seat. In the middle. It seemed the 'right' place to be. Protected. Demure. Bashful. Like one of the seven dwarfs. Would San Francisco and Chicago be the bookends of a life in miniature? Here a highway, there a road. Is that a lane? A dead end? Two-lane blacktops or concrete freeways. I looked at the itinerary for details. We were flying everywhere once we finished in LA. Well, that made sense. This was a big country.

We prepared ourselves for the first show at The Boarding House in San Fran. The tickets were subsidised by Chrysalis at only $4; we wore the black-and-whites and walked on to a full house.

What is it, when a moment predicted as mundane turns into euphoria? Confronted by 300 San Francisco residents who, over the years, must have seen and heard it all and more, I anticipated a struggle. It was not to be. From the first note they beamed with delight, whooping, laughing, intense and wide-eyed; at the final, crashing chord of 'Another Great Divide' they rose to their feet, shouting and cheering. And we were only halfway through the set! We had scooped them up and taken them to another place.

The real spirit of the performance came from our desperation at the whole Los Angeles media focus on haircuts and zaniness, wackiness and silly clothes. Here, tonight, we were going to prove that we could overpower the whole theatrical monster we had created and drive home a bunch of songs that would prove our musical worth. Songs—words and music—that we loved. And we did.

Backstage after the show, a long-haired chap with a Stetson hat walked into the changing room and exclaimed, 'You guys are good. I want you out of town by sunset!'

'Mumble mumble . . . ha ha . . . mumble mumble.'

'You guys know who I am?'

Noel replied, 'You're not anybody if you don't have our record.'

Presumably the bass player for The Tubes grooved on the flippancy. (We didn't know his name, but apparently he was Rick Anderson.) He hung around. We liked him. He was tall. The Tubes had hit records.

The next day in the breakfast room of the hotel, surrounded by fake palms, blueberry short stacks and bottomless coffees, we read the *San Francisco Examiner*.

> Last night at the Boarding House as they played I wondered why this septet, calling itself 'Split Enz', monkeyed around the stage like a collection of idiot robots. But popular music has always had more than its share of pseudo-freaks, the down-groups, the anything-for-a-buck (and maybe success) ensembles . . . Tom [*sic*] Finn, vocalist (with the most ridiculous of hair arrangements) prattles on endlessly between tunes, spouting silly poems and making like a Shakespearean jester . . . Better the embarrassingly contrived dance steps and amateurishly handled lighting effects had been lost.

Shortly after, Tim went on a TV show. He was all in costume, made up and his hair coiffed, quaffed and quaint.

Interviewer: 'About your hair?'

Tim: 'Yes, it is *about*, isn't it . . . an approximation of a hairstyle that I'm working towards.'

'How would you describe your music?'

'Neoclassicosmoidalcosmeticmental rock.'

'You oughta try a little calamine lotion.'

'I don't know what that is. We don't have that in New Zealand.'

'Classy group . . .'

There it was. That media focus was neatly maintained by the US behemoth for virtually the whole tour. And Tim was always in the firing line. How would he deal with this? He would make it through. He knew exactly what was going on. He had always had the *quest* written in his head.

In San Francisco, I was asked by the local Chrysalis rep about Tim. How did he find the energy for all this?

'He seems permanently alert!' she said.

'He was the halfback in our first fifteen,' I said. 'He directed the play. The ball went where he decided it should go.'

'I don't know what you're talking about,' she said.

I was OK with that. I was really talking to myself. I was finding confidence in that man. My old classmate. He could do it. Radio, TV, record companies and all their bullshit or cynicism; sceptical in-jokes.

There was only one place where we were held up high: the FM radio stations that broadcast contemporary, new music. New Zealand was still seven years away from having FM. I sat in a car with a Chrysalis rep listening to 'Stranger Than Fiction' as it was played on the radio. I was deeply moved. All the flim-flam, passing traffic and buses and sidewalks of people, heads down and full of purpose or lost in their meanderings—none of them mattered. A radio station on the US West Coast was playing our song. It was magical. It was the only time I ever heard one of our songs on the radio.

During the next stop in LA for shows, Tim walked into the lift of the Hyatt, where a gent with a London accent put out his hand and introduced himself.

'Hi, I'm Ray Davies and I'm a fan.' Ray Davies. The Kinks.

Davies spoke to Tim about how he liked the album and that he had friends, serious music lovers, who liked it too. He suggested to Tim that when he was next in London he look him up. Tim walked off to his room a few centimetres above the orange, purple and mauve carpet. When Tim told me, I was high on it too. If Ray Davies thought we were OK then we must have been OK. But then I thought, 'We know we're OK.' We were just on a treadmill, and it was coming down to how we were presented on broadcast media. And we made it easy for them to take the mickey out of us.

Over the previous twelve months, as the pressures of realising whatever it was we were striving for—*fame?*—bore down on us, we put on more makeup and hairspray and turned into wags and jesters while failing to extend our repertoire. We were arse about face. Apart from cool FM radio, which I suspect had very small listener numbers, the rest of the United States knew nothing about us.

But that didn't stop our golden horde from charging on. We played three nights at Huntington Beach. Juddsy left the stage during one of the shows—he said his guitar was out of tune, but he'd left to seek refuge. I could see it in his eyes, his not wanting to be up there. Up there in his painted face and clowny suit. The great contrast: on that stage was the only place I felt safe; he felt vulnerable.

We had three days to kill. Sight-seeing? What's that? The Chrysalis lass, Linda Steiner, knocked on our door at the Hyatt.

'Hey, we've got free tickets to the Blondie showcase gig at the Roxy tonight. Their first LA show. You want to come? Another new band, Tom Petty and the Heartbreakers, are supporting them.'

Juddsy looked at me and I looked at Juddsy. We both

declined the offer. It seemed a simple thing to say, 'Ah, no thanks.' It seemed almost necessary, as I'm sure it was for Juddsy. Just to stay put. Keep still.

While the rest of the band went to the show, we watched television. There was a beauty pageant. The host asked one of the potential queens, 'If you could, how would you make the world a better place?'

She stared at him. He stared at her and kept his cool. There was silence on the television. They were staring at each other. Juddsy and I were staring at them. There was silence in our hotel room. Real silence. The queen-to-be never said a word. She was frozen in her stage fright. Juddsy and I just watched it. She left the stage in her dumbness and presumably went back to her small condo in West Hollywood and cried the night away.

I turned the TV off. We both wrote postcards home. I didn't tell them that I had said 'No' to the Blondie and Tom Petty concert, with its free tickets and best seats in the house. I would have had to tell them the truth. How I deeply regretted that decision. How I knew that going to that show was what you should do. And all I'd achieved, in this nondescript, tasteless hotel room was to fall further under the tidal wave of fear and exhaustion that my life had become a target for.

I took another pill so I could float above this freaky town and lift myself into a beautiful, dark space high above. Or was it down below? I guess Juddsy did the same thing in his own way. He had a small bottle of brandy. I could see him sipping away at it. He never saw me slip a pill into my mouth.

Why were we unable to talk to each other about the inner wars we were engaged in? But then, when did any of us ever talk? Did we subconsciously think, 'If we talk we might crack open the thin shell that surrounds us and holds us together. And all of us will fall out into a vacuum and suffocate in a matter of seconds. All die on the rugged treadmill that we are currently trying to stay on. Possibly. Probably.'

How to talk? What was talk? We were Tweedledum and Tweedledee. And the next morning we awoke and just got on with it.

Next day we flew southeast. We scraped through small, diffident crowds in Houston, although having Boz Scaggs turn up to watch us was cool. And then Dallas. Things were going awry.

At the Texas Opera House, Juddsy would stop playing at seemingly random moments, and his guitar parts took on an increasingly abstract tack, trembling and reeling as if out of control. A window into his turning mind, I thought. He was by now failing to sing with Tim at all. Tim was seemingly unable to confront Juddsy about this, and drove himself onstage like a fanatic, clamping his eyes shut and pounding the floor.

Once again, Tim's despair was contagious. That was the thing about him—his emotions ran wide like a net and it was impossible to avoid being scooped up in it. When he was cooking, we all cooked. And when he was down we would find ourselves struggling to stay afloat. The power of the man.

The next stop was Atlanta, Georgia. Four nights at the Great Southeast Music Hall; two shows a night. Another Holiday Inn to lie on your bed in. Somehow I got a room to myself. Paradise. I turned on the TV. A soap opera. I turned it off and turned the radio on. A Christian station. The evangelist was after money.

I turned it off, went downstairs and we all went off to the gig. Over the four nights we were lucky to get more than six people a night. One night there were two. Tim called out, 'You having a good time?' in his best Lynyrd Skynyrd scream. Both punters sat there and said nothing. Tim screamed back, 'Well we are . . . and majority rule.' We laughed about it backstage. We also reflected on Juddsy leaving the stage during the second show.

The morning of the third day I woke very early and went outside. I saw a taxi (cab?) and hailed it.

'Is it far to the Peachtree Center?'

'No, son. Hop in.'

The glistening shops and skybridges of the Peachtree Center were of the future to this skinny kid from New Zealand.

I wandered down the sidewalk. The place was virtually empty except for two Greyhound buses going in different directions. Should I have hopped on one? Just sat down with a transistor radio in my ear and slid along Interstate this and Interstate that while patiently waiting for a place where I wouldn't need to take tranquilliser pills? Could I find such a place? Both Greyhounds went on their merry way, leaving me behind.

A steel-and-glass building was in front of me. Someone walked in and disappeared. Where were they going? What would they do when they got there? Did they own oil fields? Did they own a string of gun shops? I saw a 24-hour café and went in.

'A bottomless cup of coffee please, and a plate of grits.'

The coffee was certainly bottomless, as I had five cups. The grits? I won't order grits again.

I sat there. I thought about Chrysalis Records. I would have loved to have been a fly on the wall of their marketing meetings: 'This Split Enz band is just sheer hard work. What can we do with them? No one's buying their records because they're not hot!'

Hot? No—we weren't hot. It's not enough that Boz Scaggs comes to see you in Houston and an FM radio station in San Francisco plays 'Stranger Than Fiction'. And the New Wave was coming up over the horizon. It was 1977. Blondie, Talking Heads and the English mob—The Jam, The Clash, XTC, et cetera. How could we head them off at the pass? I guess we'd have to make decisions.

I can make decisions. I ordered a sixth cup of coffee and looked out the window as more and more people passed by. They all had flared trousers on. There was bad fashion on the move down both sides of the street. A lot of platform shoes.

I looked down at Jerry's black leather shoes on my feet. Maybe Texans thought I was a priest. A professor of Classics. A nobody. Maybe I should go back outside and drag some cheerfulness from these people. Draw it out of them.

The morning sun was warming everything. No need to be ceremonial about it. Take it with a flick of my moppy hair. Say 'Good morning' to people. Listen to the footsteps. Give the shoddy, shabby beggar a dollar note. A greenback. Watch him spend it as fast as he can. God bless him. There he goes; a slouching outcast with an extra dollar to his name. And look! A pleasure-seeker with huge cleavage strutting on past, strutting on down—all at the wrong end of the day. Maybe she's going to the Great Southeast Music Hall to queue up for Split Enz tickets. She's urgent. She doesn't want to miss out. What's her name? Dawn? There is a dawn not long past, here on the sidewalk on this sunny day in this town with the passing parade with their clicking heels and shimmering hair and long, wide cars and taxis that seem to float off the ground.

A taxi?

I hopped in and went back to the Holiday Inn. And the day began.

H alfway through the second show that night Juddsy left the stage again. How often was this going to happen? I had an idea—'Let's talk about it'—so we did. Backstage. And not with Juddsy. It was a playground discussion.

'Is his guitar really out of tune?'

'Let's go and check it.'

So Eddie and I went out and checked it and it was in tune. But we all knew his guitar was never out of tune. Juddsy just wanted to get off that stage.

Eddie and I came back and like good lads, like on-the-ball policemen, we reported to Tim and the others: 'His guitar is in tune.'

Juddsy walked over and Tim stared, and in a slippery, sardonic voice half-shouted, 'Ooo! My guitar's out of tune.'

Juddsy punched him, a good right hook in the face. Eddie and I held Juddsy back. There were about five long, long seconds of silence. Seconds that stretched out. Seconds that let us all know the truth. They weren't seconds of a secondary nature. They were potent. And Juddsy burst out, 'I'm leaving the band at the end of the tour.' And he walked away. He was setting himself free.

Back on my Holiday Inn bed I just lay there. The TV and radio were off. No one knocked on the door. There was a true sense of something about to happen. What were we all thinking? Tim—he must have known that it was up to him. He would be the one to write the new songs. A band with no songs isn't a band. If you have no songs for a new album then 40 minutes of silence isn't going to sell very well. And the rest of us? Well, apparently there was another album to record for Chrysalis. Back in London. Buckingham Palace. The Queen. Lord's Cricket Ground. Squirrels. The sun setting at 3 p.m. The rumbling tubes and grinding double-decker buses.

We might have been thinking about all these things. That may well have been the sum of the parts of our collective, tweety, foraging mindscapes. We were, after all, a bunch of twits. In the suppressed environment that we had somehow managed to sustain for so long, and with the external forces now so in control of our movements, Juddsy was unable to confront the situation and we were unable to help him. There was no one he could turn to and I believe he felt victimised. A scapegoat for the drudgery we were steeped in.

So Juddsy was leaving the band. No more brandy at midnight. No more crowds staring at him like some wacko prog-rock band member. What was he really? It was all writ on the stage at Levi's Saloon in Auckland. Those January 1973 shows where a purity of musical adventure was throwing out songs like golden apples to whoever was in the room, people who would carry them off in excitement and bravado to keep them in their heads.

It should have been like that forever. Juddsy must have wanted that purity. A life of songwriting and performance with no media nonsense. No record-store appearances, no vans scouring UK motorways and departure lounges day after day. But it can't be like that. It just can't.

The next day we flew to Boston, where Juddsy announced to us all that he was officially leaving. He would meet Julie and Amy in the UK and live there.

The rest of the band got together to talk about the 'next move'. There we were. A meeting. It happened!

We decided to follow Eddie's suggestion of asking his old Orb cohort, Alistair Riddell, to join us as Juddsy's replacement. Tim backed it but said virtually nothing. In earlier times, he would have been shattered. But now, weary with the struggle that this US trip had become and more confident in himself, in his ability to focus the direction of the band, he accepted it. There was no contemplation of an end to Split Enz by virtue of Juddsy's departure. There was a definite will among the rest of the band to carry on. Tim would have to carry the writing role on his shoulders. We knew he had the confidence to do it, I guess. Did I? Confidence? Yes. Stamina? . . .

The rest of the tour slipped by. There were nights when crowds in small numbers shifted aimlessly. And others, like The Bottom Line in New York, where as support to Polish comedian Henny Youngman (!) we played our hearts out, seemingly free as birds and without a care in the world, to an enthusiastic reception. And in Boston's Paul's Mall we nailed it. Maybe that was right. We were all facing, with certainty for the first time, a new frontier within ourselves. Instead of asking 'Why, why, why?', we were asking 'Who, what and where?' The uncertain future we faced on arriving in the States had been replaced by a different uncertain future; one in which the band had to change within, as opposed to just another reshuffle of the external circumstances it found itself bashing its head against.

In the meantime, there was publicity to be had. Linda Steiner—the Chrysalis promotions woman—Tim and I boarded the train to take us from Washington to Philadelphia, PA, on a clear D.C. day. I hadn't been on a train since Wally Wilkinson and I had shared a double bed on the overnight train from Auckland to Wellington for the filming of the *New Faces* heat in 1973. This time there were no beds. Just carriages of seats all worn and rugged, taking us on a nor'western route as if to stake claims on lands of brushweed and loblolly pine, a stone's throw from the Mason–Dixon Line or at the foot of snow-capped mountains hovering over Benjamin Rush State Park. Clearing the land so that sycamore and walnut trees might find root and climb to the sky. But I didn't know anything about trees or soil, so I stared out the window. It all came down to the simple, rewarding skill of analysis. Those backyard strips of fences, dogs and rubbish skimmed along in their deeply monotonous repetition. The blue sky found them sparkling in an almost appealing way, though a downpour would have turned them into their real, dowdy, abandoned selves. They never changed.

Onwards to Aberdeen, Maryland. All the houses were painted in tartan and the kids in the backyards were tossing cabers. I thought of Paul Simon's song 'America' and wrote a new verse for it.

Timmy, I thought, as we rattled through Elkton.

That'll do. A line. Not a verse. And there it was. The backyards of Elkton. It flashed and was gone. And then I drifted off to sleep. I was in a movie. *Strangers on a Train. Murder, She Said. Von Ryan's Express*. But I wasn't acting.

I have no memory of doing the radio interview in Philadelphia, but I do recall Linda asking Tim and me if we wanted to go to the ice-hockey stadium at the Wells Fargo Center to see Genesis in concert. We had VIP seats, and as we watched these English lads do their thing—without Peter Gabriel—we could see that they were in control, with musical dexterity and a colourful Gabriel hangover. I thought in a simple, impressionable, matter-of-fact way, 'What are they doing that is so much more advanced than what we do?' May I say that to you, dear reader? True— there were about 10,000 people in the stadium. And if we were to stage a concert in the same place, there might be 100. But the craft, the teamsmanship, the lyrics, the melodies, the musical prowess . . . I watched Tim watching them. I bet he was thinking the same. The climax of their show was 'Supper's Ready', from the Peter Gabriel-era album *Foxtrot*. I had first heard it standing in Alastair Riddell's outhouse with Eddie Rayner. That was 1974. Now it was 1977. A thousand years later.

At the end of the show Linda took us backstage to meet the band. We walked into the green room, which was cavernous. As I went through the door I looked across at their bass player Mike Rutherford, who was just leaving. He stopped for about half a second and our eyes met. He plays a Rickenbacker

4001 with roundwound strings. I think he knew which band I came from, but he wouldn't have known what bass I played. Then he was gone.

I looked around the room. There were French champagne bottles and acres of spring water bottles (Perrier?). Sandwiches. There was a peaceful, considered air to it all. What I would give to be Mike Rutherford. But maybe he takes tranquillisers all the time and fades into grey as the night closes in. Mind you, I bet he loved the stage. How could he not?

And the next morning the intrepid three of us returned to Washington.

A t Washington's Cellar Door club we peaked—the crowds gave us long, zealous receptions. Juddsy never left the stage early, and we played wildly and exuberantly, shaking off the stigma of Chrysalis's zany emphasis. We focused back on the material and fired. There was change in the air and this American tour was now just a ride. The natural development of Split Enz, from its beginnings at Levi's Saloon in Auckland to The Bottom Line in New York, had taken so long in so many different markets that we were now defeated. We had pushed the one particular concept to such an extreme that it had to explode. Implode? And Juddsy lit the fuse.

On 11 March, 40 days after our bubbly arrival at Los Angeles airport, I flew back to Auckland. We had gathered without Juddsy and decided that I would fly to Auckland and ask Alastair Riddell, whose Space Waltz band had shut up shop, if he wanted to join Split Enz. None of us really knew if he'd work out. But the thought of auditioning dozens of English rock guitar players filled us with dread.

Eddie and Tim flew to Baltimore to write songs at Tim's uncle's house; Juddsy and the rest of them sloped back to London. I don't believe we knew what Chrysalis Records were thinking. They would have been talking to Michael Gudinski, and I'm surmising that *that* dialogue would have produced a headache.

Off I flew. Two pills down, a panic attack held at bay and a dream looming. A window seat. As far as I was concerned, there was no one else on the plane with me.

Chapter Sixteen
Around the World in Eight Days

On the evening of Sunday, 13 March 1977, I caught a taxi into Auckland town. I knocked on the front door of Paula's family home and it opened. The father was back. A surprise arrival. Playing a trick? Something like that. 'Here I am!' That kind of said it all. 'How are you all?' Maybe I hadn't told them I was heading home. Details can settle into dust. I just didn't have much to say. I was on a diplomatic mission to find a guitar player. But really, I was back in Auckland because I wanted to feel that slow peace settle inside my head. Release.

The three of us drove along to Von and Jerry's on Parnell Road. I put my key in the door and walked in. More surprises. I was almost dead on my feet. But I had to move on. I was coming home.

Von and Jerry were mightily pleased to see me. Von told me that in three hours Geoffrey, Neil Finn and a couple of other lads calling themselves After Hours were playing at the Maidment Theatre as support for Waves, the new band formed by Graeme Gash. (Yes, these names keep popping up!) Deeply curious, I went along to the Maidment and walked in as they were starting. And there was Geoffrey: acoustic guitar and singing. Neil on piano, guitar and singing. Mark Hough on drums. Alan Brown on bass. And what was it like? It was remarkable. In a word, remarkable. Neil and Geoffrey had forged cool songs and the arrangements were engaging. The audience listened in absolute silence. They were almost as silent as the cowboy and cowgirl that came to see our own show in Atlanta, Georgia. (That's meant to be funny!)

I went backstage after their set and surprised them. I told them how much they'd surprised me. There was warmth in the air. They were curious about the US journey; I skimmed over it. Well, I told them about Juddsy's exit. That was good gossip, in their assessment. And I did tell them I was in Auckland to ask Alastair Riddell if he wanted to be our guitar player. And then I asked them some questions. I was curious about their 'where to next'. Where to from here, lads? And they pretty much skimmed over that. It was early days for them. You can predict, but you can't be sure. So you charge on, grabbing every stage and recording studio and any public attention you can get. As we all knew. You're on your own. And we left it at that. I was jetlagged. I was drifting off. I caught most of the Waves show—they were bloody good too. I slept well. And I woke on a mission.

'Hi, Alastair, it's Mike Chunn here. I'm back from the US tour and we have a question for you. Would you like to join Split Enz as the guitarist to replace Phil Judd?'

Alastair said he'd have think to about it. Consider it. I guessed that made sense. He'd have to consider many things. Putting on makeup? He'd already done plenty of that. Playing electric guitar with a panache of his own? He could do that. Would we want him to be a singer? He could do that. Other things? Help carry the speaker boxes from the stage to the van? Stuff.

I went downstairs. Alastair wasn't rapid in responding.

While waiting for Alistair to call back, I soaked up New Zealand. Although it had been only two years since I'd lived in Auckland, the country had changed considerably. Oil shocks had shuddered the economy; inflation, having spent decades as a simple, dull statistic for the Treasury, now burgeoned into the headlines. Each week price tags were scribbled out and another dollar or two added on. Muldoon was in power and the austerity resulting from protectionism, prohibited export of money out of the country and increasing unemployment all added up to a new buzzword—recession.

This of course meant that New Zealanders wanted some entertainment to soothe their stressful lives. The pub-touring circuit exploded and zigzagged across the country, allowing a whirlwind of new bands the opportunity to play regularly. This beery environment encouraged guitar bands to flourish, and very soon Hello Sailor was the country's top draw. As well, the punk movement was filtering through via the UK music press and there were rumblings in inner-city Auckland. Who would be first to dress up and be a punk?

In essence, though, I found myself not wanting to leave New Zealand. Back home in the security of family and friends, I found myself emerging from the cocoon of Split Enz. It quickly dawned on me how repetitive, frustrating and mind-numbing the seemingly endless pursuit had become to me. All weighed down by the tranquillisers, which worked their numbing magic so that panic attacks were very rare. But it was a hollow victory.

And now, here in Auckland, I realised that my susceptibility to panic attacks was much less. Why? There must have been a reason, but I still hadn't figured it out.

*R*ing ring ring. I was on the phone to Alastair. He had decided not to join the band. I wasn't really surprised. He knew Split Enz was a kaleidoscopic array of characters, egos, personalities and freaks. He wouldn't have been able to predict how it would go. Would Tim want to sing Alastair's songs? Who would be the frontman? Would there be two? If so, Alastair would be some light years away from the Juddsy persona. And with Juddsy out of the band, in which direction was Split Enz going to go? I guess we the Enzer lads were asking ourselves the same question. In our own, silent way. Luckily Alastair didn't ask me about that.

I thanked him for his consideration and phoned Eddie, who was still in Baltimore, to tell him that Alastair had said no. We poor sods had no choice but to put a 'Guitarist wanted' classified ad in the *Melody Maker* music rag in England and see who turned up. Eddie responded in a similar 'This is going to be painful' way and we both hung up. I had four days till my flight back to England.

Here I was, standing on some Auckland footpath. I was in this Split Enz band, and up onstage we were a tightly wound musical concoction and proud of it. Maybe I could just stay on the stage. Be a stage-bound bachelor. Sneak out to bars and hamburger spots and meet the locals. Then blink and be at the next venue and walk onto the stage. The stage. The wooden stage. The warm, worn, wooden stage.

I sat in an upstairs room at Parnell Road. It was Von's study, out of which she ran the Auckland Medical Bureau. All very cool. The wallpaper especially.

I could hear a distant sound of loud music. You know, hard rock that's been sifted and softened by hundreds of trees. From the university quadrangle? Was Tim Shadbolt still there climbing up on the soapbox and making a fine job of keeping our attention? He probably was. Did students still go into the clammy, ramshackle, tawdry darkness of O'Rorke Hall and take drugs, have sex, think for a few seconds about the world around them, then traipse down Symonds Street with long hair and sandals to a room with a large blackboard and a fog of information, words, numbers and lines swimming in front of them like a galaxy of the future forming from dust?

There would have been a few punks. Punk rockers. The anarchists. Good on them. We thought we were anarchists in our early days as we learned and played our songs on the verandah of Tim and Juddsy's flat, Malmsbury Villa on Kohimarama Road. Just over four years before. And now? A new album to record. A dazed and confused record company. A Juddsyless band. A new electric guitarist currently sitting in a greasy spoon somewhere like Putney, not realising that his life could soon be up in the air. Such is fate. Big Fate. Fate the dickhead. Maybe Fate would just pick me up and toss me away.

Chapter Seventeen
Around the World Again

The day of my flight back to London via Los Angeles arrived and it was just a matter of walking on board. I made my farewells, but I'd taken my Michael's Little Helper a tad too early (I was very nervous about this flight) and the farewells were dreamy.

Sitting in the departure lounge, I stared at everybody like I always did. Were any of them fans of our music? I finished my orange juice; I hadn't drunk alcohol since that night of terror in August 1974. I was sure it would bring back the fear, the horror, so I never touched it. But I've told you this.

A voice rang out asking us all to board the plane. So I got up, floated along the floor, walked in and sat down.

The flight from Auckland to Los Angeles might take twelve hours, but then it might not . . . it might take a series of dreams, an interminable line of questions. Questions coming quietly to you under your blanket of numbness. Somewhere far off a baby cried. It had a tune. A melody. Reminded me of 'What Shall We Do with a Drunken Sailor?' I liked that infant, wherever it was. That was the first song I learned on the piano.

Los Angeles was where I had to stop. Last time all we

needed was to take over the place. Conquer it. Seemed possible. Probably not probable, but very possible. But we didn't. This time I'd be one of those passengers who gets off and doesn't have to prove anything. I didn't need to imagine, make plans. Just charge ahead. Just be who I am. A who? A what? I could jump in a taxi and maybe just tell the driver to go south for a few days . . . and you never know, we might have ended up on a Mexican beach with rolling metre-high surf. I had plenty of tranquillisers in my cargo bag, happy-go-lucky down in the hold among my clothes and guitar picks.

First, though, I needed to go and pick up a guitar from the offices of Chrysalis Records, before catching the flight to London the next day.

In front of me was a Customs desk with a surly man at it. He looked formal. Bored. So did the two cops to his side. One was very tall and had a gun. I thought of asking him if he would let me hold it. I had never held a gun and perhaps it wouldn't matter if I never did. But I wanted to. It was shiny and black and looked heavy.

'Passport, arrival card and visa.' The Customs man had spoken.

I gave him my passport and arrival card.

'Visa?'

Visa. What visa? 'I don't have a visa . . . well, I'm in a band that had visas when we came here to perform on a tour recently and I've just been home to New Zealand to—'

'No visa, no entry. That's how it works.'

'So what do I do?'

'You go to the transit lounge and when the plane you've arrived on leaves for London, you get on it.'

I get on it!

'What about my cargo bag? Can I get that?'

'Sorry, no. It stays in the hold until you get it in London.'

Everything freezes. I have nothing to say. I can't speak. My tranquillisers are in the hold. How can I board that plane without them? I can't. I will be cast under the spell of a huge panic attack. I will shiver in that quick rush of terror. I *have* to have a tranquilliser to get on that plane. What if it's delayed? Will the panic arrive as I'm seated in the transit lounge? Will I shiver? Vomit? Uncontrollable terror spinning through my head. Thoughts round and round and round . . . People will look at me. They'll whisper.

A thought. Do I have a tranquilliser on me . . . in a pocket? Hope. I start searching. Searching. In my trouser pockets? Nothing. In my jacket pocket? Nothing. In my shirt pocket—*a half pill!* Oh Christ . . . a half pill.

That must work. But when to take it? I can't take it on the plane. I won't be able to board the plane without *knowing* . . . *sensing* its dream state working. Can I sit in the transit lounge and keep my eyes shut and fifteen minutes before the boarding call take it? Can I?

Ninety minutes later I was back on the same plane, in an aisle seat. Was the pill working? Could I *feel* it? I must. Surely. People were going up and down the aisle. I wanted them all gone. I had to shut my eyes. I did, and a thousand images screamed through my head. Spinning, spinning. My imagination was a monster. I opened my eyes.

'Would you like the fish or the stew for dinner, sir?'

She hovered above me like a demon, her eyes from a witch's coven. I shook my head.

'Nothing, thank you.' I closed my eyes. I had to fix on something. Stop the racing. The endless motion of my eyes, fingers, feet.

And then I feel it. It moves through me. It was only half a pill . . . but it's slowing me. I settle into the seat. I unfold my arms. I listen peacefully to the sound of the engines. The hum of the engines. Keep that sound alive. As all else drifts backwards. Push it away. Can I do that? Keep my eyes shut. The sound of the engines. The soft roar of the engines. I pray that the person next to me doesn't speak. All I can hear is the roar of the engines. And the half pill is working.

I jerk upright. My eyes open. I look around, senses knowing the rumble. The plane has landed. I have slept. How long? I don't care. I am in London. I will have my bag soon. I will have my bottle of pills. The cure. The drifting ersatz sense of normality that I can fool myself with. I know I will be able to keep the onset of terror at bay.

I take my case off the carousel, kneel down, open it and eat two tranquillisers. I will survive. I will live.

The black cab skirts the dreary shopfronts from suburb to suburb, early-morning apathy in a grey summer world. We drift into the southeast London suburb called Catford. I knock on the door of a two-up two-down in a street I have forgotten the name of. Tim and Eddie are there. I'm shown up the stairs to a room. I go in. I close the door. It is a monotone room. It's also monotonous. I open the door and go back down the stairs. I make a cup of instant coffee. It's April Fool's Day 1977.

'How was the flight?'

'Fine.'

'You get your guitar from the Chrysalis office?'

'I didn't have a visa. They wouldn't let me in.'

'We're at the rehearsal rooms this morning. Geoff Emerick's coming in.'

Geoff Emerick is coming in. He was the engineer on The Beatles albums *Sgt. Pepper's Lonely Hearts Club Band* and *Revolver*. He would have been sitting at the recording desk in Abbey Road Studio 2. Once. Soon he will be sitting somewhere with us—that Split Enz band—offering suggestions. 'Mike, that bass line you're putting between the middle eight and the chorus. Did you rip that off McCartney?' Or will he wonder why I've fallen asleep on the couch behind him? Seemingly distant and vacant?

I go back upstairs and wait till 10 a.m. Then we walk down the road to the tube station. We go up the up-up to Caledonian Road, up and out onto the footpath and walk to the E-Zee Hire rehearsal rooms. It's a blessed path, one we walked—strode—down in 1976, last year, in anticipation.

A jet flies overhead, filled with happy passengers. Maybe one of them is terrified. Is that person in an aisle seat? Hiding in the toilet? I thought of doing that. They would have come banging on the door. Opened it with a crowbar? The broken-wheeled clouds block my view of the plane. The clouds' reflections shimmer in muddy puddles. I see my own reflection in grimy shop-front windows. My body is thin, my face is pale.

'Mike, let me introduce you to Geoff Emerick.'

'Hi, Geoff. Nice to meet you.' We shake hands. Those hands. Magical. He sits down next to me, a notebook in his grip. My mahogany Madill bass is on my lap. Ever since I was fourteen I have rehearsed while sitting down. I don't stand up. The only motion I entertain is a nodding head. Apparently all bass players nod their heads when concentrating. I should ask Geoff E. if McCartney always rehearsed sitting down. Did he nod his head? But McCartney isn't really a bass player. He is a guitar player who became the bass player because no one else wanted to play the bass.

I look at Geoff E.'s fingers. Think about all they have done. He's not doing anything with them at the moment. He's just sitting there, listening. Tim is having us start to learn a song he turned up with. It's called 'My Mistake'. He's asking Mal Green on drums to bring in a disco beat. I'm hoping I don't have to play a disco bass. What would that be? Geoff just sits there. Maybe the true talent of the man is that he knows how to listen.

The song starts to come together. The tranquillisers have folded me into a tissue state. I can't think of what to play.

In a couple of days, some guitarists are coming round to audition for the guitarist's slot that Juddsy vacated. What will that be like? They'll have flared jeans and wispy beards. Dreamers. Battered guitars like crippled furniture cradled in their arms or slung over their shoulders. Their eyes looking for that easy answer. That gig up the M1, down the M25. The full-house sign. An ad in the *Melody Maker* with their name on it? A ferry ride across the channel to Amsterdam? A ferry across the Mersey?

I want to lie down and forget them all. There must be an easier way.

Through the fog in my head a clever little idea forms and forges through to my mouth. We're back in the two-up two-down. Time is dragging its viscous, deliberate way forward.

It's 4 April 1977. I turn to Tim.

'Neil should be the guitarist.'

Tim and Eddie pause. They don't need to speak.

I can tell they think it's a brilliant idea. And another idea comes to mind. It too sprints from my inner mind to the outer perimeter of my murky means of communication. It is urgent. Pleading. Unstoppable.

The Judd era is over. Neil Finn will turn this band upside down, shake out the dross. But how long, how long, how long can I be the bass player? I can keep a peaceful place in this line-up, but how many more pills do I have to take to flatten me? To keep me submerged in that muddy creek, out of sight of terror? I can't get answers to anything. Everything is fragile.

This endless haze had slowly shut me down as the tangible rewards of our hard work continued to evaporate like a desert mirage. I had to come to grips with the reality of life with a mental disorder. The homelessness of touring coupled with the myriad changes that the group was undergoing was too much. I had endured enough of my own private hell, and the glorious moments onstage were now too few and far between. I fully understood Tim's commitment. Having conceived of Split Enz, led the group for so long and now developing a song-writing talent without Phil, he had to forge ahead and prove himself. His dedication was now as much his own personal thirst for success as for the band's. And he wasn't torn by family commitments, as were Phil and I. I had decided that at the right moment I would make my exit. It had to be. And that moment had arrived.

I turned to Tim again.

'I'm going to leave the band.'

I echoed that back to myself. The time had come. I'm going to give up. My head has won the war. My heart has been torn apart. The dream has been poisoned.

No one tried to talk me out of it.

In less than a day a new bass player had been found. His name was Nigel Griggs. He was a mate of Malcolm's. The next day he reported into E-Zee Hire for a rehearsal. I went along to check him out.

As I stood against the wall, watching the starts and stops, I can't say I didn't sense the dispossession, the sad forfeiture of my special corner of the rehearsal room. It seemed too simple a solution as I stood in the quick vacuum I had created. The gradual inevitability of my departure contrasted with an inner wrestling spirit (my heart) that wanted to remain firmly rooted to the spot, to lift the guitar strap over my head and throw off a costume drenched in sweat at the end of each night. But the resistance from my soul (my head, in fact) was too deep; my weary being was battle-scarred and desperate for home. I knew one thing for sure, though: the times I had shared with this crazed bunch had created an extraordinary web. For 5 years, across 460,000 kilometres, more than 270 gigs, on 112 stages and in 7 recording studios I had walked the earth with these men.

Neil arrived on 5 April, eighteen years old, completely free of any expectations and happy to take whatever circumstances he found himself in. He was in a state of high excitement from the moment he set foot on English soil. It was straight into rehearsal.

On 15 April, my suitcase and I climbed into a black cab

headed for Heathrow. I never went back to E-Zee Hire or saw Geoff Emerick again. I never played 'My Mistake'. I said goodbye to the city of my birth. The one and only London town.

I wound down the cab window. I watched it all. And I listened. A Cliff Richard song crept out from an upper window. It was spring 1977. A sports car with the top down. A Sloane Ranger with the top off. Who were these bodies and faces, distant memories all plodding into the present and out again in their mechanical Rolls-Royce Spitfire way? Grey suits and long dresses. Platform shoes. Incongruous. So much of it like me: pathetic.

I wasn't going to taunt Mr Terror or Master Panic again. With a double hit of tranquillisers and a dark coffee—a short distance from black—at the Heathrow departures area, I thought about the band I'd left.

Juddsy. Where was he? Would I ever see him again? Would he keep writing songs? Tim would be out front. The ringmaster. The town crier. Rallying all and sundry to that unique, special place at his feet. Eddie controlling it all in his unique subterranean way. Noel the intelligent, masterful jester. Mal, the one on the drumming stool. Rob blowing his horn. And now the unknown factors, Neil and Nigel Griggs, playing in a band I would never be part of again.

Would they miss me?

'Would you like the fish or the chicken curry, sir?'

'Neither, thanks.'

She slipped away and I smiled. I turned to the window and looked out at the long, blue sky and fell asleep.

Chapter Eighteen
The Pavilion Revisited

My taxi drifted down Manukau Road to Parnell. I was home. Each building was a welcome. Each set of lights beamed at me, and our driving past would find them smiling. Why did I feel like this? It was as if I didn't want to be anywhere else. Would evening merge out of the day and find me nervous and wound up? Until I took another pill? And then would I settle down? I would find out soon enough.

I climbed out at 469 Parnell Road, took the ever-present front-door key out of my pocket and went in. Paula was there, and Von and Jerry were sitting at the breakfast table under their Dick Frizzell painting. Once again I hadn't told them what day I was coming. I'm a surprise man. A practical joker in a sleepy disguise.

My return was welcome, though. We talked about the flight. There was no talk about the band and how it was coping with Juddsy gone. I didn't tell them about Geoff Emerick or 'My Mistake'. We didn't talk about 'What next, Michael?'

The door opened and in walked Geoffrey. He and I went and sat in the lounge. He had lost his band member Neil Finn. I had suggested Split Enz steal him and they had. What did Geoffrey think of that? I didn't ask; he didn't say. He must have hated me. He said he had been writing songs, and took a cassette out of his pocket and gave it to me.

'There are three demos on it. One's called "Julia". Have a listen. It's starts in French.' And he left.

I went over to the cassette deck and started to play it. I listened. It finished. I played it again. I played it again. It was magnificent. I rang Geoffrey at his flat.

'Let's meet up and talk about all this.'

Von and Jerry went about their business. They'd seen all this song focus many times before. Jerry, I imagine, was keeping an ear out for lyrics.

It was about three or four days later that Geoffrey and I met up. I said 'Julia' should be recorded. (I don't remember the other two songs, sorry.)

'Yes,' said Geoffrey. Then he said, 'I have another song I've written.' And he picked up his guitar and started to play 'Good Morning Citizen'.

'Holy shit,' I thought. 'We'd better make a plan.'

Let's form a band. Let's make it simple. Guitars, bass, drums. Chunn Brothers. CB.

'Have you got more songs?'

'I do. I will.'

As Geoffrey sloped away to write, write, write, I went down to Mandrill Studios, where I met with co-owner Glyn Tucker. I knew Glyn fairly well, from the days before we'd moved to Australia. I said, 'My brother and I are wanting to form a band, and would you like to record us here—at Mandrill?' To cut to the chase, Glyn said yes. I went back to Parnell Road and sat in the lounge. And thought.

What am I doing? A new band? Playing shows. Recording. Getting a record deal. Touring. Touring? A tour manager. A manager? Vans? Aeroplanes?

But what about the *stages*? The sheer joy of the stage. The wooden boards. The green rooms. The sound. The lights. The instruments. The people. The audience. How can I not return to the stage? Can I just keep the travelling, the hotels out of it? And being in a band: the childhood dream.

Geoffrey and I decided on Citizen Band as an appropriate name, forged from the conglomeration of its various elements. Like a good chemical compound. Acronyms: Chunn Brothers; Citizen Band radio. And so on. If you're not careful, deciding on a name can take forever. And it never seems 'right' at first. When OK Dinghy changed their name to Dragon I bet they thought, 'That's a crap name.' But we, they, hundreds of thousands of people got used to it. Now it's just Dragon. Citizen Band would just sink in.

And it's not the name in the end. It's the songs, first and foremost. That mysterious craft. It's so easy to write a song— one that no one wants to listen to. So difficult to write one that thousands of people listen to over and over again.

Geoffrey and I had started playing 'Julia' together. I was on my Madill bass, Geoffrey on his Gibson acoustic. Here was a song that thousands of people would want to hear over and over again. I knew that. I just did. And Geoffrey had new songs rolling in. 'Out in the World'. 'In a Lifetime'. 'Counting the Regiments'. 'Blue Lagoon'.

We knew we couldn't go out like a Simon & Garfunkel duo, though. We needed a band. I had played with guitarist Greg Clark and drummer Brent Eccles when I played bass on that New Zealand tour with Space Waltz three years earlier. They were now both in a covers band called Voxpop. So we went to a bar to check them out.

Geoffrey and I sat there in the presence of sublime excellence. Both Greg and Brent had forged true mastery of their instruments. We needed to get them away from that covers band nonsense. They needed to be in our band.

'Hey, lads. Want to be in our band? We're Citizen Band.'

'Yes.'

'Yes.'

And so we existed. We gathered for rehearsals somewhere that has faded from memory and started learning songs that we would eventually record at Mandrill Studios.

While I was still carrying tranquillisers in my pocket thanks to Jerry's continued belief that I was stricken with an enduring 'stage fright' syndrome, I occasionally forgot to take them. And nothing happened. I was gently content. I started to think, 'I'm cured. Maybe it's gone.' What was it anyway? In reality? A chink in my psychic armour that had—well—repaired itself? How would I know? Did it matter any more?

Days rolled around. That peace of mind stayed with me like an invisible cloak. I smiled. Was I being presumptuous? Was my mind the emperor in his new clothes? But where was the fear? The sudden rush of heartbeats screaming up to 160 bpm? The thoughts racing in their manic, terror-laced hurricane? The running to seek dark corners where no one would see me? How long had it been? I must be cured. But I kept the pills in my pocket and, if I thought about it, I took one half. Each morning. Each evening.

It was in that easy-keys, soft-breeze condition that I went

to the Auckland Town Hall to see Split Enz on 15 September. I can't say I felt like I was missing out. We CB lads were building up a head of steam. And in talking to Eddie before the show, his summary of future dates, cities, nations and so on exhausted me, though I didn't say so.

During the show I watched Nigel. He had a B.C. Rich bass. His strings were roundwound. He used a pick. They had new costumes; he wasn't wearing one of mine. They were up there doing their thing. They had a full house. I dawdled home thinking about the debut performance of Citizen Band that was looming. I had walked out one door and soon there would be another. Life does that to you.

The first-ever Citizen Band show was at the Island of Real café in Auckland's Airedale Street on 9 October 1977. New Zealand had a world of young rock bands playing their own songs. Hello Sailor had been part of this rush, and when they booked the Gluepot in Ponsonby and filled it with around 750 people we all knew something was up. And we wanted a piece of it. Bands surged forth. Street Talk and Th' Dudes hit the ground running.

I went to the Island of Real one afternoon when Th' Dudes were playing. They were, in essence, a bunch of Sacred Heart College lads. That was cool enough. When they played a song that their guitarists had written called 'Quite Frankly', with its long-tail lead solo played by a platinum-blond kid called Dave Dobbyn, I thought to myself, 'Uh oh. These guys are good. Like . . . *good.*' It was obvious that the competition was going to be tough. And then when I saw Hello Sailor at the

Windsor Castle not long afterwards, that impression became even more pronounced. The standard out there was *high*! We had to get out there and play.

Auckland had a flurry of live venues appearing—the Globe Hotel, Station Hotel, the DB Windsor Park in Mairangi Bay, Mon Desir in Takapuna, Gluepot, Mainstreet, Windsor Castle and more. Brent got on the phone, and the Globe and the Windsor Castle were our first bookings.

The liquor licensing laws in those early days were draconian. Bands started playing at 7 p.m. and had to be out of there by 10 p.m. (Eventually the closing time became 11 p.m., but not just yet.) So they played in bars filled with evening sunlight. Not very rock'n'roll at all. But the crowds turned up.

While a Sunday afternoon doesn't lay much of a rock'n'roll foundation for a debut live gig, it didn't matter because we were all buoyed with anticipation and hope. We walked on and took our places. Nothing was said. We knew enough about what to do to just do it. We plugged in, looked out at what seemed to be a full house.

Mr Eccles tapped his hi-hat. Geoff and Greg strummed the A chord in a distorted, orderly climb to a crescendo when Brent screamed 'One! Two! Three! Four!' and BANG! the four of us hit our start buttons right on time. Geoffrey stood close to his mic and belted out the opening line to 'Good Morning Citizen' and we were away.

Now what? I *watched* it all without looking like I was. I used my peripheral vision to view a kaleidoscope of revelations and impressions.

We had the prescription for forward motion. There was no inertia; there was only acceleration. Here we were on a small stage in a small venue with the time-honoured line-up: two guitars, bass and drums. I knew what that could do. We had to take our vision and materialise it, forge it and set about pinning the punters to the spot. We had to make sure that they set their eyes and ears on us and never wavered.

The crowd were all on their feet. We were winning.

Maybe I had started this new journey thinking we could achieve some subtle musical thing reflecting our past. Something to leave the tortuous Split Enz route behind. After all, that's why I left that band. I was dying. It was killing me. And now we were taking what we had been as musical dreamers and were set to move forward once again. Keep close to the ground. No risks. Could I do it like that? And not fall into black holes?

That afternoon in the Island of Real, that Sunday afternoon, we saw the light.

In mid '78, after recording and releasing a song Geoffrey wrote called 'In a Lifetime', which failed miserably, we booked into Mandrill Studios to record an album. I had the same impatience during recording that I'd had during the *Mental Notes* and *Second Thoughts* sessions. But it wasn't really impatience. I just felt trapped in a studio. I used to think, 'We play these songs live. Count in one-two-three-four and play them and then they're done, surely? Let's just play them live in the studio.'

But we often recorded instruments one by one. It wasn't the gelling of a united band—it was like Meccano. Piece by piece. Well, that's just how it was. Everyone was doing it in the era of multi-tracking. But we knew we had cool songs. You have to have the songs; they are the life force. Geoffrey wrote songs that gave us weapons to fling across New Zealand. Songs that captured the attention.

Eccles and I played as a single instrument. We were tight. Greg soared on his lead guitar. Geoffrey put down rhythm guitar in simple, energetic chords of distortion and melody. And then one day it was done. Glyn Tucker had licensed it to Phonogram Records; we called it *Citizen Band*. In our minds that made sense.

It was released on the same day we started touring New Zealand with British band Graham Parker and the Rumour, 3 September 1978. Connections. Phonogram Records were Parker's label and I presume they asked him nicely if the New Zealand act they'd just signed (us!) could tour New Zealand with them. So we did. And we took off . . .

It was in Wellington, the scene of my first violent panic attack back in 1974 in the Waterloo Hotel, that my arch-enemy returned. The show was about an hour away and I was suddenly filled with fear. Why? I don't know why. But there it was. The racing mind. The rush for the toilet.

My acting was brilliant. No one noticed. I dived into the bottom of my pocket, extracted the tranquilliser and washed it down with water from the toilet sink. I went back into the cubicle to wait. There was now a pattern. If I 'knew' a tranquilliser was going to be arriving in the bloodstream soon, then I could achieve some kind of anticipated calm. As that knowingness slowly eked its way into my head, I crept out of the toilet and back to the dressing room.

It was alive with pre-show banter, tuning, humming,

drinking. Not me. I still hadn't drunk alcohol since my first panic attack.

Graham Parker came in. I sat and watched in silence. I had nothing to say. One thing I knew: I had to take tranquillisers morning and night if I was back out on the road. Nothing had changed. On the road was on the road and what must be must be. But what was it? Madness? Simple brain damage? I might never know. I'd just be the pathetic dribbler in the corner of the asylum when I was 80 years old. If I got that far.

We walked out onstage at the Wellington Town Hall. I'd been there before, eighteen months before. Another world, back in time. In a medieval costume. Here I was neatly sedated and ready for a full house. It was Parker's full house. I didn't care. I looked out; they were all there to see Parker. I didn't care. We played well. And afterwards I sat in the dressing room and a comfortable stillness came over me. No need to do or say anything. You can see it on this book's cover.

Our album was out. The first single was 'I Feel Good', our cover of the Larry's Rebels 1966 single, which was itself a cover of an Allen Toussaint song, but that's all irrelevant. It had received a snowflake of airplay, had a live screening on the *Ready To Roll* television show and slipped away over the horizon. It didn't make the Top 40. We were going to get used to that.

The tour rolled through New Zealand, and we ended up back rehearsing at Brent's father's factory, within walls of sanitary pads. He ran a business sterilising them for hospitals, and they made great soundproofing.

Our next big gig was the 1979 Nambassa festival, in January. We'd played at Nambassa the year before. At midday.

One of our first gigs and we didn't garner much attention. Geoffrey asked the crowd if they knew where we could buy a mince pie. The hippie ethos was grandiose and shambolic. There were no dressing rooms. You took the stage with dusty fingers sticking to guitar strings. No sound check. But you did it because, in New Zealand back then, that's what you did.

This time, Split Enz were in town, and after having all their equipment burned in a fire, they borrowed a big pile and took the stage with a blinding set. It had been virtually twelve months since they'd played live. They nailed it.

I sat up in the rafters above the stage. They had drilled a lot of energy into their new songs. They'd had a hard time of late. And there's nothing like a big stage, bright lights, big sound and an adrenaline rush to catapult your entity out into the crowd.

The Citizen Band version of that didn't really work. We were on after Enz. It was late. Something was adrift. My bass fell off my shoulder in the first song and crashed onto the stage. That was uncool. How did *that* happen? I looked out into the crowd and couldn't see anything. It wasn't overly clear whether anyone was there. Was I in tune? Maybe not. Maybe the audience realised I was out of tune. My A might have been closer to Bb. No matter. Enough about that Nambassa show. It was an Enz triumph and I loved them for it.

Shortly after retreating back to Auckland, we started rehearsing a couple of new songs—'No Stereo' and 'City Slitz', as I recall. Geoffrey's lyrics were maintaining their focus on words that told stories. Words that pinned you to listening so you never pushed the stop button. I listened to them as they arrived in our world. How did he do that? It's mysterious.

A few months earlier Brent had had the idea that we should be playing lunchtime concerts at Auckland secondary schools. 'Make them free,' he'd said. 'Play for twenty to thirty minutes. It will be the highlight of their day.'

So off we went. Phone calls to school secretaries who beeped through to the principal. The principal usually said yes because it would mean no truancy on that day. Over the next six months—the autumn and winter of 1979—we played around 40 lunchtime shows in Auckland schools. The students rocked out (that's rock jargon for we blew their minds!). We could see what was happening. Twenty minutes in a school day was a cool break from Physics and Maths but they wanted more. They would have to wait.

While this was going on, our gig sheet grew and grew. *Radio With Pictures* was playing us regularly, and that meant national promotion. Venues all over New Zealand came alive to meet the demand from young New Zealanders for local bands playing live, as their primary means of having a good time.

In Christchurch we teamed up with promoter Jim Wilson (more on him later), and played the Hillsborough Tavern a number of times. When we went to Christchurch we stayed at the Ferry Road Motel. We called the owner Oddjob; I'm not sure why. One time we were booked at the Hillsborough for two weekends in a row, so we flew down on a Thursday and went to the Ferry Motel to stay for ten days. We played the first Thursday to Saturday, then Sunday rolled around. We were sitting in the Ferry Motel. Sitting there. In Christchurch. We would be passing time till the next Thursday when we went back and killed them at the Hillsborough again. Sitting there.

It started out as a quiet brook, grew into a stream . . . a river . . . then a raging torrent of terror. I was trapped. I was in the Ferry Motel. Where could I go? Walk down Ferry Road for a few kilometres. Go to Sumner Beach and lie on the bottom of the sea as waves came and went over me? Get out. Walk back again. I didn't have a room of my own.

I knew what I had to do. I feigned a cough. I acted out a simple, 'I'm not well, boys. I've got a headache. Sore muscles. Hey, guys, I think I've got the flu.'

I taxied out to Christchurch Airport and flew back to Auckland. Ran into the house on Brighton Road where I was living with Paula and Nikko and locked the door. I looked in the mirror. There he was. The bass player who was insane.

I flew back down to Christchurch the following Thursday morning.

'Hi, guys. I'm better now.'

That night I played my heart out. New songs were arriving. 'Another Night, Another River'. 'No Stereo'. And one called 'Acrobats'.

It was during this song that I realised that my madness was probably permanent. I just had to live with it. That Thursday night at the Hillsborough, as we played 'Acrobats', I retreated from everything around me. The world, the country, the city, the people, the audience. Everything. I shrunk into what had evolved for me into a perfect world. A supreme place. And this song was the pot of gold. I was up on the stage.

Such great lyrics. Geoffrey's encapsulation of the acrobat, the high-wire victim, the one to be shouted down . . . each of us probably in one interpretation or another knew that man.

I joined in with Eccles with my long, deep notes. Geoffrey had written a beautiful melodic array to go with his story. His journey in words. And Greg Clark had written a lead solo that to this day fills me with joy. A melodic translation of the entire song.

Magical. I had taken my rotten self up onto that stage and become a better man. Our quartet of adventurers was untouchable up there.

While we were treated with respect and admiration by Jim Wilson and the Hillsborough Tavern management, things could be different elsewhere. We were booked into a Rotorua hotel not long afterwards, and we checked in at reception and asked for four rooms.

'Sorry, bands aren't allowed to stay in the rooms.'

'But we'll pay for them.'

'It's the rules of the hotel owners. No bands are to stay in the rooms. We have accommodation in the staff quarters.'

I had an idea of what would happen next.

'OK then. But we'd like to reserve a table for dinner in your dining room and we'll pay for the meals.'

'Bands aren't allowed to eat in the dining room. We provide meals in the staff quarters. That's just how it is.'

As we drove out of Rotorua the next day, we vowed never to go back to that hotel—and we never did. Small-town mentality. Musicians were lazy bastards who didn't have a real job. They smoked drugs, had group sex all the time and were idle.

'Snotty layabouts. They're probably on the dole as well. They get up onstage, strutting away, sing stupid songs and expect to get paid inordinate amounts of money. God knows what these young punters see in them.'

We'll show them.

The Sandown Park hotel in Gisborne was different. The manager, Alan Sciascia, was cool. We had our own quarters—a small house, let's call it—and I had a single bedroom to myself. And we were allowed to eat in the dining room and the meals were free. Paradise.

I remember Brent starting the show. We were all backstage and Brent had a microphone, beaming out to the crowd. (Man, we got big crowds.) He put on a very creditable Robert Muldoon voice.

'Arh . . . Good evening. Welcome to the Citizen Band show at the Sandown Park. Yesshh . . . Now people are asking me why the government has started issuing toilet paper with a map of New Zealand on it. Well, the answer is simple. We think New Zealand is pretty good on the hole.'

We fell to the floor. But he wasn't finished.

'And . . . yesshh . . . now it seems people are talking about how I'm not circumcised. Yesshh, true . . . They say I'm not circumcised and that there's no end to the big prick.'

We were little boys lying on the floor. And we walked out and took the stage and wallowed in a high point of a glorious era in New Zealand rock'n'roll. A time when young New Zealanders who didn't have sport on night-time television, pokie gambling rooms, café society or multi-channel TV broadcasts all hit the road down to local bars to see New Zealand bands playing their own New Zealand songs. It was a special time.

In April 1979, Split Enz passed through Auckland to play two nights at His Majesty's Theatre. Eddie rang me and asked if I'd like to hop up and play 'Time for a Change' with them. And I did. I walked onto the stage and Nigel handed me his bass. The B.C. Rich. Yes—roundwound strings.

'Time for a Change' is a very simple song to play on bass. For the first half of the song I play nothing. That's really easy. It was a perfect chance to take it all in. I looked around the stage. The rest of the band were all looking around the stage. Poised for action. Waiting for the referee to blow the whistle.

What about the audience? I looked out. They didn't seem so different from the last time I'd been up there with them in early 1976.

Tim finished off the first half of the song. And then we were in. Neil played the solo on guitar that Miles Golding had originally written on his violin. He played it very well. They all played their parts very well. And then it finished. I took the bass off, handed it back to Nigel, called a soft thank you across the stage to them all and went back to my seat. Luvverly.

A few months later, in June 1979, we started recording our second album at Mandrill Studios. We had attracted the attention of CBS Records under John McCready, and they brought in Jay Lewis from LA to produce it. In our minds Jay was cool, as he'd played on an American record that we'd actually heard: acoustic guitar on Albert Hammond's 'It Never Rains in Southern California'. He might have the magic touch.

A few weeks before the sessions started, Geoffrey had

brought a new song to rehearsals. It started with a B strummed four times and then an F flat strummed four times. Many of you readers can do that. It's easy. That went on for a while, then Geoffrey hit a G. Ah. That was a cool thing to do. And then an A. Doubly cool. Over in the corner Greg had come up with a riff for the B–F flat. To this day, when Geoffrey plays those two chords and Greg plays his riff, whoever is in hearing distance will know that they are playing 'Rust In My Car'. There is something unique and matchless about watching a song come to be in the evolution of a band's rehearsals.

When we put it down at Mandrill with Jay Lewis, we knew we had something that would last. We might even get in the charts. We also had some live dates looming before the album release. Two of them were at the Last Resort café in Wellington.

The band room at the Last Resort was accessed from the stage. If you were in the band room and wanted to leave the venue, you had to go across the stage. It was after the first set that we descended to that room and it hit me. Why? I was trapped. To have even a temporary escape for air, or a chance to hide, I had to walk across that stage in front of a full house. People. Eyes. Voices. Motion. I couldn't do it. I took a second pill. There were twenty minutes to go before we started again.

I went and wedged myself against the wall. I panicked. Would this be like that night in Wellington in 1974? Vomiting? Diarrhoea? The familiar screaming thoughts all totally out of control? I took a third pill. They were taking too long to act. I pretended to be half-sleeping. Rather have my eyes shut and the speeding sensations than the thought of people talking to me, watching me. Asking questions. Why can't we just go out there now? Start the second set early? Why?

I can't say anything. I can hardly breathe. I should stop breathing. I should will my own death and be rid of this hell . . .

'OK, boys. We're back on.'

As usual, the panic left me the minute I walked back onstage. And the tranquillisers played havoc with my consciousness. I missed intros. Hung on long notes wondering what might come next. An F maybe. No! It should have been a B.

The show ended. I gathered my blue bag and went outside. There was a taxi. I gave the driver an address, and then in seconds, it seemed, I was in a bedroom in a house where I was staying. Do you call it a billet? I don't remember who owned the house. It was a double bed. There were green curtains with shifting light beams from passing cars and their almost inaudible hum; a Doppler effect riding up and over from the hill outside. It was winter but I wasn't cold.

I lay on the bed. I shifted into the middle and the mattress and base crashed to the floor. I was left suspended in the air. I floated in slow motion—down, down—like a drifting dandelion. I settled into the mattress looking up. A beautiful green light hung up there. It was floating across the ceiling. And the green leaves in the planter-box over on the windowsill. They were all leaning in my direction. They were offering. They were moving gently from side to side. The window was open. The Wellington breeze off Cook Strait, no doubt. Is that where I was? Did I need to know where I was? I wasn't down below the stage in the band room in a cage of speeding fear. I could be happy. I could be wherever I wanted.

I am here with the green lights knowing that I will survive. The light flickers and I trust it. I murmur to it. It responds by hovering above me. I am happy. I am saved.

Chapter Nineteen
The Cool Craft
of Lying

C BS released the album titled *Just Drove Through Town* in early August 1979. The single release was 'Rust In My Car'. Here was our chance to reach the New Zealand Top 40.

The first week it came in at number 49. The second week it had vanished. (I have to admit now, dear reader, that of the 24 singles I've played bass on, none has ever made the Top 40.) We were unperturbed. Maybe having a Top 40 record would have been too much of a discombobulating rift in life. A speed wobble? Anyway, off we went to promote the album with live shows. Ezy Promotions put together concerts in the South Island, and Neil Ronald in the north. But concert halls and theatres drew meagre crowds. After two years of venues where drinking was a priority, our fans found it hard to sit and act sensibly in theatre seats. We were learning. And then we hit Auckland.

On 14 September we played the Auckland Town Hall. It had been sold out for a number of days. The Eccles philosophy had triumphed: the crowd was virtually entirely teenagers. To sum it up, we had the equivalent of a hyper-enthusiastic school lunchtime audience, numbering 1800. Now it was time to reap the seeds we'd sowed.

We walked out on that stage and it was overwhelming. The place was riotous. I went to the mic and I'm pretty sure I said, 'Hey! A full house! How's that?' But I probably sounded like, 'Hee . . . Sher shee sha shoo!' I was shaking with joy. This was the *Auckland Town Hall*. This was where The Beatles played in 1964. They had a full house. This was where Split Enz played in 1975. We had a full house then. Now it was our turn.

I added a little bit more volume to my amplifier and we took off. It was a peak moment in the more than 650 times I have taken a stage with Enz or CB. Blissful.

For a while, the New Zealand and Australian CBS people had talked about a plan to have *Just Drove Through Town* released over there in Aussie. And so it came to be. In early November we flew to Sydney and found rental accommodation on the North Shore. Neil Ronald came with us and we were represented by an agent who started looking for shows.

I went in to CBS to check out their vibe. It wasn't very welcoming. It was like CBS Australia was just doing CBS New Zealand a favour. The promotions lad behind the desk said, 'We won't be seen to be promoting your album.'

'Oh, that's good,' I thought. 'That'll save me from having to look for it. Promotion—what's that anyway?'

While we waited for live bookings to come through, I went to Bondi to meet Tim. Split Enz were in town and had just finished recording their new album, which would be called

True Colours, for Mushroom Records in Melbourne with producer David Tickle, who had produced their song 'I See Red' in 1978, in a one-off session. Tim had a glint in his eye. He took a cassette from his beach bag (let's call it).

'Here's our new album. We're thinking of making "I Hope I Never" the first single off it.'

I looked at the list of songs written on the cassette slick. 'I Hope I Never' was number six on side one.

It was good to see him again. We didn't talk about Juddsy. I took the cassette back to the North Shore, and when the four of us got together we played it.

There was a unanimous impression that the Enz should go with the second track on the album, 'I Got You', as their first single. And that's what happened. It wasn't telepathic transfer. It's just what happened. And the rest is history. 'I Got You' became the band's first number-one hit, in both Australia and New Zealand.

Meanwhile, CB had some gigs coming through from our agent. We had a hire car and off we went to Goulburn, southwest of Sydney, to play at the Mustang Car Club social. We started off as we usually did, but the Mustangers all shifted to far, distant corners of the hall and tried to talk to each other. Eventually one of them came up to the stage and looked at us, so we stopped.

'I think there's been a miscommunication. We were after a covers band to, like, play stuff we know.'

I looked at Brent. Geoffrey looked at Greg. I looked at Greg. Brent looked at Geoffrey.

'OK,' said Brent.

The next song we played was 'Proud Mary'. We played it

very well. We'd never played it before but we knew how to. And then when the gig was over we drove back to Sydney.

Sometimes when we went to a gig down the line, we'd catch a train. Luckily it was summer time, as we'd go to the train station after a gig and stand on the platform for about an hour waiting for a train. The platforms were always empty. Everyone in Australia drove cars. They even had car restaurants where, presumably, cars went for meals and coffee. That's cool.

The CBS Records 'not promoting' strategy was very successful. *Just Drove Through Town* was never seen. There was no single release off it. There were days when we didn't have gigs. One of them was a sunny, warm day, so I hopped on the bus on Military Road to go to Manly Beach for a swim. As we puttered along I started thinking about it all.

Here I was with a band that had a record company and a tour manager and an agent. We got to play at the Mustang Car Club. Why was I here again? Hadn't I been here in this huge country a few years before—two, actually—playing full houses, going on television, getting great reviews in magazines . . . all over Australia? Having the guy from Roxy Music want to produce an album with us in the UK? Weren't we with a record company that wanted to be seen to promote us?

Here I was again. At the bottom.

And then it hit me.

I pushed the stop button on the bus and stood by the door as it cruised to the next stop. I ran from the bus and stood on the footpath, my head spinning, searching. There it was. I ran to the public toilet, opened the door, locked the door in less than a second and then vomited. I was shivering. Here in a muggy, hot-day toilet about a kilometre from Manly Beach.

I found a pill in my pocket and took it. I drank the sink water to get it down as fast as I could. Then I sat on the toilet and waited. No one appeared. I knew I would come right. I knew it.

After about ten minutes I headed out into that beautiful weather Sydney has a hold on and walked the rather long distance to Manly. I thought back to the *Mental Notes* sessions at Festival Studios, when I'd taken off and just kept pacing, pacing until I got to Bondi. Thank God this distance was somewhat less.

When I reached Manly I just kept on walking until I was submerged in the sea once again. I was going to be OK. I caught a wave. I stood up. In the distance I heard Mi-Sex playing on a transistor radio. It was 'Computer Games'. I looked around. This was their audience. It was about to be a Split Enz audience. Dragon's audience. I thought, 'I can never make it. If a bus trip throws me out into the street like a pathetic rag of a human being, what next? How low will this town take me?'

At our next rehearsal, Neil came up and said he'd had contact from a guy called Daniel Keighley back home. He and some others were putting on a three-day festival at Ngaruawahia which would be titled Sweetwaters. They wanted Citizen Band to play at it, and the fee was a good one that would easily cover airfares home, et cetera.

There wasn't a sense of 'Yes, we must play that show' in the room. They wanted more details, to follow due process and discuss whether it was worth going back. But my head was screaming, 'Get on that plane! Get back there! It's the only way to get home!'

I said, 'I think we should do it.'

That didn't seem to generate much excitement. I repeated myself. I had to get back home. I had to get back to Auckland. A decision had to be made, as the festival was only a few weeks away.

'I think we should do it,' I said again. 'And I have to tell you that I want to leave the band. I want to get back home and this festival will get us there. And then you can find another bass player.'

The air in the room chilled. I could read the signs. They were thinking my commitment was a shallow trough. They were thinking, *knowing*, that I couldn't summon the energy, the fight to give CB a fair go.

We'd only just got there. We had an agency. A tour manager. A label as such . . . although a label that wished it didn't have us.

The band was pissed off, but no one tried to change my mind. I had to hang in there. I had to get home.

Our Sweetwaters set was booked for the Saturday night, as the sun was setting. Well over 40,000 tickets had been sold. Split Enz were co-headlining with Elvis Costello and the Attractions, and Juddsy's new group The Swingers were booked to play as well. Juddsy was back from London and living in Auckland. I hadn't really kept in touch with him, but I knew from reading *Rip It Up* magazine that he had put together this band with Mark Hough (of my brother

Geoffrey's band After Hours, who was now calling himself Buster Stiggs) and Wayne Stevens (much better known as Bones Hillman, who became the bass player for Midnight Oil, lucky bastard). They'd supported Split Enz at the Auckland Town Hall on the 'Give It A Whirl' tour in 1979, but I'd never seen them live.

Backstage we all congregated and flitted across each other's radars. Tim was buoyant. Radio in Australia had jumped on 'I Got You' and it was looking like big things would happen. The album *True Colours* was about to come out. Then I happened on Juddsy. The Swingers were moving ahead, with new songs rolling out of that man's deeply fertile mind. I'd get to hear some when they performed their afternoon spot.

I can't deny thinking how we were all in that same band. Once. Out on the verandah at Malmsbury Villa, playing all those cool songs that no one seems to know. Songs about beach walls, being outside the times, watching flowers hit the floor. But I guess every forward motion has a kick-start. An emergence from the dark into the light. The revelation. This festival might well lay out where that revelation had taken us all.

First up were The Swingers. Juddsy was singing so much better than he used to. It was his role now to carry the vocal melodies, sharing the words to his cool new songs. 'The Jinx'. 'It's All Over Town'. 'Certain Sound'. I wasn't to know then, but we would meet over a couple of these songs in the not-too-distant future.

CB was on in the evening. We walked out to face a sea of heads a long way away—a huge crowd who had drifted in from their tents, long-drops, sleeping bags, empty cans, smirks and teenage ramblings. I don't know what song we started with. But there was a sense of discipline over excitement. The guys weren't impressed with my walking away. Geoffrey threw in a few lyric changes that told me what he thought of me. Best to know these things. And a good place to pass them over. No way to start a conversation. Around 40,000 punters out there. They don't care. They just want the next song.

'Rust In My Car' maintained its pride of place as the one they sang along with. That's always a moving moment—when a song you've written stays alive in the mob and they throw it back with you high in the air.

It seemed a clear-cut conclusion to this life in a second band. This final retreat. Nothing goes on forever. Geoffrey and I and all those hours in the Otahuhu Pavilion. Onstage at Sacred Heart. The Split Enz triumphant buck-a-head. The Citizen Band full house at the Auckland Town Hall. Another dream come true of my fourth-form essay to Brother Stephen.

I looked out at the Sweetwaters audience, now silhouetted against the evening sky. A high wall of moving heads. Shimmering. Listening. I whispered to myself, 'I love you, Geoffrey, but this is goodbye.'

We finished our set and retreated to the dressing room. Well, a tent. I took off my sweat-drenched clobber and folded it up and threw it in the rubbish. This needed to be final.

I went to the Split Enz tent. Smiles and handshakes.

I spoke to Nigel. We talked about bass guitars. They were minutes away from playing. They were distracted and poised. I knew that feeling, that anticipation. I left them to it.

Split Enz came out and played a set that showed they knew the album they were about to release was going to catapult them into the stratosphere. They played like masters of the universe. And that's what they became in a matter of days. Songs we heard live for the first time. 'What's the Matter With You'. 'Poor Boy'. 'I Got You'. 'I Hope I Never'. Beautiful.

While we were standing around after our slot at Sweetwaters, Neil Ronald had come up and told us that Charley Gray, who had managed both Island of Real and Th' Dudes, was keen to book us a February 'final' tour. We weren't sure about the 'final'. My final, sure—but not a CB final. But we were keen to do dates. They would differ, I suspected, from the Mustang Car Club show in Goulburn.

During February we skedaddled around the North Island playing here and there. Full houses everywhere. A consolidation. We played in Hamilton and, as usual, a pill was taken at 4 p.m. But being close to Auckland I decided not to stay overnight. So I drove back around midnight. At least three times I found myself heading towards the centreline barrier as the drug tried to make me go to sleep.

Driving *to* a gig caused the real tension. Take the pill, and the effect found me on a level playing field as evening came on. But returning from it, back to Auckland—where was that tension? I wound down the window. All the windows. Deep-breathing to ward off the incoming sleep. Just as well

I was the only one in the car. As I cruised up the motorway offramp towards home, I knew I had been lucky to stay alive.

The tour hustled on. We played in Rotorua. We didn't play in the hotel that wouldn't give us rooms; we played to a full house somewhere else. We stayed in a motel with a spa pool, a rumble-tumble spin-off to the true nature of life on the road. A life I would soon be leaving behind.

This tour was a revelation after Sydney: people actually wanted to hear us play. The guys were going to return to Sydney after finding a new bass player. Who would that be? Would he change my lines? What bass would he play? Roundwound strings? Flatwound strings? A Peavey 210 amplifier? Time would tell. What was I going to do? Be an engineer? Build a bridge? Concoct a computer program for dredging harbours? I wasn't going to pack suitcases and check in at airports; I was going to lie low.

The weekly *Radio With Pictures* show on Sunday nights often had a documentary segment, made by the maestro Dylan Taite. He recorded an interview with me backstage at Sweetwaters. Word had got out that I was leaving the band. It goes like this:

Q: What's made you again turn your back on success?
A: Well, touring and playing—you either finish a gig, I really enjoy that—or you find sometimes you do and sometimes you don't and you just stick to it 'cos you know it's just something you're working at. And if you find you're getting nothing out of it, most of the time, then you think it's time to step out. It'd be the same in any job, surely. I'm not getting anything out of being

in a band that's touring a lot . . . that's on the move, a transitory thing all the time.

Q: Does it mean it's the end of your career as a playing musician?

A: I'd like to think not. I'd like to do little things here and there . . . on recording. Recording is the one aspect of the music industry and playing in particular that I enjoy most. And getting behind the desk in the recording studio which I've tried—producing. Just stay in the music industry. I don't want to get out of the music industry.

If I may, I will respond to Dylan Taite's questions here with the truth.

Q: What's made you again turn your back on success?

A: Well, I have a madness. A mysterious—let's call it a disorder, which I don't understand, although I think it came from drugs. Probably stress, in fact. But I deny that. But others were there as I fell apart and nothing happened to them. What it means is that I find myself in the most torturous situations where I have absolutely no means to deal with anything. I hide, I crawl, I lock doors. And it's always when I'm out on the road. When I'm away. I have to be able to retreat. To escape. To turn around. To reverse. To accelerate.

Q: Does it mean it's the end of your career as a playing musician?

A: Dylan . . . I set my sights as a young boy on being a performer in a rock band. I was going to be a Beatle.

The thought that I may not play again fills me with dread. I will keep on playing. I don't know how. Or who with. I don't think it will be far away. But I will. Especially when I find out how to cure myself.

Chapter Twenty
The Revelation

I took a phone call in February 1980 from one Arthur Baysting. I knew him from when the dance/music troupe Red Mole supported Split Enz on the 'Courting The Act' tour in 1977. They did fire-breathing and a parade of left-of-centre things. Arthur was on the sideline there. It wasn't clear what his role was, but it was something creative.

'Hi, Mike. Did you see The Crocodiles at Sweetwaters?'

I had. They had played in the afternoon. Their lead singer was wondrous. Her name was Jenny Morris. Most of the feedback, though, was around their bass player, Tina Matthews, who wore see-through harem pants. You get the picture. They had some hooky songs with colourful lyrics. Tongue-in-cheek.

'Yes, I did, Arthur.'

'Well, can the band and I come to see you? They're looking for a manager.'

'Of course.'

And in they came. Bruno Lawrence was with them. He was their drummer. In my mind he was Mr Cool, as he had played drums with Quincy Conserve and wrote their hit 'Ride the Rain' in 1970. It featured very cool bass-playing by their man Dave Orams; it sounded like he was using flatwound strings on a Vox 'teardrop' bass. Supreme. At the time I dreamed of playing like him.

Anyway—The Crocodiles. I agreed to be their manager. After all, getting a job as an engineering graduate was not to my liking. I had no idea what being a manager really meant. I guessed it was like it was in Citizen Band during times when we weren't on the road. Making phone calls and booking gigs.

A day or two after that first get-together I met with Arthur and band members Fane Flaws and Tony Backhouse. Flaws, Arthur and their keyboard player Peter Dasent had written ten songs and recorded them at Mandrill Studios with Glyn Tucker. Arthur was like their spiritual guidance officer, and the co-writer of many of their songs. I was given a cassette of their debut album, and told that they intended for the song 'Tears' to be their first single. It was track number four on side one. (As you track-listing experts know, track four, side one held pole position on most albums.) And off they went. There was no talk of live shows in the first instance, but I knew that must come.

Now, after some seven years bearing witness to the wobbly, discombobulating arena of the New Zealand music industry, I'd picked up a thing or two. The main one, particularly in relation to where I was right then, was that radio stations tended to avoid playing singles by New Zealand artists that weren't in the Top 40 chart. Hello Sailor's 'Gutter Black' and Th' Dudes' 'Be Mine Tonight' walked onto playlists because they each had a large fan base who bought their records via word of mouth, putting them in the charts, so radio played them and they sold more records.

The Crocodiles didn't have a fan base. But, lo and behold,

I knew one of the people at the radio station 1ZM who was doing research into what the public thought of particular songs. That research would tell 1ZM if they should play a song or not.

First, I applied to be one of the punters out there being rung by the researchers. So my friend rang me. What followed was banal.

'Hi, Mr Chunn (*snigger snigger*). Thanks for agreeing to be on our research group. I will play you excerpts of songs and you tell me on a scale how you rate each one. One means you really dislike it. Ten means you love it. Or you can say "I don't know it."'

'Thanks, dear researcher (*snigger snigger*). Off you go.'

I heard about ten seconds of 'Crazy Little Thing Called Love' down the telephone.

'I don't know it.' It sounded terrible.

About ten seconds of 'Woman in Love' by Barry Gibb and Barbra Streisand. That sounded terrible, too. (It was coming down a telephone line, after all.)

'I don't know it.' *Snigger snigger snigger*.

We hung up. OK. I saw how it worked. A song like 'Tears' would get rafts of 'I don't know it'. A song like 'Crazy Little Thing Called Love' would likely get screeds of 'ten' ratings because the video was on TV a lot and 1ZM had already started playing it because it was a hit overseas.

I had a plan.

I met with my researcher friend and the concept was simple. For every person she rang, no matter what they said, she put a ten in the column for 'Tears'. Within a week, 1ZM was playing 'Tears' every four hours. It went into the Top 20. Excellent.

The Crocs did have a few dates that they'd booked around the time of Sweetwaters. The first one was at a bar in Manukau City. I put Fane Flaws, Jenny Morris and Tony Backhouse in my back seat and drove them down the Southern Motorway. They started to sing in three-part harmony.

Oh my God! It was one of the most glorious, musical, vocal moments of my then-bumpy ride through life. How do people do that? Like—well—The Beatles did.

The members of The Crocodiles had voices of the highest order, and at the show that night I was mesmerised by them. Their songs had cool humour all through them, too—a cleverness that weaved crazy stories around clichés that weren't clichés but you thought they were, that made you smile.

They soon recorded a video of 'Tears'. Those were the days when TVNZ made the videos for free, and paid artists the musicians' union rate into the bargain. It was a good deal, but the resulting videos were terrible. And with 'Tears', the video clip paled in comparison to the song. I couldn't help thinking they'd have been better off without a video. But videos were de rigueur! If you had one that truly 'related' to the song, like Split Enz's 'I See Red', then well and good. But if you didn't, then the video distracted the viewer from the song. Not good. That's my view of all that; and here, decades later, I'm sticking to it.

The Crocs album was released by RCA Records in April 1980 and reached the same chart position as the single— number 17. On the back of the energy that both created out there in the marketplace, gigs started to come in.

I'd seen Juddsy around a bit, as a few of The Crocodiles

were living in his flat in Grafton. His band The Swingers were to have their debut single 'One Good Reason' released on Ripper Records, which was a label started by Bryan Staff, who had been a radio announcer. Bryan invited me to join him as a co-Ripper guy. I said, 'Of course.' An informal partnership, let's call it.

Juddsy had asked me to produce the two tracks 'One Good Reason' and 'All Over Town' with him and his band at Mascot Studios. I said, 'Of course.' I had no experience of producing apart from being produced. I'd been in a studio. How hard could it be? I now know that production is actually a mixture of science and psychology, of getting people to work together in the best possible way.

The two songs were hooky and vibrant. Juddsy had returned to his mastery of the three-minute song that propels you with it. It was exciting. My contribution as producer was minimal and really, in the end, it might well have come out better if I hadn't been there. But I was, and it was a joy to see and hear Juddsy, my old bandmate, doing this new thing.

He asked about a producer's royalty for me, but I said, 'That's too fussy. Who's going to calculate it? All that palaver.' I suggested that if The Swingers recorded and released a future single then Ripper Records would have the rights to release it in New Zealand. That was easy—written on a single sheet of paper, probably worth about one cent, we both signed it.

The two Swingers tracks were released as a double-A-side single in April 1980 and reached number 19 in the Top 40. Around this time Juddsy told me that he was planning to take the band to Australia. The Enz's album *True Colours* was selling a massive number of copies on both sides of the Tasman, and

I sensed that he had his old label Mushroom Records in his sights. And Mushroom's boss Michael Gudinski had his eye on Juddsy. Why wouldn't he? It seemed to me a logical progression.

Juddsy kept writing and The Swingers went out gigging. And in the not-too-distant future they flew across to Melbourne to record for Mushroom. They had a new song called 'Counting the Beat', which was going to be produced by David Tickle, who had produced Enz's *True Colours*.

And, while fate was lining up all these ducks, I rode shotgun with The Crocodiles as their manager. But as gigs got booked it started to dawn on me that I should be a proper manager and travel with them. Gigs were booked in all sorts of towns and cities. Back on the road. The white lines on the motorway.

The first time we took off touring, I felt much less tense than if it had been with Enz or CB. Why? I knew. If I started to feel that swell of panic and terror looming, poised to attack me, I could just make up an excuse: 'I've just forgotten that it's my mother's birthday and I need to get back to Auckland for her dinner party.' It could be that easy. But what if it happened at night? The gig finishes and I'm in a candlewick-bedspread motel unit with instant coffee and non-dairy whitener. How do I explain a sudden exit and drive back to Auckland at 1 a.m.? I knew the answer to that, too. Take tranquillisers at around 5 p.m. every day; not in the morning. That would work. So I did that. And it worked. Almost.

We all boarded the Cook Strait ferry in Picton to get to some bookings in Wellington. About two kilometres out into the Marlborough Sounds it hit me. Came rushing into my head. Where had it been hiding? Why? It wasn't even 9 a.m.!

Another 'oh dear!' revelation. I knew I couldn't dive off the side of the ferry and start swimming back to Picton.

I moved swiftly to the toilet and on the usual shivering, 160-bpm highway of terror, I vomited. I took two pills. They would take 20 to 30 minutes to work; I had to hide. I went to the far corner of a row of seats, burrowed myself into them, closed my eyes and pretended to be asleep. I waited. Waited. My thoughts doing their usual constant streaming with nothing to hold on to. Spinning. Whirling.

And then the drugs hit and I fell into a deep sleep. Jenny Morris was shaking me. She could hardly wake me up. They gathered around, bemused by my soporific state. I explained that I'd taken a seasickness pill and it had made me very drowsy. I apologised. Their blurry manager. They believed it. I was now a true master of disguise.

The Crocs gigs went on, and I sought refuge in the tranquillisers if there was no way I could return to Auckland. I virtually never flew. Ferries were out. Give me a car! I can turn that around.

In mid 1980, down in Wellington, The Crocs had a night off so I went to the Last Resort café to check out Barry Saunders' band The Tigers. As I walked in and sat down—there weren't many people there—I was socked in the jaw, smashed in the face and tossed against the back wall. That night's support act was performing, and the power, the supreme musical coherence of their arrangements, their energy—I couldn't take my eyes off them. I turned to the lad who was mixing their sound.

'Who's this band?' I asked.

'Pop Mechanix,' he said.

Pop Mechanix? Who were they?

'Where from?'

'We're up from Christchurch.'

After they finished their set I went over and introduced myself. Each had their own identity. The drummer—he looked like a drummer. The bass player—eyes that went back about a hundred miles. Suspecting. Wary. Their lead guitarist—like them all, hard to read. Their personality entwined with their fingers. The keyboard/guitarist, the one who looked about five years younger than the others—jerky, happy. And the lead singer—the main man. I walked up to him.

'Hi. I'm Mike Chunn.'

'Hi, I'm Richard Driver. They call me Dick.'

And that's how I met Pop Mechanix.

'I'd be keen to be your manager.'

'OK,' said Dick. And from then on I was. How would I do that? Where were they going? Where did they want to go? Would they want to get on ferries? How do you manage two bands?

Pop Mx, as they came to be called in industry shorthand, settled into Auckland. First things first—let's record a single.

They had one tumultuously hooky song called 'Now', so we made plans to record it at Mandrill Studios. I would produce it and Ripper Records would release it. (After The Swingers session I had produced three more tracks for Ripper, all of which solidified in the back of my mind that I was good at being superfluous. 'Suicide 2' by Proud Scum and 'Short Haired Rock N Roll' by the Terrorways were released as a double-A-side in May 1980, and 'Lifetime Occupation' by The Whizz Kids, featuring Andrew McLennan, better known as Andrew Snoid, on vocals, was released double-A with the Spelling Mistakes' 'Rena', produced by Bryan Staff. Anyway, back to Pop Mechanix . . .)

The recording of 'Now' blew my mind. That band had a mastery of how far to push performance so that you were hanging on every note and every word. It all felt like it was going to go! And then Dick announced he was leaving the band. But his voice was on the track. Mmmm. Where to now, St Peter?

Paul Scott, the bass player and magician of the band, came up to me. 'We're going to ask Andrew Snoid to be our singer.' They asked him. He said, 'Of course.'

So we brought Andrew into the studio, pushed the 'record' button and Andrew's new vocal wiped out Dick's. We mixed it and it was done. Ready to go!

It was released on Ripper in September 1980. Radio wouldn't touch it. There was no official video. It drifted out over the horizon and was gone. But the demand from live venues was strong because the band was starting to grow a fan base. So I got on that phone. Bookings were made far and wide. We were moving on. And sometimes people rang me. One in particular.

The phone would start ringing around 2 a.m. The first time went like this.

'Hey, Mike Chunn. It's Kim Fowley here in Los Angeles. Have you heard of me before, Mike?'

I had heard of Kim Fowley. He co-produced a song in 1960 that went to number one in the USA. It was called 'Alley Oop' and was a novelty song. But more recently, and in a more groovy way, Fowley had put together an all-female group called The Runaways. I saw their show in a nightclub in Dallas, Texas, on the Enz tour of 1977. The room was filled with young men (that included me I guess; I was 24) and we were all fixated on this very rocky band playing in their underwear.

'Yes, I've heard about you, Kim. I saw The Runaways in Dallas. In '77.'

'Ah, man. I was there. They rocked. OK! We're off to a good start. Now, you manage Pop Mechanix and you produced their single "Now," and I have a copy and they will be New Zealand's Beatles. That's how I see it. Can we talk?'

I can't deny that being woken at 2 a.m. became rather enjoyable after a while. Kim Fowley was colourful, vehemently enthusiastic and on a mission. But I never met him. He never met Pop Mechanix. He came through the telephone lines and . . . well . . . went. And time kept moving on.

The decision was made to record another Pop Mx single, so they went to Stebbing Studios with the ex-Dudes guitarist Ian Morris producing. They recorded 'The Ritz' backed with 'Brains Are Dumb' and 'Talking'. This was a magnificent trio of hooky songs. 'The Ritz' got a smattering of airplay and then it all drifted out over the horizon to join the graveyard of New Zealand singles, which was becoming more and more voluminous.

I kept booking gigs, and I found myself sticking more to life in Auckland. No trains or boats or planes. And always a bottle of pills, safe in my pocket.

By the end of 1980 both my acts were making moves to go to Australia. Pop Mechanix had interest from CBS Records in New Zealand and, on a sympathetic vibration, interest from their Sydney office. And The Crocodiles had a lad in Sydney—Terry Condon and his Stunn label—so both decided that New Zealand's circuitous route of playing venues here and there was getting too repetitive. Both were booked to play at the 1981 Sweetwaters festival: The Crocs at around 2 p.m., Pop Mx just prior to Split Enz in the evening.

During that slide to the end of the year The Crocodiles recorded a second album, titled *Learning To Like Ourselves*. As always, the songs were hooky, lyrical and sung beautifully. But it lacked a focused producer and it sounded awful. Glyn Tucker at Mandrill Studios, where it was recorded, said the album was 'way below par' and should be withheld. If it was released he wanted the studio's name removed from the cover. He was right, but how could I go to the band and say it was a thin, tinny-sounding record and out of time with all that was happening in the era of New Wave? I was their manager. Don't managers step up to the plate and do what has to be done? Talk reason? Discuss in economic language the realities of a band's situation? Talk about prospects, strategies, necessities? Of course a manager does that. But I couldn't. All year I had avoided any confrontation, no matter how much I needed to engage in it. Dialogue. Communication. Rapport. How do you do that?

I did what I did. I rang a sales rep at RCA Records and said, 'Mandrill Studios thinks the album shouldn't be released. What do you think of it?'

'I think it's great,' she said. Of course she would. She had probably never heard it, I suspect. It would be mean to say,

'Don't release it.' No skin off her nose. So I handed over the master tapes and the album artwork and RCA made a bunch of records and talked a few stores into stocking it, and it sold nothing. It ran as fast as it could to the horizon and dived over the edge.

At the same time The Crocs took off on a national tour (I stayed in Auckland). Full houses everywhere—and then the Auckland Town Hall. It had been just over a year since Citizen Band triumphed there. Now it would be The Crocodiles' turn. They had a hit (of sorts) with 'Tears', didn't they? They'd been on TV now and then. So why not the Auckland Town Hall? How foolish could I be? There were about 40 people in the 1800-seat hall.

Soon afterwards the band lost members. Tina ran. Fane was gone. Bruno had been gone a while. New members came on board. They played Sweetwaters on 4 January 1981 and I was on bass. Yes, really. Why was I on bass? With my head spending most of its time sitting comfortably on its botty in Auckland, my heart could march to the front line again and shout at the top of its voice, 'We're going back onstage! We're going to play the bass! We don't care who with!' And it led to nothing and The Crocodiles flew away to Sydney.

Pop Mechanix, meanwhile, triumphed on the Sweetwaters stage. Andrew Snoid zipped and curled out front cajoling the crowd, and the band was monstrously good. They were socialising with Split Enz backstage, and Pop Mx were offered a support slot on Australian dates if they got themselves across the Tasman. We talked about that, and, in the aftermath of Sweetwaters, plans were made. They were going to fly away too.

I walked away from Pop Mechanix thinking that my time as an artist manager was something I must never try again. My ability to stand up and fight for my artists was bordering on nil. My communication skills with the artists themselves consisted of a smiley silence with virtually no feedback, as I was terrified of getting into an argument. That word again—confrontation. And what good is a manager who goes travelling only if he has to, and then takes tranquillisers all the time so that as everyone else perks up he mellows out? It was too hard and I didn't have the balls to just knuckle down and do it well.

And then I got a call from John McCready, the managing director of CBS Records. He invited me out to lunch at a restaurant in Newmarket.

'Mike, I'd like to have you join CBS as A&R manager. Sign new talent to our labels. Are you interested?'

'Of course.'

I wobbled out into the street after our lunch. John and I had had Irish coffees. It went straight to my head. I hadn't drunk alcohol since July 1974, nine years earlier. As I've mentioned, I was certain that it would bring on panic attacks. Why did I think that? I had never worked that out. Now—on the footpath in Newmarket with a big grin on my face, a soon-to-be corporate animal, a man with a budget, a company car!—a panic attack seemed a very unlikely event.

A short time later, Michael Gudinski from Mushroom's head office in Melbourne visited me at my home. He was buoyant, with *True Colours* being so successful. He had a copy of The Swingers' new single 'Counting the Beat' and was certain it was going to be a smash hit in Australia. He played it to me and I was shocked. It was freakishly good. Juddsy had captured the perfect elements of a hit single—the melodic mastery of weaving together words and music—and laid them all out in a row on this recording, which was certainly bound to be top of the charts. Gudinski was going to have the single released in New Zealand on the Mushroom label, with RTC Records distributing it. He returned to Melbourne and had the tape masters sent to me for delivery to RTC. I didn't hand them over. I had a piece of paper. I took the single to my new boss John McCready at CBS and said, 'I have the rights to this single. I have an arrangement on paper signed by Philip Judd and myself. Can you put it out on Ripper?'

John listened to the cassette I had with me. He thought it was a smash. I left it with him.

The phone rang that night around 2 a.m. 'Ah,' I thought. 'Good old chatty Kim Fowley wants to tell me again how Pop Mechanix will be the next Beatles.'

'Chunn, it's Michael Gudinski.' He was in Europe. He was vehemently angry.

I listened to him, noting just how good he was at telling me how I'd been a conniving, traitorous individual. Which I had been. Why hadn't I told him about this piece of paper signed by me and Juddsy? I had been too scared to.

'It's not worth the paper it's written on,' he said. As the phone call tapered to an ending—not a conclusion—I thought, 'You know, Michael, I wish this wasn't happening. Mushroom Records and Mike Chunn go way back. You always had time for me. You supported me in the Enz days and understood what drove people like me.' But there I was in my pyjamas on Brighton Road listening and not saying anything. And then he was gone.

I got a call from McCready the next day. 'The single is in for manufacture. Gudinski rang me this morning. He's a tough negotiator but we've sorted it.'

In a couple of weeks 'Counting the Beat' came out on Ripper Records, distributed through CBS. It went screaming up the chart to number one. I thought, 'Juddsy, you've cracked it. This is monumental.'

It was one of the most successful singles I had ever been involved with, even though I hadn't really done anything. I didn't make a penny out of it; it was just exciting to be part of its phenomenal success.

About three weeks later I went in to the CBS Records offices in Falcon Street, Parnell, to start my job there. I was assigned a desk with a phone, an office chair and an IBM golf-ball typewriter. The office was essentially open-plan and there was a hum of voices.

One thing wasn't as expected. On that first day John McCready announced he was leaving to go and run CBS Australia, and a young guy called Murray Thom was coming in as managing director. All good. A company has people in it. I presumed they came and went. Finance people. Promotions people. Sales people. Manufacturing people. Quite a mob. And me. Looking for talent.

Murray and I talked about checking out a band called The Gone.

I said, 'Shall I go see them?'

He said, 'Of course.'

So I looked up where they were playing. It was in Christchurch. I knew I should go down there. That would be fine . . . with a few pills in my pocket. Back on a plane = pills.

I went up the road to my father's surgery and shuffled into his office. He was sitting in his cool Scandinavian desk chair. (The one I am sitting in right now, as I write this.)

'Jerry, I need some more Serepax.'

'You've been taking them for quite a while,' he said. 'I wonder if you shouldn't go have a chat to a psychiatrist about this stage fright or whatever it is that makes you nervous. You're not in a band any more.'

Clever man. No, I wasn't in a band any more. But what could I say? This? 'Jerry, it's not about going onstage. I've been lying to you for seven years. It's about what I'm presuming is a drug-induced madness from taking LSD and Thai Sticks all mixed in with stress about my beautiful band losing its drummer. My brother. I can't go on a plane and fly away without taking one. It's just . . . how it is.'

Instead I said, 'But you never know, I might be asked to play bass for someone somewhere and I'll need them so I can take the stage with confidence.'

'OK,' he said. 'But I'll call a psychiatrist who I recommend to some of my patients. I think you should go and talk about this with him.'

So I did.

'Hello, Mike,' said Mr Psychiatrist. 'Your father said you have some problems with fear overwhelming you when you have to take the stage. Tell me about it.'

So I told him my lies and outlined one of my panic attacks—the onrush of terror and what it did to me. I didn't mention Class A or B drugs. Or stress.

I finished and waited for an answer.

'Well, it sounds to me like something you'll just get over one day.'

'Thank you,' I said, and left.

I went to the chemist, got my pills and floated off on an aeroplane to Christchurch to see The Gone. I can't recall the venue. They played bloody well with a post-New Wave, edgy, melodic impact.

I was with the CBS promotions rep from the South Island. Her name was Brigid. It was her job to go to Top 40 radio stations and drop off new singles on the CBS label. She looked at me to see if I was converging on some sort of decision about The Gone. Would I or would I not sign them?

I thought about it. They had songs. They sang well. Did they like each other? Were they getting ripped every morning and stealing food from supermarkets? Did they have convictions? If I offered them a contract, did they have the family solicitor of one of their parents poised to pore over every clause? Did they have parents who thought being in a band was a life well wasted? How would they perform in the recording studio? Would they have red-light syndrome, and freeze when it came time to lay down their tracks? Did any of them have panic attacks?

'What are you thinking? Do you want to sign them?' Brigid asked.

'I don't really know anything about them.'

'Isn't what you've just seen and heard enough to tell you?'

'But I watched the audience. Some danced to them. Some were talking. Some left the room. Was that audience completely taken with that band?'

'But isn't that our job? If you like their songs, then we get radio to play them and TV to show them and then people will buy their records.'

'No,' I said. 'That's wrong. No member of the public who hears a song on the radio suddenly walks zombie-like down to a record store, goes in and pulls five dollars out of their pocket and says "I must have The Gone single. I have heard it on radio. I must have it." They only go and buy it if they like it.'

'Well, will people like their records?' she said.

'The way I saw it, not enough people in the room were taken with them. I think it's risky. CBS could spend thirty thousand dollars recording tracks and videos and there's no guarantee they will sell records. When that band has crowds of people fixated on them—cheering and going crazy—then you know something will happen. You need both. A big stash of fans who pour into your live shows, and then a record comes out and goes Top Ten. And then radio will play it and the momentum builds. It is exponential. It's about playing a role in the foundation of a band's long-term career. It has to be a long-term strategy.'

And the conversation slowly closed. I watched the band getting their gear unplugged and ready for loading. Brigid went and paid the bill. I watched her over there . . . paying the bill. It was just a bar. But I wanted to keep looking at her.

The next morning I took another pill and boarded the plane back to Auckland.

I had imagined that being an A&R man would mean going to see lots of exciting new bands play live. My role at CBS turned out to be largely sitting in my office listening to cassettes from acts and bands, all looking for a record deal. I felt the weight of their urging. I knew the dream they harboured and what it would mean to get a record deal with CBS. But I wouldn't sign anyone who didn't have the crowds pouring in and going crazy. I'd seen how it worked with Hello Sailor and Th' Dudes. The fans were there at the ready. They made moves the minute a record came out. They ran off down the road and bought those records. I was convinced that was how it must be. And so I listened and watched and analysed and didn't sign anyone. I hated saying no to people, but I knew that I knew a good song when I heard one and I wasn't hearing any. I wasn't going to sign a band just because they were trying really hard.

Then Billy Joel came to town. Joel played a show at the Logan Campbell Centre to a full house and his performance was sublime. The sound was amazing. Technical expertise all over the room. I was in a flash seat, as Billy Joel was a CBS Records artist. At one stage he screamed out to his drummer Liberty DeVitto, 'NEW YORK!' I knew that tone. I recognised the facial tics. It was the last show of a global tour and he was desperate to get home.

CBS hosted a post-gig function at the White Heron Hotel in Parnell. There was hubbub and dialogue, gentle motion around the room and well-deserved praise. I was standing alone when Joel walked up to me.

'You're one of the CBS people, yes?'

'I am,' I said. 'Can I ask you a question?'

'Sure,' he said. 'Are you a journalist on the side? Moonlighting?' He smiled. If anyone knew a journo's face it would be him.

'You screamed out "New York!" to DeVitto. I recognised the look on your face. And the tone of your voice. Are you desperate to get home?'

A pause.

'I sure am,' he said.

For around twenty minutes we talked about the road. The only difference between what each of us had experienced was that he had been to hundreds of cities and had millions of dollars, a manager, a staff of minders, tour managers, et cetera. But he still had to queue at airports. Take things out of a suitcase. Do sound checks. Kill time.

This whole fame thing: Joel was drenched in it. During his press reception someone had asked him, 'Is life so different at the level you're at?' He answered, 'Well, I have an obscene amount of money.' But talking to me, he seemed like he'd had enough of the travel. And this despite having limos and minders and people to carry his suitcases. Perhaps he thought, now and then, 'I'd like to carry my own suitcase. I'd like to go to a café and just sit there and have a bottomless cup of coffee. Think about what's been did and what's been hid.' He was like you. He was like me.

And then he was gone. As he walked away with his band to slope off to their rooms, I watched his every step.

B y August 1981, eight months after starting at CBS, I still hadn't signed anybody. I met with Murray Thom in his office. He had that look on his face and, I guess, so did I. He thought I'd been achieving very little. I was thinking that I'd achieved very little. It didn't take long to agree that I would depart from CBS.

I thought about next steps. Where to? Do what? Things were changing: I had separated from Paula the month before. And now Brigid had appeared on my horizon.

A week later I walked out of the CBS Records building and dawdled back home. Back out into the wilderness. But, as one finds in life, there's always something around the corner. This time it was a magazine. In the barber shop.

I don't recall what the magazine was called, but it was from the UK. The article that I had flicked upon was titled 'Phobic Disorders'. It said:

> A phobia is an irrational fear of something that's unlikely to cause harm. The word itself comes from the Greek word *phobos*, which means 'fear' or 'horror'.

There were around twenty phobias listed. Some rang bells.

> Claustrophobia [Down in a tunnel stuff—I liked that. No worries]
> Acrophobia: Fear of heights [That's me]
> Arachnophobia: Fear of spiders [Bring them on]
> Haemophobia: Fear of blood [I love blood]
> Koinoniphobia: Fear of rooms full of people [I'm into crowded rooms]

Ophidiophobia: Fear of snakes [No thanks]

And:

> Agoraphobia: A fear of not being able to return to where you feel safe. A safe haven.

Oh my God! *Not being able to return to where I feel safe.* Like what? Like being side-stage at a gig in Wellington and not being able to leave and go . . . where? Being on an aeroplane flying between Christchurch and Wellington and not being able to go . . . where? Driving in a van to Sheffield from London and not being able to go . . . where?

I knew where. I sat back in the barber's waiting chair. He called me over for my haircut. I stood up and walked out the door.

I was shaking with relief. There it was. *Agoraphobia.* The irrational fear that I wouldn't be able to get back to . . . AUCKLAND. That's where I am safe. In Auckland. I looked back at the article (I had stolen it). It said:

> Those with phobic disorders sometimes have panic attacks when in particular situations. These panic attacks can be so terrifying that people, in their day-to-day lives, do everything they can to avoid them.
>
> Phobic disorders are not uncommon but generally sufferers are embarrassed or confused by them and don't report them to their doctors.

NOT UNCOMMON.

I went to a coffee bar and sat in a window seat. I was still shaking. *Phobic disorders*. I had agoraphobia. *Not uncommon. Embarrassed by them.*

I knew what I had to do.

1. Avoid leaving Auckland.
2. Take tranquillisers when I had to leave Auckland (and never when I didn't).
3. Clarify in my mind that I had a disorder just like . . . who? That woman walking past the window? She might have one. It's OK.

And from that day of revelation I have never taken a tranquilliser when I've been in Auckland. Auckland is the soothing voice, the warm hand holding me. I can live. I am free. The rest of the world? I can deal with that in my sleepy fashion. But what matters most is that I may well live the rest of my life never having another panic attack. I won't ever will for my own death again.

Chapter Twenty-one
The Exponential Mushroom

I was sitting on the deck at Brighton Road thinking about the future. About the next day. The day after the next day. About a job that would send me off to Christchurch now and then. I could handle those trips. Christchurch. Brigid was at Canterbury University. And the phone rang.

'Hi, Mike, it's Doug Rogers here.' Doug was the lad who had started Harlequin Studios in the '70s. 'I'm looking for someone to come help manage the studio and I hear you're leaving CBS.'

'I am.'

'Are you interested?'

'Of course.' And a fortnight later I was in there.

The first person I saw was up a ladder painting a wall. She had long, bouncy black hair and her name was Debbie Harwood. She was 21 years old and was working there after arriving in Auckland from Taradale. The studio had some cool, contemporary artists booked in for sessions. Blam Blam Blam. Geoffrey's old bandmate Graeme Gash. And it seemed that more would be around the corner.

Doug sat down and said to me, 'You know, we should have

a record producers' seminar series here . . . in the studio. Get New Zealand producers and those who want to be one to come along and watch an expert in action.'

I thought that was a cool idea. 'Who?'

'We should get Roy Thomas Baker,' said Doug.

Roy Thomas Baker? Eek! How would we do that? He'd produced 'Bohemian Rhapsody'! In fact, all of the Queen albums. He'd been producing The Cars—making hits all over the world.

'He's in Boston recording a new Cars album. The place is called Syncro Sound. Give him a call.'

To cut to the chase . . .

'Good evening, Syncro Sound.'

'Hi, my name's Mike. I'm calling from Harlequin Studios in New Zealand. Is Roy Thomas Baker there?'

A fairly long silence. Then, 'Just hold the line, please.'

'Hello, it's Roy Thomas Baker here.'

Right on! I got him. I suspect he only took the call because he thought New Zealand was a distant place with palm trees, white sandy beaches and hula girls. He was curious. I asked him if he wanted to come down and run a studio producers' series of seminars and he said yes. There he was a few weeks later. He brought an engineer with him: Ian Taylor.

The producer series was a revelation. Roy did very little on the recording desk—Ian did all the twiddling. Roy spent most of his time throwing out comments to the performers, acts like Dave Dobbyn's newbie group DD Smash and Blam Blam Blam. It was all devoid of rocket science because everything was analogue and down to 'what you heard'. If it sounded good, you'd keep it. If it didn't, you did something about it.

After about ten days Roy and Ian flew to the UK to tell everyone, I'm guessing, that New Zealand didn't have palm trees, white sandy beaches and hula girls. I could be wrong.

Then Doug sat down again with another idea.

'You know Michael Gudinski. Give him a call and ask if he's interested in us running a Mushroom label in New Zealand out of Harlequin. And, if he is, we can go to DD Smash through their manager Roger King and see if they're interested in signing to it.'

Ah, such a cool idea. Harlequin would be the studio that bands recorded in, and Mushroom would put up the cash. I rang Michael Gudinski. Our last phone call, as you know, was fairly one-sided, during which I silently applauded Gudinski's talent in using the right language to say exactly what he felt.

'Hi, Michael. It's Mike Chunn here in Auckland.'

'Hi, Chunnie. What's up?'

Chunnie! Ah. Time heals. He called me Chunnie just like he did back in the mid '70s.

Two days later, after immediately agreeing to the establishment of a Mushroom New Zealand record label, Gudinski turned up at Harlequin with an artwork design and a question.

'Have you got anyone in mind for the first signing?'

'We do, in fact. DD Smash.'

'Who?'

We met with Roger King, who said yes to signing to the Mushroom New Zealand label, and Dave Dobbyn and his mob booked in to Harlequin to record what became *Cool Bananas*.

I would drop in on the album sessions and just watch. Well, once I did say to Dave, 'I can't hear the kick drum', and he reached over and turned it up. (The track was 'Solo', and the producer was Ian Morris again.) It was clear that DD Smash had stored up a repertoire of songs that, en masse, would go out and terrorise the country with energy, skill and cool language. They already had a large fan base from their national tour supporting Dave McArtney and the Pink Flamingos.

Mushroom New Zealand released their track 'Repetition' as a single in late 1981, and the album *Cool Bananas* came out in early '82. In its first week of release, it entered the New Zealand album charts at number one. It couldn't have been a better start.

Debbie Harwood joined in promoting the album and its singles here, there and everywhere, and it reached platinum sales status (15,000 at that time) in a few weeks. And out on the road the band was filling houses every step of the way. I stayed in Auckland, clean and all-knowing.

One day the phone rang.

'Hi, Mike, it's Jim Wilson.'

Ah, ye olde Jim Wilson. He of the Hillsborough Tavern in Christchurch and our Citizen Band gigs. The man with a bird's-eye view of what was happening in all things Cantabrian and rock'n'roll.

'Hi, Jim. What's up, me old fruit?'

'There's a band down here you must come and see. Their lead singer's name is Luck. That's all you need to know.'

Travel. An aeroplane. I could do that. And this was Jim Wilson, who knew what was going on.

'When are they playing next?'

'In two weeks they're at the Hillsborough supporting Hip Singles. Your name's on the door.'

'What are they called, Jim?'

'Dance Exponents.'

It was March 1982. I rang Brigid. She could join me at the gig. I booked a flight, took a pill, put another few in my pocket and flew to Christchurch.

The Hillsborough Tavern was full. A stirring mass. We took up a spot where we could look across and see the reactions of the crowd.

Out came Dance Exponents, looking like schoolboys in their last year at school. In fact they were slightly older than that. I remember Jordan Luck was wearing tartan trousers (or was it a kilt?) and had a floppy haircut.

From the first moment they played, the crowd seethed. Shook. Hopped. Skipped. Jumped. I kept watching them. I looked at the stage. Listening all the time. Concentrating. I looked at the crowd again. They swayed slowly in deep concentration when a song called 'Victoria' started. Simple guitar lines. Then two guitars. Then singing. Then their drummer came in with the bass and the crowd was propelled to movement and started to sing along. They knew the song. They loved the song.

I kept watching the crowd. They never took their eyes off that band. No one talked. No one left. It was a perfect realisation of how words and music can bring a large audience into a unified state, but one where each of them also has their aloneness—at one with what is coming from the stage.

After their set we went backstage and introductions were made. They were drenched in sweat. I had a sudden flashback to how Tim used to leave the stage in a similar state. I thought, 'This is a good sign.'

I asked them if they wanted a record deal with Mushroom New Zealand and they said, 'Of course.' The next morning, a Sunday, I went to a flat somewhere in Christchurch where they were waiting for me. I said that I'd like to offer a deal where Mushroom New Zealand would record and release two singles and then, if we were all getting on like a house on fire, Mushroom would finance the recording of an album.

They said, 'Of course.'

I said, 'I think the first single you record should be "Victoria".'

(I'll tell you why. This band had a legion of fans who would buy a debut single no matter what was on it. A song like 'Victoria' was outside the common thread at the time of the emerging melodramatic stuff that was proliferating in the charts, the New Romantic artists like Duran Duran and Human League and the grandiose puff of the likes of Survivor and Toto. 'Victoria' was a song with a cool, brave evolution. It started with one simple descending guitar line. And it grew and grew. The lyrics told an evocative story of Victoria, the girl next door. A hooker? And if you put in a string quartet to give the recording a Beatles-esque reference, then it just seemed to me to be a good idea. The thing is, I didn't really know anything. Every single I'd played on had disappeared from view without any discernible impact. But, as we all are, I was aware of hit singles and how one stands out from others. Here in 'Victoria' there was a song that told an engaging story with a musical setting that was truly dynamic and evolved beautifully. I just felt it. It had to be 'Victoria'.)

'I think the first single you record should be "Victoria",' I repeated.

'Do you really think so?' said one of them. Maybe more than one of them.

'Yes, I do,' I said. We shook hands and I left to fly back to Auckland. And that was OK with me. I knew I'd be clean up there.

Mr Terror was out there somewhere. But he was chained. I knew what it was. It had a name. Agoraphobia. *A fear of not being able to return to where you feel safe.*

On the plane I closed my eyes and thought about the Hillsborough bar. And the landscape of Auckland.

A few weeks later, Dance Exponents hopped into a van and came to Auckland, where they went in to Harlequin Studios to record 'Victoria' with producer Lee Connolly. It was released in mid July 1982 and debuted on the national singles chart at number nineteen, moving up to number six in two more weeks. People were talking about Dance Exponents.

As the second single, 'Airway Spies', was released, plans were made to record their album *Prayers Be Answered*. Australian Dave Marett was brought in to produce.

All around these recording dates, the band kept playing shows. The crowds grew in size, and soon it was a string of full houses. I would tag along now and then, drive down to here, maybe there. Fly to the South Island. Brigid would buy drinks at the bar. It was always the Hillsborough Tavern. I was a bachelor now following my separation from Paula. This whole new life, this understanding of what was wrong with me had put my past years on freeze-frame, along with the fog of fear that had swirled around and through me. I could watch it dissolve. Slip away. A new existence was emerging. New faces. And Serepax outside Auckland.

About this time my days at Harlequin came to an end and I started running Mushroom New Zealand out of my pad on Parnell's Brighton Road. I had a new phone, with an answerphone plugged into it. Very modern. Mushroom New Zealand records were distributed by Festival Records over in Newmarket, and their promotions person was Debra Mains. She was good at it.

However, in the winter of 1983 she was raped at knife-point by the Parnell Panther, Mark Stephens. Debra was in a bad way, so she moved away from the high stress of promoting international acts at Festival and came to work with me in Brighton Road, promoting the Mushroom singles.

Back then, getting New Zealand radio to play local singles wasn't easy. The US magazine *Radio & Records* would list all the songs American radio was playing and New Zealand stations would just imitate those playlists. But Debra went in and shook them up. DD Smash and Dance Exponents singles were getting played. And the very cool *Radio With Pictures* music show on TV gave them solid support.

The year finished with Dance Exponents supporting David Bowie at Western Springs, where around 80,000 people turned out. *Prayers Be Answered* sold more than 30,000 copies in a matter of weeks. Michael Gudinski was a very happy man.

I went to the Mushroom Records conference in January 1984 on a farm outside Melbourne. I was adrift on a sea of tranquillisers, but no one in the Mushroom Australia mob knew because they didn't know the normal me—I'm sure they thought that I was just the shy, retiring type. I always went to bed first and fell asleep like a puppy dog. It had to be that way.

While Dance Exponents was shaking up New Zealand, DD Smash had based themselves in Sydney and were recording their second album, *The Optimist*. That produced some cool hits—'Whaling' and 'Magic What She Do'—but my involvement was minimal as Mushroom Australia were on their case now.

Along the same lines as my time at CBS Records, I kept getting cassettes from artists who wanted a record deal. Some of the young singer/songwriters were tenacious. One in particular had a really cool phone manner. I wanted to say, 'Hey, Russ, I'm not going to release your recordings and there are a number of reasons why, but I do have to tell you that, listening to you on the phone, you are one truly convincing guy!'

The phone calls stopped when Russ le Roq went to Sydney to take a lead role in a stage production of *Grease*. Over there he reverted to his real name, Russell Crowe.

Chapter Twenty-two
Exit Stage Left!

In mid 1984, I got a phone call from promoter Mike Corless.

'Hey, Chunn. Have you heard of the Party Boys tour in Australia? A collection of members of different bands putting together a show and touring?'

'I have not,' I said.

'Well, we're doing one here. Dave Dobbyn, Graham Brazier, Jenny Morris, Dave McArtney and Peter Warren. Do you want to play bass?'

I felt my heart surge. My head sat back, knowing that it wouldn't take too long and a bottle of pills would keep the peace. And what the hell, the poor little bass player hadn't played bass for some time and . . .

'Shut up!' said my heart.

'I'm in,' I said, and the Party Boys tour was put together. I would be playing bass again. Each singer chose a few songs they would take lead vocals on, and therein lay the repertoire.

It was the first time I'd got together with McArtney and Brazier. How come? Well, in the busy golden era of 1978–79 we all had gigs virtually every night so we never got to check out each other's bands. As well, we would often be in different towns so between-band socialising was limited. Virtually nil.

But I really took to those two lads. They were scallywags. They were larrikins. They were bright, intellectual masters of the song, of the stage.

I knew Jenny Morris, of course, from The Crocodiles. She had gone on to dominate the Australian music industry as a solo artist with her beautiful voice and original songs. And Messrs Dobbyn and Warren were of course from DD Smash, which was still alive and very much based in Sydney.

We hopped into hire cars and off we went. My promotions person Debra was now with Peter Warren, and they were going off to Sydney together. Good on them. It meant I needed to find a new promo person when I got back to the big smoke. The town with no pills. Auckland.

The purity of being onstage with artists I had never played with before but who shared a love of performance was new to me. It was magic. Yes, I was finally in a covers band. But when Dave McArtney stood at the mic and sang The Beach Boys' 'Darlin'' with glorious harmonies from Graham, Dave, Jenny and Peter, what can you do? You are within an enchanting season that you never knew about, that you never thought would be part of your life but it becomes real and wraps itself around you. It holds a place between spring and summer. With the silent communication that true talent brings to the stage, you all relish each note, each beat, each falling drop of sweat.

That's how it was. Night after night after night. And with the bass strap around my shoulder I felt like I was back in the womb.

The tour finished at the Mainstreet Cabaret in Auckland, then everyone drifted away. I turned around to check out the Mushroom lay of the land. I needed a promo person. So I went to Radio Hauraki and into the office—well, not an office, the funky space—of the Hauraki music director Ross Goodwin.

'Hi, Ross. You know, when I was fourteen I used to listen to you on Radio Hauraki, when it was a pirate station.'

'Ah, cool,' said Ross. And it was cool. Here he was in the flesh.

'I'm looking for a promotions person. Someone who a music director like you—who is a tough bastard—can't say no to.'

'There's only one person who can push me to play singles. She's at EMI Records. Her name is Bridget de Launay.'

'Thanks, Ross.' And off I went to see her.

'Hello, Bridget. Would you like to be the promo person for the Mushroom New Zealand label?'

'Of course,' she said. And so it came to be.

I joined Bridget a few times when she went into music directors' personal spaces, and Ross Goodwin was right: they couldn't say no.

But in the world of Mushroom not everything was going so well. In essence, both DD Smash and Dance Exponents took on Australia and lost. While they were over there, I became isolated from their activities, and that distance and lack of involvement found me thinking more and more about where the hell I was going in this life.

Brigid had vacated Christchurch. I would now watch her buy drinks at various Auckland bars. She would stand up there. At the bar. I would watch her.

So there it was. I could live in Auckland pill-free. I could be normal for once. What to do?

Well, why don't we go and see Split Enz?

The whirly-gig, helter-skelter, up-hill-and-down-dale life of Split Enz in the Neil Finn era saw them achieve great things. A Wikipedia investigation will see you right. But let's cut to the chase. Tim had officially left the band in mid 1984. He had released his first solo album the year before, and was on his way to the UK with his partner, Greta Scacchi. The others were at loose ends. (Some not for long.) Neil had taken the helm, but the band had finally come to an end and released its final album, *See Ya 'Round*. In December 1984, they toured Australasia for 'the last time'. The 'Enz With A Bang' tour was put on the road to a long and vibrant string of full houses. I went to the last show, at the Logan Campbell Centre in Auckland. They were playing four full-house nights there. And at the right moment, in the right place—they ran onstage.

Suited in wild colours and hopping, skipping, jumping, lurching and leaping about the stage, Split Enz gave the town where it all began a warm, luscious, emotional send-off. Neil's final effort in the single stakes—'I Walk Away'—kicked off proceedings and struck an immediate chord. (I think it was C major.) Their new drummer, Paul Hester, was inextricably immersed in the Enz spirit, and his performance out front on 'This Is Massive' was masterful. Nigel poured thick molasses bass all over our ears. Tim was springing around, his frenetic stage persona of the '70s a shadow on the back wall. He was now level on the stage with the rest of them and they looked, sounded, smelled like a unit . . . a one-piece shot of exultant musical superiority.

Tim sat at the piano and tinkled a few notes in E major,

a sure sign he was heading into 'Time for a Change'. He spoke: 'This song is dedicated to all the past members of the band who are here tonight. They know who they are.' And he started to sing lyrics from the nineteen-year-old head of Phil Judd.

It was uplifting. I flew around the hall for a while and slid out the door, sailing out over the city. The Wynyard Tavern was murmuring with a few hither-and-thither conversations; Levi's Saloon was thundering to the sound of a hundred Space Invader machines, which had long replaced the video table-tennis ones. A quick right turn and it was down to the beach at Kohimarama where the footprints of the band remained etched under a thousand tides. Like every note etched in my head, their heads . . . a nation full of heads still oscillating to some, a few (all?) of Tim, Neil and Phil's words and melodies. Eddie's notes. Noel's magic vision. The lot of them. Putting on the headphones, standing in a line.

'Charlie', off the *Dizrythmia* album, with its timeless allure brought a huge response. Tim's vocals, precisely in tune, and Eddie's cascading piano frills drowning us all. Pouring out of the speakers like beads of emotion. 'The Woman Who Loves You' brought Noel out for his final spoons love-affair with the public. His legs buckled, flew out to the right and left, his head statuesque and grim. Unique.

The final encore was 'Hard Act to Follow'. Tim's sweat flew all over the front row and Neil squashed his distortion pedal. As the final chord reverberated around they came to the front of the stage and lined up. They'd had a good show. Who would follow them?

As they wandered away to the waiting blackness side-stage, Eddie paused and struck a piano note. Neil noticed this and came back and punched out another one. As the younger Finn then left the stage, Eddie ran back and quickly pushed down a key. I think it was an E flat. It sang out over the sustained applause and stamping feet. I caught it as it went by and put it in my pocket—the very last note ever played by Split Enz. And it was Ed—it *had* to be Ed—who played it.

I went home and put Eddie's note in my bottom drawer.

The Melbourne Festival Hall and Auckland Logan Campbell Centre shows from the 'Enz With A Bang' tour had been recorded, and a double live album was released in early December 1985. It was titled *The Living Enz*.

At this time in my life, I had been writing the odd record review. Out of the blue I received the Enz album in the mail. Ignoring the arm's-length distance I was supposed to have, I absorbed the record and wrote a review. Maybe the madness and tranquillised state of my four-and-a-half years with them had ground my recollections down to a powder. Mind you—I loved writing this.

> Most New Zealanders who have been motivated to witness live music have at some time or other been to a Split Enz concert . . . From the first performance in a coffee bar in December 1972 to its final concert at the Logan Campbell Centre in December 1984, Split Enz toured New Zealand 13 times (give or take the odd burst in the early days), playing to more than 200,000 people

(excluding the Sweetwaters and Nambassa festivals).

Since leaving the band in 1977, I have seen them perform on all but one of their tours and the overriding factor has been their consistency. The costumes, stage sets, choice of songs and gimmicks have always provided colour to varying degrees—but the band's unwavering high standard of musical performance has never been less than excellent. That is why very, very few people have ever left a Split Enz concert unsatisfied. At the very least, people got a musical hammering that could not fail to impress.

In many respects, Split Enz broke the rules. Its democratic musical process avoided the usual pitfalls of over-indulgence and the internal rapport was so acute that the band could sway the most blasé listener with its combined sense of fun . . . and sense of purpose. Spurred by Tim Finn and Noel Crombie, who were chiefly responsible for the band's initial dedication to 'excellence onstage', Enz members never forgot their dictum: 'the people have paid for this—we are here to entertain'.

Whether it was wholesale laughter as Crombie played his spoons, banging heads to the raucous 'I See Red' or shutting eyes to Tim's plaintive 'I Hope I Never', the audience displayed a wide spectrum of emotions throughout any performance—proof of the musical power and entertaining glory that was once theirs . . .

The only sad thing about this record is that it is the end—the last album for the band that in 1980 surged to the top and, while retaining its unique musicality and integrity, won over a whole nation. In April 1976, Roger

Jarrett, then editor of New Zealand rock magazine *Hot Licks*, wrote a review of the band's concert at His Majesty's Theatre and took the opportunity to farewell the group on its trip to Britain. He signed off with: 'Thanks for the vision, thanks for the trouble and thanks for the time.'

To Tim, Eddie, Noel, Neil, Nigel etc., I can only say 'Hear hear!'

At the time the album was released, over a year since the band had last performed, Noel was interviewed by Colin Hogg for *The Auckland Star*. With a comment that stands perhaps insignificantly on this page, Noel put the entire Split Enz quintessence into one simple, direct and perfect sentence. He said: 'We are all still inextricably entangled—Split Enz isn't just something you can walk away from.'

In 1985 a new Party Boys tour came to be. This time the line-up was Dave Dobbyn, Neil Finn, Peter Warren and me. Neil had put together a trio that he called The Mullanes. When we met he gave me a cassette of their demos. One of the songs was called 'Now We're Getting Somewhere'. I listened and thought, 'Yes, I think you are, Neil. I think you will.' I still have that cassette. And we took off in a car down the motorway to play some shows.

The songs were time-honoured ones written by Neil and Dave—Split Enz, Th' Dudes and DD Smash hits, plus Neil's new song 'Now We're Getting Somewhere'. This reconstituted bass player was in heaven. Firstly, I was playing with one of the great drummers. Peter Warren has a percussive skill that makes the bass player sit tight and ambitious within his rhythms and motion. And secondly, there were the songs. 'I Got You'. 'Message to My Girl'. 'Be Mine Tonight'. 'Whaling'. It doesn't get any better. My heart was on fire. My head was fine, with evening pills calming the cerebral nerve-wracking. Every house was a full house.

And then it was over. A lot of things were over. Brighton Road was quiet. I had resigned from Mushroom New Zealand and Bridget de Launay had taken it over as general manager. What to do? Where to go? What was out there? Might I have to wear a tie? There must be a position that had my name on it, a pendant with my photo on it . . .

I had a degree in Engineering Science. Surely I could get a job. Might someone want a lapsed Catholic? Maybe I could see the wood *and* the trees? Maybe?

I could stay on the ground, without planes, trains and ferries, and avoid the faltering world of decision-making that the music industry was. Still is. I knew what to do. Go to a recruitment consultant company, tell them who and what I was and see if they could wave a wand and find employment that would give me peace of mind. Something that utilised whatever it was I had. A fear of confrontation? That's me. That could prove useful.

The HR consultant told me that my CV and work experience was so unusual that there was nothing they had to offer me, nor did he think anything would be likely to turn up.

'Am I unique?' I said.

'Sadly, you are.'

I went down in the lift.

I felt I had to just go somewhere, despite my agoraphobia. So we did. We? Brigid and I married and made plans to get out of town. I booked tickets and we boarded a plane to London. That's the short version.

We were leaving the past behind.

Chapter Twenty-three
Hopping, Skipping, Jumping

The Air New Zealand 747 trails a vapour line across the cities of the world. We fly for another night, over another river. Two oceans. All is left behind in New Zealand as if we will never return. There's a Brighton Road mailbox has been nailed shut. The lawn cut one last time. There's a bottle of pills in my pocket. I look out from my window seat.

'Come and get me,' I whisper. 'Come on—come and get me.'

And then we are on the ground. As grounded as any shiftless wandering pair might be . . . Picking up a suitcase from a carousel. From the merry-go-round. Then outside in a shafting, chilly sunlight queuing for a cab.

The black cab, solid and square. Like an English rugby player. Like most of the buildings. Those buildings of grey paint and concrete façades. No sharp edges anywhere. No glass buildings—yet. Hyde Park is losing its hue in the gentle escape of a cold summertime. The teased and gelled hair wisping and floating in this, the great hair decade, over great coats. Everyone flush with New Romanticism, or smiling because their passion for The Smiths makes them special.

London is confused and wayward. But that doesn't matter. Nothing matters. Not whether these people in their ambling and stalling pedestrian vagueness turn left or right or wish for nothing. May they rest in peace when they die.

I'm OK. I will be the lead item on my own newsy proclamations. The late news about this and that. I can relate to rumours and hearsay. Oh God, yes. I'm here in London. No one knows me. I am innocent. I can make my mark.

But really, am I just another prodigal son? Maybe I am hollow. A hollow man. Look at me. The bottoms of my trousers aren't rolled up.

I reach down in the cab and roll up my trousers. I feel I have gathered a name to myself. What is it? Something special. And soon I can be launched.

I've always done things quickly. London is a centre-point in the global spin of record companies. I've signed two acts in New Zealand that went on to multi-platinum sales. They won awards. Here in London, the drummer from The Fourmyula out of Wellington, Chris Parry, signed The Jam and The Cure when he moved here a while ago. It can't be impossible.

W e moved into a flat off Lavender Hill in Battersby. Gazing out the window, I thought, 'This is the city of my birth. This is where I arrived 34 years ago. This may well be where I live for the rest of my life.' I took the bottle of Serepax out of my pocket. I read the label. I took the lid off and looked inside. There they were. Yellow pills. A torn piece of paper was taped to the outside. I had snipped it off Jerry's *British Medical Journal*. In small type it said:

Serepax contains the active ingredient oxazepam, a benzodiazepine. Physicians may use benzodiazepine to treat severe anxiety, phobic disorders and other conditions. In general, benzodiazepines should be taken for short periods only (for example 2 to 4 weeks). Continuous long-term use is not recommended unless advised by your doctor.

I had been taking it for nearly twelve years.

I thought about this, as I had done before. I let it pass. If I was a madman because of it, it was a preferable malaise to the madness I had without it.

I was watching the browning leaves on the tree outside get ready to fall for the winter. Brigid was at a Tesco supermarket. I was alone. I wasn't lonely; I've never been lonely.

I spent many hours alone as a boy in our bedroom out in Otahuhu. A true Gemini, I could abandon the noisy, whirling language, action and social mayhem of day-to-day life as a child and retreat. One day I could be one of me. The next I could be the other me. It was natural.

In that Otahuhu room I was in pursuit. An explorer out in the wilderness on his own. I used to send coupons off the back of comics to order plastic Civil War soldiers. They would arrive in the mail with cool postage stamps shouting *USA!* from the top right-hand corner. I stared at them. Or I would read a Famous Five book. (I read all 21 of them.) Or a *Mad* magazine. Or my Hayley Mills scrapbook. A chemistry kit, where purple crystals appeared overnight from a mystery world of dangerous substances like potassium permanganate crystals. The marvel of science afoot as I magically made them. Always engaged. Always imagining. It was easy to do.

I decided that breezy afternoon as I sat in silence with a temperate view of the future that London could be my safe haven. I was born here. I 'came to be' just over there at Hammersmith Hospital. It's home. So the Serepax can go in the bottom drawer and I won't take any while I'm here, in London. I am safe here. Surely.

So I put that bottle in the bottom drawer. And I started to live like a normal human being just like I had in recent years in Auckland.

What if I were to leave London and go travelling? Well, maybe I just wouldn't do that. We'll see. But first, I'd better get a job.

I went about contacting record company after record company to see if I could seduce one of them to take me on as an A&R lad. I could 'identify' a young band who was drawing crowds and who ticked all the boxes. I knew what those boxes were. (No need to repeat them all here.) I started putting pen to paper and letters drifted away to various men—no women running record companies back in the mid '80s—to see what gave.

I was fairly sensible in ascertaining that such an A&R position wouldn't turn up overnight, so I got a copy of *The Times* and scrolled through the Situations Vacant looking for a temporary job. There was one! I applied. I got it. Working at a press-clipping service.

Every weekday I was woken by the alarm at 4.30 a.m. A deep silence all around. I clambered up towards Clapham Common to wait for and catch the 4.50 a.m. bus to Vauxhall

Station. There were about twenty of us on the bus. A lot of high-fiving and faint traces of late-night reefer. I wondered where they were going. They might have wondered where I was going. I could have told them but no one asked.

I caught the tube from Vauxhall Station to High Holborn, climbed up to the surface footpath of the human trail to weave my way to the PR company that had its own press-clipping service for its corporate clients. Got that?

On the dot of 6 a.m., I sat down with about ten different newspapers and scrolled through, looking for any mention of the specific clients I had been allocated. There were four of us sitting at a long table. We drank tea. We didn't really connect, because if we did we ran the risk of missing a 'Barclays Bank' mention in an article in *The Sun* about someone trying to rob it. And so the day dragged on.

Morning tea was the peak. At 10 a.m. the four of us trotted up the road to a greasy spoon, where we all bought different things. Mine was always the same: a hot sausage sandwich in the whitest bread, with lashings of HP sauce and pepper. Sometimes I would buy two. Then it was back to newspapers and more detective work, slowly grinding us under the bright wash of fluorescent lights.

At 3 p.m. we spilled out onto the street, squinting under a setting sun soon to be victim to the winter closing in. Buses flicked their red images in and out of shop windows. Red was almost the only colour. Red noses. Red lips. It was cold. The gutters were slowly filling up with Burger King wrappers, just like they had a decade earlier, except back then it was Wimpy burgers. The slow-motion horde had plenty to spit onto the footpath. As I weaved around this party on the footpath, I absorbed them all and exhaled frost from my mouth.

I returned to High Holborn, to Vauxhall Station and down to Lavender Hill to see if there was mail. Brigid handed me a lone letter. She had got a job teaching at a private school. One of her pupils was the son of Christopher Reeve (Superman). Apparently Mr Reeve was profoundly handsome in the flesh. Now the letter.

Dear Mr Chunn

Thank you for your letter regarding employment opportunities in the Artist and Repertoire department of Fast Bucket Records. Unfortunately we are unable to offer a position at this moment in time. We will keep your details at hand in case this changes in the future.

I ended up with 22 such letters. Eleven of them came after interviews with record company personnel. The general manager of this and the managing director of that. The A&R director. CEOs didn't seem to populate record companies. Maybe they did but I was too short to reach their height. Perhaps the New Zealand accent put them off. And so the whole affair started to fade away.

As winter and its complicated weather came over the horizon, Brigid planned a holiday to the south of Spain. Did I want to go? Spain? Pills. Aeroplanes. Buses and a *casa* just a short walk to a cobbled stony beach. No surf? Pills. I declined the trip. I was sick of pills. I had an option. I could make a choice. The dreamy state was a hollow victory; not for me. Brigid flew away.

I sat again on the couch under the large south-facing window, and the soft murmur of the Lavender Hill traffic crept in under the door. Then the phone rang. It was Jenny Keath, boss of Mushroom Music Publishing in Melbourne. She managed the business careers of songwriters signed to the company. I used to do that too, at Mushroom New Zealand. She was very cool.

'Mike, I'm in London. Let's meet up at the Bayswater Hotel.'

'Of course,' I said.

Jenny would travel here and there around musical hotspots looking to sign songwriters or their publishing agents to Australasian deals. Presumably she didn't suffer from agoraphobia. She didn't look drawn and haggard. She looked alert and sharp. As well as business, she always had the latest gossip.

'Mike, have you heard?'

'I haven't heard much lately. Tell me.'

'Crowded House. They're taking off. Capitol are releasing the album soon. It's going to go. There's talk of radio playing their single. I have a press release.' She took it out of her bag.

Oh yes! Neil Finn and his merry band had an album out and it was *going to go*.

I looked at the list of songs. There it was: 'Now We're Getting Somewhere'. Track three, side one. The Mullanes had turned into Crowded House and their future looked perfect. And the single? 'Don't Dream It's Over'. I'd never heard of it. No matter, I'm sure I would. And as you would expect of an album's premier track, it was track four, side one.

Jenny and I covered off some more Mushroom matters. Mushroom New Zealand had closed, as Bridget de Launay was moving to London to work for A&M Records. Excellent. We could meet up. Talk shop. Dance Exponents was also heading to London, after spending a few years in the musical wilderness back in New Zealand. And DD Smash had dissolved, with Dobbyn going solo to write the music for the animated movie *Footrot Flats*. And then Jenny was gone.

I stayed put in that Bayswater Hotel chair. Dance Exponents was coming to London. I must find them.

The phone rang.
'Hi, Mike here.'
'Flip, me old friend from far away. Here *we* are! Where are you?'
'I'm in Battersea. Where are you, Mr Luck?'
'Camden!'
I descended the stairs (I ran down the stairs) and strode down Rush Hill Road, along Lavender Hill to Queenstown Road and onto the 87 bus. Hopped off the bus at Charing Cross Station and got on the Northern Line to Camden Town station and ascended to the mayhem of the markets. Brothel creepers and hookahs. Punk-hangover clobber and dishevelled New Romantic swish and glamour. Stands of counterfeit albums recorded on cheap cassettes. I paused then. Out-takes of Beatles' sessions from the *Revolver* album. Presumably an Abbey Road engineer snuck them home and copied them and returned them with stealth the next day. (Maybe it had been Geoff Emerick?) What a find!

And then onwards through the throng until I found the address that matched the one written on a piece of paper in my pocket. I rang the bell and went up the stairs.

Jordan stood there in front of me with the look of a lad who had been at the front and returned alive. It was and always had been in his eyes. We embraced. Some of the others lingered in the vicinity. There was no excitement as such. No superficial palaver. No boisterous shenanigans. London will keep you from being so foolish. But facts are facts.

'What's up with you guys?'

'We have some new songs.'

Songs. New songs. Songs fuel any artist, act, band—whoever stands up and charges off down the road in this wacky music industry. Songs. The life force.

'When can I hear them?'

'We're playing a show at the Empire Ballroom in Leicester Square. You must come along.'

'Information please.' I took out my piece of paper and my trusty pencil and wrote it down. We drank tea. We reminisced in a fashion. I could see that the past was another country and they didn't really know the language any more. It was about the future in their eyes, in their plans. They were like coiled-up springs with something to prove that only they knew about.

I gave each of them a hug and went back down the stairs. It was so good to see them. I felt like a kindly uncle. Out towards Camden Market and down to Camden Town station. Charing Cross Station. Out and onto the 87 bus. Off at Battersea and slowly ascending to Rush Hill Road. Onto the couch in the light shadows of the tree outside the window.

Winter had passed. Months had gone by. There was another letter from a record company. There was no opening for an A&R person in their world. On their planet.

I turned on the TV. It was an old black-and-white model. A contemporary music show called *The Wire* was screening. It was engaging. The host knew his stuff. It played music videos, yes, but it also covered news, interviews. It was a vibrant window into the world's new music. I thought, 'We don't have anything like this in New Zealand.'

Then news came from Brigid that we were to be parents. Ah. Parents. Life. New life. In August! A parent again . . . It just seemed *right* to get back to New Zealand, the three of us. There was no way we were going to be tossed and turned in London town with a pram . . . a baby. We made the easy decision that the future was in New Zealand.

There was time to save up for the trip home. A job? A job!

I had to do something. I had to join the mob. Many New Zealanders landing in London acted on a pre-arranged, almost robotic set of instructions. I knew about it even before flying out of Auckland. Now I really had no choice. So off I went to an HR consultancy for the financial industry.

'Hello, my name is Mike Chunn. I'm looking for a job. I am halfway through an economics degree and I know how to use Lotus 1-2-3.'

The woman looked at me, reading facial tics to make sure that I was really lying and, armed with that knowledge, gave me a job that required only common sense.

'I have a three-week temp job for you at Merrill Lynch in the City. Be there at nine a.m. on Monday and ask for Ian in the Twiddle Your Thumbs section. If you arrive at eight a.m., however, you can have breakfast at the staff smorgasbord restaurant. It costs 40 p.'

A 40 p breakfast! Golly gosh. Would it be on a par with the hot-sausage sandwich at the High Holborn greasy spoon? I would find out.

Monday morning in my grey suit, white shirt, leather brogues and 1950s recycled tie, I boarded the 137 bus to Marble Arch and then down to the Central Line station, from whence I tumbled along to St Paul's. All quite simple really, and with enough time to make serious inroads into the wonderful *Independent* newspaper. A hop, skip and jump down to Merrill Lynch at EC1 and in I went. It was 9.10 a.m. I'd missed the breakfast. Damn! I'd have to get an earlier bus tomorrow.

So I stood there waiting for the security guard to get off the phone. I looked around. It was all glass. I asked for Ian, who knew I was a fraud and was expecting me. The security guard made a call and Ian arrived.

'Hi, Mike, come with me.'

We hopped in a glass lift (Oh God, I was freaking out. How many floors up would this death trap go? . . . Only two) and we moved into a large, open-plan office. I was shown to a long desk (a table, really) at which were seated three other gents. They all had suits, ties and leather shoes, too. It was like a scene out of the movie *Wall Street*. All these people. Is greed good?

I listened to Ian tell us what we were supposed to be doing. It seemed to be all about scrolling through ink-jet printouts from massive computers in the hope that we might pick up things he had asked us to look out for. For a while I thought I was meant to be finding the missing one billion yen that

Merrill Lynch was supposed to be paying to Deutsche Bank. I'm not sure I found it.

But let me tell you about the next day. The Tuesday morning. The smorgasbord breakfast.

I turned up at 8.01 a.m., swiped my super-security pass over the reader and shuffled in. I took the Sony professional headphones off my head and slipped my Aiwa walkman into my jacket pocket. I had been listening to the Madness album *Keep Moving* and would repeat-play the song 'Michael Caine'. I would sit on the bus thinking, 'How do you write a song like that? Something that makes me want to play it again and again and again?'

I asked directions to the staff café. I slid through the glass-lined monolith that was Merrill Lynch. And in I went.

'How does this work?' I asked.

'You take a tray, son, and go down the aisle there, know what I mean, an' put anyfink you want on a plate and Bob's your uncle.'

I thought about my uncle. His name was John. Was? Yes. He'd passed.

'Thank you.'

'Oi. You from South Africa?'

'Yes, I am. On contract from the Smith Pilling bank in Cape St Frances. Six months.'

'Never been there.'

'No. Not a lot of people go any more.'

'That'll be forty p.'

'Cheers.'

That morning I had scrambled eggs, bacon, baked beans, a sausage, two fried breads, some creamed corn and a large mug of coffee. And then I was ready for anything up there in the mayhem of lost funds, misplaced two-way swaps, a collectivised death warrant and a collateralised obligatory hedge. Actually, I thought we would be dealing with exotic financial instruments but in fact we were brought in to clear up the mess post the City's 1986 deregulation of broking commissions. A whole lot of foreign banks moved into London, employees were hired into positions for which they were not qualified, and hence accounts became a mess. Well, I knew what a mess was. So what were we doing there? Merrill's auditors would not sign off their accounts because there were a lot of accounts with dodgy entries. I asked Ian about all this and he said it was a vacuous trade indicative of a long short. You get the picture.

The basic rule was stock bought, stock sold, profit booked to P&L. So I turned to my desktop computer and hit the space button on the Lotus 1-2-3 thingamajig so the alarm went on and on and on. It was mesmerising. I tapped out a rhythm so that the blend was mystical. And at 4 p.m. the four of us went to the pub.

I was there at 8.01 a.m. each morning for quite some time. I put on weight. Whether or not the four of us found the financial failings and subterfuge we were looking for . . . Did we? Maybe we did . . . Well, to this day I suspect none of us really knows. But we were all there on time for a big breakfast every day. And the weeks rolled by. The three-week temporary assignment turned into an eight-month one.

And then the Leicester Square ballroom date arrived in my Filofax and we went along. Dance Exponents was on the bill but renamed as The Exponents. I thought that was a good idea. Put a line in the sand—between the present and the past. And these new songs that Jordan had talked of. What were they? Would we hear one?

We walked into the ballroom. It was time-honoured. You could feel it. It became best known for Liz Hurley and her dresses—or lack of them—at film premieres. No matter. The Exponents walked out. And they killed it.

The crowd was admittedly mostly ex-pat New Zealanders, but their enthusiasm was immediately clear, and the exuberance in that large room was a joy to behold. Mr Luck strode the stage, rising from the ashes of the band's decline.

Jordan had that unique connection with the audience where his long arms reached out from the stage and enveloped everyone in that cavernous room. Every punter on the floor or in the circles believed—rightly so—that they had been drawn close to the heart of that man. All knew that they were loved by him and his merry band. And they played a new song.

'Here's a new one for you all! It's called "Why Does Love Do This To Me".' And they played it.

I stood there reliving that moment in the Hillsborough Tavern in Christchurch in 1982 when they played 'Victoria'. The sense that here was a song that would live in the hearts of everyone at that show, and beyond. A song that had the power to go on forever.

I was very excited by this. Here was a 'new' band. Here was a group of lads who had endured, frozen and starved in this miserly city, only to gather around the songwriting mastery of Mr Jordan Luck and emerge from the pale corner into the light. This bright light of a Leicester Square night of triumph. I ran backstage and raved about that song.

'We're taking it back to New Zealand,' said Jordan. 'We're The Exponents now.' There was a glint in his eye. Their eyes. They were going to re-emerge and do it just like they did the first time. They knew they had an audience waiting there. They wouldn't take any prisoners.

'Hey, Jordan,' I said as the night dwindled away. 'We're returning to New Zealand, too. There's a baby due in about six weeks.'

'Flip! What are your plans?'

'I don't know.' And I didn't know. That insecurity of life, its sharp left turns, its flagrant disregard for anyone who has plans. Brigid and I dawdled down Charing Cross Road. Two of us had arrived in London and soon three of us would be leaving. Plans?

As we were waiting for the lift to come and slide us down deep into the tube station, we stood there watching the television in a Dixons shop window. It was screening *The Wire*, and the host, on a neon-lit street, was with Crowded House. They were in Japan. Neil was talking to him but we couldn't hear it. What would he have been saying? 'Well, it looks like we're getting somewhere'? Of course he would. Because they were.

I'd seen them a few weeks before in London, onstage and in complete control. I went with Tim. We went backstage after the show. The contrast between Neil on the Party Boys tour with his cassette of Mullanes demos and his Crowded House band with record sales all over the world was very clear. And there he was on this chilly night on *The Wire*. In Japan. On *The Wire*.

Rumbling and swaying on the tube train heading to Battersea, I had an idea. I knew that TVNZ had dropped all its music-video shows because record companies wanted to charge them for the right to play their clips. There was a stand-off.

Alongside this was a letter I'd had from my dear ma, Von, telling me how her friends Marcia Russell and Tom Finlayson (along with some other colleagues) had won the right to launch a third television channel in New Zealand, which they were going to call TV3. I started thinking how TV3 could scream in and start running a magazine show where contemporary music and accompanying video clips were the focal point around which dialogue, interviews and news could gather to make something that was interesting and of the moment. Just like *The Wire*.

When we got back to our first-floor pad on Rush Hill Road I sat down at my Amstrad PCW 8256 computer and started writing a letter to Marcia and Tom. I talked of TVNZ and its abandonment of contemporary music and how, in the UK, they had a show called *The Wire*. I outlined its cool format and said that TV3 had the perfect opportunity to offer a show just like it. And hey—what about this?—I could produce it for them. And I posted the letter off.

With London only a one-hour flight from Paris, we decided to check out that city of lights before the arrival of a baby and the long hop back to New Zealand. Twelve thousand miles. We might never return. So we booked flights and a hotel room.

When I saw the itinerary, a cold chill went through me. I had been pill-free in London; I had avoided travelling. Could I do it? Could I board a flight to Paris, stay in a hotel and fly back again without the small yellow Serepax pills?

I decided to give it a day or two to see if the tension eased. It increased. If I boarded that plane without the pills—well, there would be no way I could do it. I would want to die rather than cross that line into the fuselage.

Two hours prior to the flight I took two pills. I sat in my seat in the familiar soft and dreamy state, knowing I would be OK. Any excitement about the trip had succumbed to the fog. The peace and murmur of the flight enveloped me. Nothing had changed. This must be how it would always be. I could live a normal life in Auckland or London; I had mastered that. But was I blind to a way out? I couldn't see it. I'd now been living with this for fourteen years.

Sitting on the minuscule balcony of the tiny Parisian hotel with the Serepax gently toing and froing, I could have been anywhere. This could be Rome. New York. Byron Bay. Stewart Island. It wouldn't be any different. Any place I could float above myself, watching myself drift off to sleep. Agoraphobia is just another bed to sleep on if you know how.

We returned to London to find a letter waiting. Tom Finlayson had written advising that they would like me to manage the music shows for TV3. He liked the concept of *The Wire* with its magazine format. He said (in essence), 'Get yourself down here and we'll sort this out.' The launch of TV3 was a few months away but they wanted everything 'lined up'.

I thought, 'This is a beautiful thing.' I had a purpose. A place to go when we got home.

I thought about The Exponents and how they would record 'Why Does Love Do This To Me' and how it would shake the whole of New Zealand and I would play the video clip for it on TV3. I would make sure that TV3 screened it first!

In mid August 1988 our daughter Georgia arrived. The three of us boarded a 747 for Auckland a few weeks later. As we drove out to Heathrow, we went past Hammersmith Hospital. I gave a subtle salute to the memory of myself. Just like the baby on my lap I would have been poised to depart, except back then in 1953 it would be a six-week boat journey to Auckland. This time, the trip would take 24 hours.

Once again the pills saw to it that I didn't have a panic attack. That I didn't run back out of the plane's interior and hide down some empty corridor in the terminal. And I had Tom Finlayson's letter in my pocket.

Auckland was sparkling and breezy as we flew in after a setting sun. The early-summer sky was a fading pale blue, and the empty streets were filled with houses with their pastel interiors. Families around dinner tables. Rubbish bins, curious cats, fences and letterboxes, curtained windows and dented cars. All seemed to be exactly the same as when we had left, all those months before. Auckland. I was home. I was safe.

I couldn't wait. The next day I rang TV3 and asked for Tom Finlayson.

'I'm sorry, Mr Finlayson doesn't work at TV3 any more.'

Doesn't work at TV3 any more? Who does?

'The president of programming is Kel Geddes. May I put you through to him?'

TOP Citizen Band performing in Auckland, 1979. (From left) Greg Clark, me and Geoffrey.

ABOVE Publicity shot for Citizen Band, 1979. (From left) Brent Eccles, Geoffrey, me and Greg Clark. MURRAY CAMMICK

TOP Dance Exponents get ready to open for David Bowie at Western Springs Stadium, November 1983. (From left) Chris Sheehan, Jordan Luck, Bowie, Dave Gent, Brian Jones.

ABOVE Backstage at a sold-out Dance Exponents and The Mockers show at the Logan Campbell Centre, Auckland, 1984. (From left) me, Mike Harralambi and Dave Gent (Dance Exponents) and Andrew Fagan (The Mockers).

OPPOSITE TOP Me with some of the Mushroom Records team, (left to right) Bridget de Launay, Debbie Harwood and Debra Mains, December 1984. This was taken backstage at Aotea Square before the 'Thank God It's Over' show—now better remembered as the Queen Street riot. BRYAN STAFF

OPPOSITE The Party Boys on the road at Matawhero vineyard, Gisborne, 1985. (From left) Neil Finn, Dave Dobbyn, Dennis Irwin (Matawhero), Peter Warren, Roger King (DD Smash manager), Mike Corless (promoter).

RIGHT On the road with a cup of instant coffee, the Party Boys tour, 1984.

BELOW APRA's early days at 92 Parnell Road, 1994. (From left) Petrina Togi, me, Donna White and Andrew Davies.

OPPOSITE TOP At the APRA Silver Scroll Awards in the early 2000s. (From left) me, Bill Moran, Arthur Baysting, Brent Eccles and Trevor Mallard.

OPPOSITE BELOW Brigid Chunn, 2018.
MARK SMITH

OPPOSITE TOP The Chunn family in 2008. (From left) me, Georgia, Johnny, Ruby, Barney and Brigid.

OPPOSITE BELOW Brigid and me with our good friends Sharon and Neil Finn.

LEFT Ready to take on the first New Zealand Music Month, 2001.

BELOW With Brett Cottle in the late 1990s, at the APRA Silver Scroll Awards.

ABOVE The Last Riot in the Old School Block, May 2014: the old boys play the Sacred Heart College hall for the last time. (Left to right) Barney and Mike Chunn, Tim Finn and Eddie Rayner.

CENTRE At the APRA Songwriting Awards show in Hamilton, 2005, with Debbie Little (left) and Lydia Gammie (competition winner).

BELOW Two of my boys, Nikko (left) and Barney. Nikko performed his fine song 'Claremont Street' with Barney and me at a special mayoral breakfast in Auckland, to an audience of around 700 fathers.

'Yes. Of course.'

Kel Geddes knew nothing about my appointment as head of music programming for TV3. He said, 'Let's meet and talk about it.' I went to Flower Street in Newton and sat down on the other side of Kel's desk.

I outlined what had gone down between myself and Tom Finlayson. Kel took it all in with grace and then explained that he didn't anticipate programming a contemporary music show in a magazine format. But he sympathised with my believing that I had a job and agreed to pay for our flights back to Auckland. I said, 'Thank you, Kel,' and went back out into Flower Street. I walked home. We didn't own a car.

The phone rang.

'Hey, Mike. Michael Glading here. You know about music publishing, don't you?'

Michael Glading. He'd taken over the managing director role at CBS when Murray Thom departed. Music publishing? Did I know about it? Yes, I did. I'd handled the publishing as well as the recording contracts in the Mushroom New Zealand days, as I've mentioned already.

'I do, Michael,' I said.

'Good. CBS Records—which is about to be known as Sony Music, I'll explain later—is forming its own music-publishing company, and each affiliate will have their own publishing department. I want you to run ours.'

Ah. A sharp left turn. A new world?

'Michael, are you guys still in Falcon Street in Parnell?'

'We are.' Not such a new world after all. Seven years previously I'd been in there as an A&R lad.

'Are you in?' asked Michael.

'Of course.'

In many ways, there in Falcon Street, with the hubbub of voices and paraphernalia, nothing had changed. CBS (let's call them Sony, seeing as they now are) still released Bruce Springsteen, Bob Dylan and Michael Jackson records. The lifeblood. But the technical aura was different. There was a laser printer (only one, mind you). There were computers instead of golf-ball typewriters. I was given an IBM grey-screen computer with a 20 MB hard drive and a word-processing software package called WordPerfect. I was away. I didn't have Lotus 1-2-3 as I didn't need it; and just as well, as despite many months at Merrill Lynch I never did master it.

I spent my time keeping an eye out for local talent. I needed songwriters with great songs, so I could sign up the publishing rights. What about The Exponents?

The Exponents had signed a record deal with Adam Holt and PolyGram Records. I suspect they had their eyes on Australia again, and Holt had good, clean lines to his Australian branch. So they made their decision.

I still went to see them live, though. And my hunch came true. 'Why Does Love Do This To Me' was a hit, and to this day may as well be New Zealand's national anthem! And more hits kept coming.

The power of songs. Where did Jordan's come from? I think he went to bed and in the morning reached out for a pen and paper and wrote down whatever had crept into his head overnight. Magical concoctions.

The demo cassettes and CDs kept coming in to Sony. I rejected them all. Where was all this going to go?

Michael Glading called me into his office.

'Sony Music in Australia is hosting a conference in the Hunter Valley and we're taking four people over there to attend. You're one of them.'

The Hunter Valley. Travel on an aeroplane. Pills. Here we go again.

I don't know how many were there in the Hunter Valley for that Sony Music conference. A large swathe of Australians and a small number of New Zealanders. There was much to discuss. This was 1991, and there was much talk about what would happen when the All Blacks met the Wallabies in the UK for the Rugby World Cup. (The Australians won, by the way.) There was a flash wine-tasting session and Cuban cigars at hand. And then everyone gathered in the large convention hall. One of them took to the lectern.

'I have here the latest market-share figures. I'll read them to you. At the bottom, RCA Records—four per cent. Fuck them!'

And the crowd roared. I looked around. Slowly. The Serepax was keeping me gentle and soft; I could quietly witness this madness. There was a Nuremberg Rally-ness about it all. On it went—the great corporate competitive war-cry, loud and clear. I'd never heard this in New Zealand. It just wasn't my scene at all. If this was the Australian music industry, then I was out.

And then the conference drew to a close and we were on buses heading to Sydney. I watched birds, wombats, kangaroos, platypuses and snakes out the bus window. They were all happy in their skins. The passing cars were long and wide and brightly coloured like the ones that had overtaken us on the Houston and Dallas freeways in 1977.

The Hunter Valley softly evicted us to motorways that took us to the hotel into which we New Zealanders disappeared while waiting for the flight back home the next day. Me? I went to Crows Nest to the head office of APRA, the Australasian Performing Right Association. I had made an appointment when I was back in New Zealand to meet with their CEO, Brett Cottle. I, and a fair few other APRA members, felt that the New Zealand APRA office in Wellington wasn't making an effort to establish, let alone maintain, communications and rapport with New Zealand songwriters and publishers. I wanted to say this to Brett, and ask if he might consider stepping in and getting the New Zealand office to change its ways.

In I went and sat down on the other side of his desk. (It would have looked a bit odd if I'd sat down beside him.)

'Mike—just before you get started, I want to tell you about what's happening in New Zealand. The Wellington office will be moved to Auckland, and the director of operations will be staying in Wellington and retiring.'

Ah. I had intended to ask Brett if he would consider moving the APRA office to Auckland. He'd beaten me to it.

'Well, Brett, you've just answered my question.'

There was a pause as we looked at each other.

'Just a query,' I said. 'Have you got anyone in mind to take over as New Zealand director of operations?'

'Well, funny you should ask,' he said.

Chapter Twenty-four
Happy Members

There is a story which is not myth. It may be legend. But right here, right now, it's the truth.

In the 1850s in Paris, two composers were having a meal in a restaurant (that's French for a diner). Let's say they were Debussy and Bach. There was a string trio there, and it played a piece written by one of the composers. It contributed substantially to the ambience of the place (that's French for good vibes). When the owner presented them with the bill, the composer who had written the piece suggested that, in light of his music being played and his receiving no compensation, they could have a free meal. The owner refused and they were obliged to pay.

The two composers gathered their thoughts and presented the French government with a plan. They asked that the public performance of music fall under the Copyright Act, entitling composers to charge fees for the performance of their music in public. Voilà! The French government, some years after the reign of terror and now focused on creativity and the arts and ensuring that the worth of creative pursuits was respected, did just that, and the public performance of music became an activity requiring the permission of the composer. The responsibility for securing this permission was the person or entity authorising the performance. So to return to the Debussy/Bach moment, the restaurateur would have had to pay for a licence to play the music—not the string trio. A simple concept. Common sense really. How to do it? Easy.

The French SACEM (Societé des Auteurs, Compositeurs et Editeurs de Musique) agreed to a revolutionary principle. All composers and/or lyricists would accept the same revenue fee for a public performance. Hence a violin sonata written by a composer would cost as much to perform as a pop song written by a songwriter. The more in demand and popular a work was, and therefore the more frequently performed, the more revenue its writer would receive. (I trust you've all got this.)

And so it came to be. Many French composers, lyricists and music publishers joined the scheme on a voluntary basis. A board of directors—all members of SACEM—put a staff in place and formulated licences that venues, promoters, authorities, et cetera were required to take out; these licences authorised the public performance of music written and/or published by SACEM members. Some staffers were licensing reps, and off they went knocking on doors asking restaurants, concert halls, et cetera nicely for an annual SACEM licence to be taken out. Presumably the restaurant where Debussy and Bach had imbibed was the first to be approached.

This copyright infrastructure is now in use all over the world. Every country except the United States has a single licensing body (a collection society), with the vast majority of songwriters, composers, lyricists and publishers signed up to the system. After all, why wouldn't you sign up? Would Debussy prefer to go around all the French venues and licence the performance of his music himself, because he could charge what he liked? No. The system worked then and it works now: here in the twenty-first century, it is the crucial backdrop to the financial strength of the music industry. (What about the United States? They have three collection societies, but here is not the place to write hundreds of words telling you why.)

When did New Zealand put this structure in place? In 1926. Why then? Because radio arrived and the New Zealand government started broadcasting all sorts of weird things, but certainly music and songs. APRA was established, which both New Zealand and Australian writers and publishers could join and have their works licensed by APRA staff. The board of directors of APRA comprised composers and publishers in equal numbers, twelve in total.

And, in a truly multilateral groove, all the SACEMs and APRAs of the world agreed to licence each other's music. Say a radio station in New Zealand plays a U2 song. APRA collects the fee and sends it to Ireland to pay U2. 'Don't Dream It's Over' is played on TV in Ireland. IMRO (Irish Music Rights Organisation) collects that fee and sends it to APRA to pay Neil Finn. That's the essence of it. In practice it's far more detailed than that . . . but rest easy, dear reader, we're moving on.

In Brett Cottle's office in 1991 he asked me if I was interested in taking over as APRA New Zealand's director of operations. I said I'd have to think about it. I walked out into the corridor and walked back in again.

'I'm in,' I said. After all, there was much to learn. And I

love to learn. And . . . I had absolutely no idea how APRA worked.

At a lunch in Auckland a short while later, after formalities had been signed off, we got down to business. I considered saying to him, 'I have no idea what I'm going to do', but I didn't need to. I sensed that he knew that already.

We got down to the rocket science of it all. Brett said to me, 'Mike, what I want from you is happy APRA members.' I thought, 'Happy members? I can do that.' Another thing he said to me was, 'There are two albums you have to listen to: Paul Kelly and the Coloured Girls' *Gossip* and Van Morrison's *Poetic Champions Compose*.' At last! Deep coolness in a CEO and his musical tastes. And then he said another thing to me: 'There are people out there who want you to fail.'

Aha! I'd been there before. But the more people want me to fail, the deeper my breathing. Throw me a poison dart and I'll catch it. Hold it high. Spin it across the room and have it strike a luminous cross.

Brett finished with: 'Working at APRA, there is total security.'

I heard that and tumbled it around in my head. *Security*. What's that? I'd never had security in anything. Being in a band, running a record label or a music-publishing company, managing a band, fatherhood, phobic disorders, sitting exams, going to Mass, marriage, playing rugby, cricket, football, league. I'd done all those. Security? I looked at him and a powerful feeling came over me. I thought, 'This is my kind of guy.'

And in time I grew to love him.

I walked outside and sat down in my car. I was thinking. Brett had talked about me going to Sydney to learn the ropes. And he'd said I'd be going to Sydney about three or four times a year for managerial summits and the like. What did this mean? Travel. Tension leading to fear leading to panic attacks. I couldn't do that. Not with my well-established strategy of a long line of tranquillisers. That would surely be obvious. I couldn't fool everyone with my 'stage fright' fraud. The dream state. The heavy lids. The slur. The struggle to comprehend. What could I do?

In a few weeks I flew in my dream state to Sydney to start my absorption of the wheels of APRA and how I might spin them back home. I turned up at the Sydney office in Crows Nest, and an evocative, exotic world of detail, facts, figures and systems was laid out in front of me. It was, in a word, cool. I related it to my time studying Engineering Science at Auckland uni all those years ago. Except back then I was alert and my capacity was capable. Now my sleepy, fading self was witnessing but not absorbing. Also, APRA didn't seem to include i (the square root of minus one).

Brett walked in and spied my lacklustre persona. He suggested I slip away to get over the jetlag. And off I went in my hire car back to the hotel.

The next day was a Saturday. Brigid was with me and we had just visited an old school-friend, Simon Downey, in Mosman. I was in the hire car driving along Military Road, thinking, 'Time for my evening pill.' After all, I was over there in Sydney. It wasn't Auckland.

I reached over to the glove box and opened it. I took out the small bottle and drew to a stop at some traffic lights. I opened the bottle and looked at those yellow-coloured good Samaritans. The light went green and I rolled on down the road. Another red light. I looked into the bottle. A sensation went through me. What sensation? It was like the feeling you have when you've been standing in the shadow of a cloud, then the cloud moves on and the sun's rays emerge and cover you.

In my head, the gentle, subdued anxiety of being over in Sydney, of knowing that a flight was looming, just went away. I felt it go. Inside my head, the sun came out.

I pulled over to the side of the road. I turned to Brigid.

'Something's happened to me.'

'What?'

'I feel different. I'm not . . . anxious.' I held up the pill bottle. 'I'm not going to take one. I don't feel the need. Something's happened to me. The agoraphobia. I think it's gone.' And I put the bottle back in the glove box.

For the next four days I didn't touch that bottle. And when Brigid and I boarded the plane to Auckland, it stayed in my carry-on bag with nothing to do, no part to play.

The plane took off and I looked out the window as the glorious coastline of Sydney waved me farewell. I waved back. I whispered to wherever my agoraphobia, my reign of terror, was down there in Sydney town.

'I can't believe you've gone. But good fucking riddance. I'm going to be normal now. I feel normal. I want this plane to fly on and on and take me to exotic places where I can walk the land, the streets, talk to the people, sit on a beach, lie on the bottom of the sea . . . and be normal. I am normal. I am no longer mad.' And I flew across the Tasman like a baby in a cradle.

How did this happen?

I thought about it. I listened to the silence. *Security*. It must be. For the first time in my life I was in an environment that wouldn't come crashing down in a slowly evolving landslide unless I let it. And I wasn't going to let it. I was going to have happy APRA members.

I had an internal confidence that I had never had before. I had always thought of myself as Mr Happy-Go-Lucky. But I wasn't. And now, I was looking forward to a responsibility and purpose that weaved my working for and on behalf of songwriters with an advocacy position where I could stand up for them in the empty and dark corners of society where no one gave a damn. Where no one 'got it'. I thought, 'I don't need to be anyone—respectful, respected, famous, arrogant or anything monumental—except a simple human being.' I needed to listen to my quiet but considered inner voice. My heart. So I did. I heard it. I was now ready. Thank God.

And so an APRA New Zealand workforce was put in place (I hired three people who I knew would kick arse—I'd never hired anyone in my life). While the building that APRA would be based in was being refurbished, the four of us sat around a desk in the garage of my home in Ellerslie. I had met with Alex Jeliba, the financial controller of APRA in Sydney, prior to our quartet gathering and was advised that APRA New Zealand had been earning $4 million a year. I thought to myself, 'Mmmm, four million dollars. That's—well—that is what it is.'

Alex had suggested we put together a budget for the

coming year, so I said we'd bring in $5 million. Why not? So off we went. One phone, one computer (no internet back then), four chairs and a desk. Donna White (finance), Liz Gallagher (licensing rep), Rufus McPherson (song-logging and other mysterious admin things) and me.

Like those revolutionary French folk we were going to charge off, ensuring that music users were licensed and that the performance fees were collected. Who were these music users? I'll tell you. Radio and television channels, restaurants, discos, gyms, live concerts, ballroom dancing, cinemas, music playing in shops, lift muzak and so on. In 1850 it was a string trio in a restaurant. In 1992 it was *everywhere*.

Up until this point, the main users who were paying fees to APRA had been TV and radio, which had mostly meant the government until broadcasting was deregulated in the '80s. Commercial TV channels and radio stations paid a percentage of their advertising revenue, and public service radio paid a negotiated fee for music performance. The other big clients had been the breweries, which owned networks of pubs and bars throughout the country and paid a lump-sum fee from head office. Now the market was wide open.

I perused our licensing contracts. They were OK. They were reasonable. Why would a gym want to kill us because we wanted to charge them a few dollars for a Jazzergetics class that might gross $750? And what would a Jazzergetics class be like with no music?

But I hate asking anyone for money. I'm dysfunctional about it. It scares me. In a word, it's confrontational: like asking a nun not to strap you. (I could never do that. I just got strapped.) There was only one way to do it: I would need tough licensing reps who never asked me to go out there in the cold wind of insistence. The gruff stare of a face well flipped. I hadn't told Brett this. Did I need to?

Eventually, the matter of licensing the public performance of copyright music and the collection and distribution of royalties (fees) cropped up at a meeting. We took deep breaths, then Liz went out into the world and began savouring the intellectual alliance of administration and the forging of human relationships. Thank God I never had to do it.

After a year or two I realised that it was these human relationships that were going to make this APRA thing work, in terms of securing fair fees for the performance of our members' music. On the other side, those music users out there—well, they deserved to be listened to and respected too. All of us needed to keep lawyers and court cases way out over the horizon. We all needed to keep a level head, and take the time.

How about an example? When we targeted the central Auckland nightclubs, they said, essentially, 'Go away.' APRA had been trying to introduce a new disco licence scheme, based on the numbers of people attending a club rather than a flat fee. This had been roundly rejected. So a meeting was scheduled at Stanley's nightclub in Queen Street. Ever been to a nightclub at 10 o'clock in the morning? There were about eight of us there. There were four nightclub owners (including Stanley), Brett Cottle, my old mate Arthur Baysting (now a writer-director on the board of APRA), our lawyer David Chisholm and me.

Dialogue started and a stalemate quickly settled in. This was going nowhere. There was a predetermined air about it all. We were offering what we thought was a fair and reasonable licensing deal; they thought it was unreasonable.

Terrified of confrontation, I said nothing. Neither did the guy sitting next to me. I'd been watching him. He was receptive in a concealed, passive way. He didn't shuffle his legs or cross his arms. His eyes did the moving. Side to side. Working out who was who; what was what; why was why. He was about 50, I guess. Back then I was 40. He turned to me.

'Who are you?'

'Mike Chunn.'

'You're not Chinese.'

'True, I'm not.'

'I thought that Chunn guy was Chinese. But I think I know you,' he said.

'Well,' I said, 'I know you. You're Johnny Tabla.'

'I am,' he said. 'Why are you familiar?'

'I used to go to your club all the time. Tabla's in Lorne Street. Early seventies. Bands like Space Farm and all that acid stuff. I used to go with Wally Wilkinson. We were in a band called Moses. I saw you there. Maybe you saw me?'

There was a pause. He said, 'Ring me. Let's have a cup of tea.'

Around a week later I went to Johnny's pad in Mission Bay and we had a cup of tea. I explained the APRA thing. Like—the whole thing. How songwriters deserve to be paid. I said, 'If you don't think so, try writing a song.' He just looked at me. We had a second cup of tea. I explained that more than 150 people worked in the Sydney head office making sure that the APRA revenue was fairly distributed to live performers and recording artists who wrote their own songs. He then stood up, went over to the phone and dialled.

'Stanley,' he said. 'We'll take out the licences.'

And so the wheel turned. The reps went out and got licences. And while this was going on and new APRA members rolled in every week, I kept thinking of Brett's wish for *happy members*.

And then there was the Silver Scroll. The APRA Silver Scroll Awards started in 1965. The scroll is awarded to the writer of the song judged to be the best of those submitted by APRA members in any particular year.

Members were able to enter as many songs as they liked back then, so often whole albums would be entered. And then on judging day a few people—sorry, not sure who—would gather in a Radio New Zealand studio and the songs would be played and four finalists and a winner chosen. So the songs were only listened to once. Then a function would be held to present the award to the winner.

As a Mushroom Records man or Sony Music Publishing lad I would go along to these awards functions in the '80s. They were usually held in a nightclub or a restaurant. There would be the 'final five' songwriters, and they were invited to the stage where they would line up (much akin to a beauty pageant) and the winner would be announced. He or she would step forward and be presented with the Silver Scroll, which they kept for a year and then gave back. There were no live performances. We all celebrated the ethos of songwriting as a classy craft and then drifted home.

My first Silver Scroll as director of New Zealand operations for APRA was in 1993, and I pondered how to make it better. We invited APRA members to send in a song they'd written (only one), which had to have been broadcast or played live. I then asked four music-industry bods—two songwriters, a NZ On Air guy and a radio programmer—to be judges, and sent them cassettes of the 70 songs rated as second-stage finalists from all those sent in and considered by us to be eligible to win. The four judges lived with the songs for at least two weeks (you can't know a song on one listen), and then we gathered at my home and they thrashed out a winner. It was all very civil. I would make coffee, hand out sandwiches and add up the votes. In 1993, they chose Shona Laing's 'Mercy of Love'. We played it again to make sure. It was beautiful! We were away.

Now what do we do on the Silver Scroll Awards night? Mmm, 'happy members', Brett had said. Free food and drink are OK. They're crucial! But what APRA members really love is live music. So we sent out invites to the top 1000 earning APRA members (free tickets for them, charge for a partner), and I took the top five finalists from the judging day and invited various performers to do their own version of each song. Bushbeat from South Auckland was keen to do a funk version of the grungy 'The Way I Feel' by Jan Hellriegel. The Jazz Committee (with Nathan and Joel Haines) did an instrumental version of the Headless Chickens' 'Choppers' that split the room. It was musical anarchy. Everyone was wide awake, forging opinions, avoiding the asparagus and taking note of what was happening on the stage. The whole thing worked. And so from then on, every year, we invited artists who were emerging or carving out their own special place to perform the finalists' songs.

It was a gas. I walked around the room and I thought, 'Happy members.'

At the same time as I was preparing for my first APRA Silver Scroll Awards night, I heard that Brent Eccles had returned to live in Auckland. He had been in Australia playing drums for The Angels and hosting a music show on Sydney's premier radio station, Triple M. And in a synchronous fashion, Sony Music had released a 'Best Of' compilation of fifteen Citizen Band tracks—all remastered.

I thought 'Why not?' and rang Brent as well as my brother Geoffrey and Greg Clark. 'Come on, lads. Let's book some venues and play a pile of Citizen Band songs.' And so it came to be. It had been close to twelve years since we'd walked onstage together.

At rehearsals it all fell into place. There was union. A realisation in our usual quiet fashion that we had cool songs. With the spark of knowing each other so well and what we could do with our instruments and voices, we charged into it, harbouring a subtle knowing that it would fire. We looked at each other in that shabby room; each standing in a shaft of sunlight; each in a corner where we harboured the past and drew it into the present. And threw what we had into the centre. There was life and resilience and assurance. That was all we needed.

The peak of this reunion series was two sold-out shows at The Gluepot. Seven hundred and fifty people a night. The equipment got loaded into a van and rolled off to Ponsonby's Three Lamps.

I walked onstage a new man. Yes, the stage was always my safe haven, but with my phobic disorder banished I felt a surety that I was in guiding hands. As a bunch of boys who had become middle-aged majors and generals we were able to bask in the lack of the wayward factors that had rested heavy on us all those years ago. We had only one priority: to be good. We had to toss our performances out into the room and bludgeon the audience with an undeniable resonance. And we did.

On the second night we were charging on through 'The Ladder Song' early in the set when I noticed two people standing down below me, about three metres from the edge of the stage. It was Von and Jerry. Their eyes were focused on the four of us. And their ears were stuffed with cotton wool. I watched them watching. Gently shuffling and sidling in time with Eccles' beautiful beat. And then they both looked at me simultaneously. I kept my eyes on them. We stayed like that for some time.

I wanted to leap off the stage and hug them. They were there. Von and Jerry were still there.

Chapter Twenty-five
The Silver Scroll and Politics

While there were happy APRA members, there was also politics. Let's give it a capital P: Politics.

When I started at APRA, radio stations used to be on a roster—a week at a time, usually four weeks in a year, where they had to type out the names of the songs they had played and send that list to us. We would send those lists to head office, and they would use them to analyse which songs would receive royalties from the licensing fees paid by radio. Radio hated this. Sitting down and typing out seven days' worth of songs, line by line, tap by tap. Insane. They knew which songs needed to be reported, because they all used a software program called Selector, which scheduled the broadcasting of the songs. (I know what you're thinking—wait for it!)

One day I got a phone call from Gus Jansen, the IT boss at head office. He advised me that Selector had a flag on it called 'Selector Report', which no one in radio-land seemed to have noticed. Gus had. He said to me, 'It's a report that lists all the songs that have been played, who sang them and who wrote them, and you can program the start and end dates of that report. Can you contact a major radio person and ask them if they would be prepared to run those reports onto floppy disks and send them to us? Let's ask for one each quarter. Four times a year. If they can or will, then I can write a program to read them and we can pay out for every song a station plays.' A thought went through my mind: 'Happy members'.

I rang Larry Summerville about ten minutes later. Larry was GM or ED—certainly boss—of a bunch of radio stations in Auckland.

'Larry—Chunn here. I have a question.' And I asked him if he would be prepared to run the Selector report every quarter onto a floppy disk and send it to me for forwarding to Sydney, thus ensuring that every song his stations broadcast shared in royalties.

'Of course. It's the fair way to do it,' he said.

And so it came to be that, within a few months, radio station fees were going out for every song they played.

Now, Arthur Baysting, who you should remember was a co-writer of The Crocodiles song 'Tears', said to me one day, 'If these floppy disk reports of all songs played on New Zealand radio come to us, we could ask head office, as they analyse them, to report to us what percentage of the songs are New Zealand songs.' Brilliant, Arthur.

Not long afterwards, Gus sent me an internal communication. (Still no internet! But better than a telex.) On it was stated the percentage of songs played on New Zealand commercial radio that were written by New Zealand APRA members.

2.9 per cent.

That is—for every 100 songs played on New Zealand's commercial radio stations, *fewer than three* were by New Zealand songwriters.

Arthur pondered. I frowned. We concluded. Then he rang me and told me what he thought should happen.

1. Government should establish a Youth Radio Network— a young-person's Radio New Zealand National, which would play contemporary local music amid a broader playlist. The idea was modelled on Australia's Triple J, which placed an emphasis on playing local tracks. It would be an outlet for young New Zealand artists to be heard.

2. Quotas should be established for New Zealand music on commercial radio, similar to what places such as Ireland, France and Canada already had for local music.

Arthur came into the office the next day. He was older than me, which meant he was wiser. His clear vision of a New Zealand where we celebrated who we are was addictive. He was also a cool songwriter. He had made the most of the '70s with Red Mole and other experimental adventurers, then spent the '80s writing songs with the likes of Fane Flaws and Peter Dasent (both Crocodiles), all the while with an eye over his shoulder for some way to convince politicians that even if they didn't understand the power of words and music they could do something about it. Or at least talk about it.

In 1993 he gave an address, saying: 'This is the cultural battle . . . to provide a national voice for young people and genuine access to the radio waves for New Zealand songwriters and musicians. One way or another, it's up to the politicians.'

A rthur was determined to make this happen. In 1995 he instigated an APRA-hosted Youth Radio Conference in Wellington. I flew down. I looked out the window.

'Okay, Mr Agoraphobia. Where are you?'

Silence.

'Where are you?'

Silence . . . and I laughed. I did. I laughed. It was nowhere to be seen.

Back to the conference. It was focused on the need for a national voice for young New Zealanders and a drive to get more New Zealand songs on commercial radio. Among those attending were the Commissioner for Children, Laurie O'Reilly, representatives from RIANZ (Recording Industry Association of New Zealand) and major record companies, Labour politicians (at this time in Opposition) and students from Wellington secondary schools. Sharon Crosbie, then CEO of Radio New Zealand, was invited but couldn't make it.

Notably, there were two commercial-radio big-wigs there— Josh Easby and Gerard Murray, from the Prospect group of radio stations in Auckland, which included Hauraki and Radio I (among others). There was a fervour in radio-land, as the industry was being deregulated and digital explorations were allowing stations to start networking and delivering nationwide programming. Very cool. And there was no government interference as to what was broadcast.

Easby sat listening to Baysting talk about the 'cultural battle'. When the APRA figure of less than 3 per cent New Zealand music on commercial radio was announced, Easby turned to his general manager, Murray, and asked, 'Why are the New Zealand figures so low?'

'Buggered if I know,' came Murray's reply.

Easby's immediate thought was, 'Let's play more then!'

On returning to Auckland, Easby called together a group of music-industry personnel, including representatives from RIANZ, APRA, NZ On Air, student radio and record companies. I was there. It was the first time ever that a group from those various environments had sat together. We called it the Kiwi Music Action Group (KMAG), and our stated goal was to work towards getting more New Zealand music on commercial radio. Easby also proposed holding a summit at which programme directors and industry folk could discuss constructive and creative ways to get more local tunes on the dial.

That year APRA calculated the content of local music on commercial radio at less than 2 per cent. Something had to change.

Meanwhile, APRA was out chasing licences for—you guessed it—the public performance of copyright music. This led to some interesting outcomes.

One—the various names I was given. In 1995 we came out with a new background music licence. If you had a bar and played the radio it was $35 a year. A stereo system? Not a lot more. We sent out licence demands all over the place. I became a scum-sucking pig; one step lower than a meter maid; an extortionist; lowlife trash; a cocksucker.

The next two results weren't abusive as such. The first was a phone call from some bloke telling us he was coming up to throw a bomb through the front door. We quickly locked it and sat at the far end of the room, waiting. I imagined a scene from the movies, with the windows blowing out. Would have been a pity. But no one ever turned up.

And then there was the phone call from *Fair Go*. They came to see me. It appeared that there was a jeweller in the Manukau City shopping centre who had received a background music licence request. She played the radio in the store. She felt that this was a matter for a *Fair Go* story. And here they were.

The reporter was pretty cool. He asked me, 'Why?' I told him it was all about happy members (actually, I didn't say that; I wanted to). I explained why and how it worked. Then he looked at me with an earnest face. 'So are you going to make this jewellery shop take out a licence?' I said, 'No.' There was a short silence. I think he thought, 'Why am I here?' And they left. The piece ran on *Fair Go* and that was that. A boring story? Yes. But it had a cool ending.

I received a phone call from Melbourne about a week later.

'Mr Chunn. It's so-and-so from Acme Jewellers. We own a chain of jewellery stores in Australia and New Zealand. We already have APRA licences for all the Australian stores. We'd like to take out licences for all the New Zealand stores.'

Mmmm. I wonder if our friend in Manukau City had managed to keep her job. And a tip o' the hat to *Fair Go* for getting us dozens of APRA licences from a whole raft of jewellery stores.

As these shenanigans were riding along, the APRA Silver Scroll became a monster. By 1997 the eclectic live performances were being managed and the guest artists chosen by my old buddy Eddie Rayner. Eddie being Eddie, he picked beautifully strange and nutty people. I recall the Albanian band who sang the finalist song they had been assigned *in Albanian*. Good on them.

Anyway—let's stay in 1997. I thought, 'Let's have a previous winner of the Silver Scroll present it to the winner on the night.' So onstage at the NZI Room in Auckland's Aotea Centre, Roger Skinner, who'd won the Scroll in 1967 for 'Let's Think of Something', which had been a number-one hit for Larry's Rebels, presented it to Greg Johnson for his song 'Liberty'. The song was performed by the one and only Mahinārangi Tocker.

I'm sitting here recalling the morning in Ellerslie when 'Liberty' was chosen as the Scroll winner. The judges were talking about 'Liberty' and for some reason I couldn't think how it went. I knew the title. How did it go? They all knew it so well they didn't play it. They'd heard it a thousand times. I was too sappy to admit my confusion.

As the session drew to a close, they shuffled out the front door and sloped away. I went back inside and took out the disc of 'Liberty' and put it in the CD player. As it played, I found myself weeping. I knew the song. I loved that song. I will always love that song. Words and music. Power. The APRA Silver Scroll. Triumph.

When we published the next of our six-monthly *APRAP* magazines for members, Paul Casserly (of Strawpeople, among other things) was invited to write up the Silver Scroll Awards event. He wrote of Greg Johnson's triumph:

I am, of course, totally in awe of Greg's ability to create such a sense of beauty and sadness in his music . . . Maintaining the drive to write and the faith that it's all worthwhile is the true skill that's been rewarded here. A prize for the basic belief that the future will be better than the past—something we all crave and need like oxygen. It's something that somehow gets distilled into art, wine and good food, and especially music.

August 1996 saw the first of those programme/music directors summits that Josh Easby had suggested. It brought together radio, recording and music industry representatives, and plans were made to put together a 'New Zealand Music Week' where radio stations spent one week in May concentrating on playing New Zealand records. Those of us in KMAG would drive it.

New Zealand's first-ever Music Week was to commence on Anzac Day 1997. This tied in with the radio industry conference for that year, at which fresh New Zealand talent would be showcased. How did that come about? In early 1997, some of the top brass from the Radio Broadcasters Association (RBA) came to see me, to ask if APRA would host a showcase of new New Zealand music talent as part of their conference. I saw this as an opportunity to get New Zealand music right in front of radio programmers, so I suggested to Brendan Smyth at NZ On Air, who was part of KMAG, that we co-manage the showcase.

By this time young Debbie Little had come on board at APRA, and she made things happen. (Still does—we've been working together 22 years now.) This showcase was held on the first weekend of May at the RBA conference. The talent included The Feelers, three young men from Christchurch who played a song called 'Venus'. We all know what happened to that song once radio got their hands on it.

With the success of Music Week and the new talent showcase, things started to happen, albeit still behind the scenes. With the departure of Josh Easby, Mike Regal, an old hand at radio, took over running KMAG. His inside knowledge of the radio industry proved very useful.

It became clear that radio was all about getting advertising. And the ratings each station secured were of prime importance, because advertising agencies took note of those ratings. To have a listener switch stations on them—that was failure. That was despair. So the tendency was to play records that were already hits overseas. They'd already been proven.

Josh Easby had known that this was irresponsible. Radio programmers had the nous to know whether a New Zealand record was any good. Just listen to it a few times. Every single day people around the world hear a new song and decide whether they like it or not. The entire history of rock'n'roll is based on that premise. Why couldn't a radio programmer do the same thing? Easby had thought, 'Programmers should just knuckle down and take note of which NZ records are *good*!' He and I did talk about making programmers aware of the release of New Zealand records in a more efficient manner, and Mike Regal was thinking the same thing.

After one KMAG meeting, Mike took Brendan Smyth aside. Brendan had instigated the NZ On Air hit-disc programme, where CD compilations of newly released

New Zealand singles were sent to every radio station in the country. It was a clever initiative in that it took a bunch of new music recordings to radio programmers on an equal basis. Every track had the same chance of being assessed. Regal said to Smyth, 'Brendan, your hit discs arrive on a music programmer's desk, where they sit for a week gradually getting buried and then they slip off into the rubbish bin. What you need are pluggers.'

'Pluggers' is industry lingo for people hired by record companies to go in and badger radio people to play their latest records: promo people like Bridget de Launay. Smyth got the message, and from then on NZ On Air had pluggers going in to radio stations making sure that the hit discs were not only kept out of rubbish bins but were heard! It made a real difference. Eventually. It was a gradual process, but it was effective, and in a slow, methodical fashion the percentage of New Zealand songs on commercial radio started increasing. A new, emerging breed of music programmers stood out. Yes, they believed that great New Zealand songs should shine and be heard, but they also deserved credit for their own grit and determination. That current of change created a cool domino effect. Radio in general started to believe that New Zealand songs and recordings needed the chance.

At APRA, we were in the perfect position to witness this evolution. We got computer logs listing every song that radio played. We could see the change. The turning season was in our favour.

The anticipation in the APRA community was tangible. It was in their eyes. At the 1997 APRA Silver Scroll Awards function, a buoyancy filled the room. There was a clarity and a coolness and light, and the hundreds of songwriters present sensed that vision and purpose of what was in essence Arthur Baysting's vision. He knew that the answer to a transformed nation of respect, celebration and reward for New Zealand songs and their writers was all about people. He knew it wasn't about formal campaigns, rigid proposals and taking to the fourth estate with proclamations. And there at the Silver Scroll function in 1997, everyone knew it when Arthur spoke from the stage. His army coalesced. His words were uplifting. The change was under way.

Late in that year, Arthur found an ally in government in the form of New Zealand First's Deborah Morris, who was the Minister of Youth Affairs in the National coalition government. She was interested in setting up a commercial-free, publicly funded, national youth radio network, and Arthur and I got called down to the Beehive for a meeting with various bureaucrats.

Morris called for a report to be written, which eventually outlined four options.

1. Fund a youth radio network (YRN).
2. Give more resources to student radio.
3. Provide more funding for youth programming.
4. Go with the status quo and do nothing.

After the relevant politicians pondered these four options, number 4 was decided on as the preferred choice and the YRN ended its brief moment of support inside the Beehive.

This *was* 1997, after all—a time when the government was intent on leaving the outside world to its own devices ('market forces' was the buzzword), and the Business Roundtable was in bed with major National Party decision-makers. Virtually no one in government seemed remotely interested in understanding or acknowledging the creative worth of a thriving local music industry.

Perhaps the defining moment in National's inability to comprehend the social benefits of a YRN and the power of local music in general came when Arthur and Neil Finn managed to get a meeting with Prime Minister Jim Bolger, on the subject of a YRN. Finn was first through the door. Bolger turned and looked Neil up and down with a studious eye. 'And you are . . .?'

It wasn't until Arthur and I called a meeting in early 1998 with more-sympathetic Labour Party MPs that we got the first taste of what might be possible. With a roundtable including Helen Clark, Judith Tizard, Dr Michael Cullen, Marian Hobbs, Trevor Mallard and Lianne Dalziel, Arthur laid out a plan to bolster the New Zealand music industry. It included those two crucial aspects—establishing a youth radio network and introducing radio quotas for New Zealand music—plus a new factor, a music industry commission. And the response was positive.

I didn't say much that day. I just knew that I was bearing witness to the right people who were waiting for the right time. Waiting for a spark to be lit that catapulted them all into a ruling government. I moved my eyes along that line of faces. A quiet detachment surrounded me, like I was in a dream. I was in a hall of depiction and revelation. It was early in my dream, however long that dream might be. The two rails of time—the past and the future—were crossing and merging such that the collision, when it happened, wouldn't surprise us. I saw a blaze of iridescence coming from the future, sweeping across New Zealand with cymbals and chants, seeing us all charging out of our houses, crossing the footpath berms—no longer moats, but bridges—to the nervous, silent halls where we would tick our votes.

I looked at those shadow ministers. The Opposition. They were listening carefully to Arthur. In 1999 there would be an election. I wrote '*victory*' on a piece of paper and put it in my pocket.

About a month later, Arthur and I were standing outside the Beehive, having had another meeting with yet another Minister of Arts and Culture who wasn't seeing our point of view, when the good doctor Cullen walked up out of the blue and asked, 'This music commission—what will it look like?'

Arthur responded instantly with, 'I'll have our document on your desk this afternoon.'

Cullen was happy with that and strolled away.

I looked at Arthur quizzically. 'What music commission document?'

'Leave it with me.'

Arthur bolted through the parliamentary doors and disappeared. He went up to Judith Tizard's office, scrounged the use of one of their word-processors and wrote off the top of his head a brief on what a working music commission would look like. Two hours later the document was on Cullen's desk.

Arthur wrote about the profile of New Zealand music (where was it?), what wasn't on radio and why not, music in education, and more. It was nothing less than a mission statement for an ideal world where music, words and recordings stood up and people took notice! For Christ's sake—these were our songs. If anyone heard them, it should be New Zealanders!

The next indication of where the future lay was a lunch called by one of Judith Tizard's sidekicks in Auckland, Paul Rose. I sat there with Malcolm Black (formerly the frontman of the Netherworld Dancing Toys, then of Sony Music), Chris Hocquard (entertainment lawyer and chairperson of bFM) and Dr Michael Cullen. Cullen asked, 'Now, tell me once again, what does this music industry need to grow?'

We rattled off a list of things. Cullen jotted it all down and put his pad back in his pocket. We kept talking. He listened. There were no promises, but I recall thinking that for the first time I was talking to someone from a political party who could get to understand the music industry. But more than that—they could encourage the exposure of New Zealand music and they could stand up and celebrate its successes.

I looked Cullen in the eye and made up my mind—I would support his party in the 1999 elections with everything I had.

Arthur then had an inspiring daydream, which led to his inviting two Irishmen who he was aware had a focus on what was going on in New Zealand to come Down Under and share their vision. The first was Niall Stokes, head of the Irish Independent Radio and Television Commission. I'd been told he was a rock'n'roll animal. He was also editor of the Irish rock'n'roll magazine *Hot Press*, so he was cool with it. In fact, Niall was cool full-stop. The second was Hugh Duffy, my equivalent at the Irish Music Rights Organisation (IMRO). His gentle demeanour masked a determination quite ferocious, I suspected.

Arthur put on a conference at the University of Auckland, which APRA co-sponsored with the Media Department there. Let's cut to the quotes.

Niall Stokes:

> Enlightened, pro-active and supportive public policies can be enormously important in creating the conditions necessary for people to make things happen creatively and culturally . . . The great Irish cultural renaissance has not taken place in a vacuum . . . the intensity of it all has been made possible through an enlightened policy of support and encouragement . . . If—as I am told—New Zealand radio stations are generally slithering between 4 per cent and a maximum of 7 per cent then they are showing a contempt for New Zealand songwriters and musicians which is deeply offensive. They are abrogating their responsibility to the community they are licensed to serve.
>
> It comes down to this. Culture is not a commodity. Music is not a commodity. And for the State to allow them to be treated as such—I believe—represents nothing less than the betrayal of the imaginative life of the people and their capacity to think and to feel and to express themselves. It is to hand over the soul of the nation to the 'greasy man and his till' for safekeeping—in what must

be the certain knowledge that he will sell it. In Ireland we decided to resist this Faustian pact and we did—and now we are reaping the benefits tenfold.

Hugh Duffy:

Music and writing have always played a central role in the social and cultural life of Ireland; not alone as a source of entertainment but also as an effective way of recording Irish history and communicating its stories widely throughout the country and the world. Internationally, the Irish nation is perceived very much through the medium of its music . . . and research has confirmed that music is one of the primary factors which attract tourists to Ireland.

Everyone in the room—admittedly, a bunch of pinkos—loved it. The media ignored it. The response from the National government was a deafening silence.

After the conference, Stokes went on National Radio to talk quotas with Brian Edwards on his Saturday morning show. Stokes talked about radio frequencies being a natural resource of any country, and how they were no different to land or waterways. They are there permanently and they are limited. Once they are sold off, they are gone.

Stokes described a wasteland where radio frequencies are sold off with no constraints on their future use. He talked of the danger of international owners just beaming in Anglo-American pop music with no reflection at all of the musical culture of New Zealand. I wrote in *APRAP*: 'The [music] industry is a flapping bird with its feet on the ground. When will it fly?'

And then Labour made their move. They released a creative industries 'white paper', in which they outlined one very relevant intention: quotas for local content. They would begin at 10 per cent for commercial radio, rising to 20 per cent over a period of time.

On one radio show, the host proclaimed that he was 'dead against' statutory quotas of local content on radio and television. He singled out music quotas. When he asked his music reviewer, a radio programmer himself, about quotas, the programmer said to the host, 'I say bring it on. Let's have quotas for all commercial radio. Then everyone will be forced to listen to low-quality music.' He was throwing down a glove. I picked it up.

At the 1998 APRA Silver Scrolls Awards, I climbed onstage (I had never previously done that) and said that I'd had enough of certain broadcasters talking about New Zealand music as being low quality. And I meant it. 'These people stand on broadcast pedestals that reach up into the clouds.' The entire Town Hall was deeply quiet as they took in a collective breath and prepared themselves to bring about change.

I was now hugely intent on having a Labour government, and I knew that the wider music industry had it in them to share that belief and make some noise about it in the twelve months leading up to the 1999 election.

In the same month, another Irishman turned up to beat the drum: Michael D. Higgins, the wild-haired poet who had become Minister of Culture in the Irish Labour government elected in 1993. In just four years, Higgins had helped take Ireland from a rural, agricultural-based society, where 55,000 people were leaving each year, to bringing culture to the forefront of new growth industries and helping revitalise a nation. It was Higgins who had appointed the cool and in-touch Niall Stokes to the Independent Radio and Television Commission, replacing a retired judge aged in his seventies.

Higgins had been invited to New Zealand to speak at a conference in Wellington called Counting the Cultural Beat, about public broadcasting. Higgins spoke of the renaissance of Irish music and the wide celebration of their songs taking on the world. He was deeply inspirational. His intellectual prowess and economy of language meant we were riveted to the spot.

Here is an excerpt from his speech.

At the bases of the choices we will make in the next few years are some fundamental value choices involving such questions as:

What value do we put on the public world?

What value do we put on issues beyond the immediate, beyond a single life span?

How do we wish to remember and be remembered?

What do we wish to be free to imagine?

Such value choices raise questions about the cultural space, its relationship to the economic space, how it is to be defined—is it to be open or closed, democratic or autocratic, fixed by tradition or flexible to the contemporary and the as yet unremembered?

One of the aims of a comprehensive arts policy might be to combat the growing compartmentalisation of the modern economic system and to restore expressive freedom to the individual, so that every man and woman can again be in some sense an artist.

Arthur took the opportunity to invite Higgins to the APRA office in Auckland to meet New Zealand songwriters. After a couple of pints, Higgins stood up on a chair and spoke— without notes or little pause for breath. As you can't get too much of Dr Michael Higgins, I want to record here what he said.

The argument about quotas is about diversity. Has new music not the right to emerge? You have to have quotas. The arguments are about citizenship and democracy and activity rather than passivity.

The value of the [Irish] music industry was around £250 million in 1995 and is now around £400 million. The right of people to hear their own stories, make their own sounds, imagine their own things, in particular make their own compositions, is not a narrow little territorial thing. My argument with narrow-minded market theorists is simply that they are bereft of imagination.

Part of the formula is the crucial importance of public broadcasting, otherwise we face the last great colonisation without arms or armies—the colonisation of the imagination. Creativity is connected to an intellectual vision of the way you are and waves of tolerance have come about as a result of different kinds of books and music and films around the world . . . If you want cultural diversity you can fund the creative society and from it will come marvellous things. But the knowledge economy as a substitute for the creative society is a disaster—it's a recipe for obsolescence and unhappiness.

Many songwriters were in attendance, including Tim Finn, who described Higgins as 'a very exciting gentleman'. Finn paid his respects by performing for Higgins 'Many's the Time', a song about Dublin which he had written and performed in Ireland with Hothouse Flowers. They shared anecdotes and embraced.

A short while before leaving, Higgins turned to me. He said, 'It is only when the leader of a nation believes in and respects its music and songs that the people will follow.'

In December 1998, in *APRAP*, Arthur wrote presciently:

There is a definite feeling that the worst is over. Conceivably, in a few years we'll look back at the new richness of our cultures and wonder what the fuss was about. We'll marvel at who we are and what we are becoming. Music, film, television, dance, theatre, literature—the language we use and the ceremonies we share—all will explode in celebration. We have already started to create our future and the future of our children. Kia Kaha.

The next year's New Zealand Music Week was a great success. But we needed some new ideas to keep up the momentum. In September I rang The Warehouse chap who handled all CD and DVD stock and marketing. His name was Terry Anderson.

'Terry, have you got any plans for next year's Music Week?'

He answered, 'Mike, a week is too short. We could plan and achieve a lot more if it was a month.'

'Well,' I thought, 'that's easy.' New Zealand Music Week became New Zealand Music Month in a matter of days.

And there was also another thing to celebrate. A few months later Labour won the 1999 election, and our supporter Helen Clark became New Zealand's prime minister. Onwards and upwards.

The new government didn't waste any time. In May 2000, Clark announced an $80 million 'arts recovery package' at a function in the Grand Hall of Parliament. I was there. I watched Helen Clark as much as listened to her. She was the Minister of Arts, Culture and Heritage. Sublime. I thought back to the National Party ministers for the arts who Arthur and I had met with—Doug Graham and Simon Upton. Meetings that led to nothing. And here was Helen Clark rolling out extraordinary support and advances, as espoused in the late '90s when Labour's white paper on the creative industries was produced.

I looked around the room. The Grand Hall. Like fragments of all our intentions and ambitions, like old dreams pinned to the wall, everything merged into an advancing army of celebration and the blending voices from all quarters were in harmony.

We all walked outside and the Beehive buzzed above us. The piano key footpath played out songs from our own footsteps as we moved ahead. It didn't matter where we were going that morning. We knew where we were headed.

I took my crumply piece of paper out of my back pocket. I read it again.

'*Victory.*'

A New Zealand Music Commission became a reality. It still wasn't 100 per cent clear what it was to do, but in general terms it would celebrate, foster and propagate the New Zealand music industry.

The new Minister of Broadcasting, Marian Hobbs, started talking turkey with the broadcasters. In March 2002 it was announced that New Zealand music content quotas were officially on the table, and would be self-regulated via a voluntary code. Starting at 10 per cent, commercial radio made the commitment to reach an average of 20 per cent across all formats in five years (formats being Top 40, Classic Hits, Easy Listening, Adult Contemporary and so on).

The official announcement was made in Auckland at a function held by the RBA at the GPK restaurant in Mount Eden. The place was packed with music industry names. New Zealand radio finally had a voluntary quota in place for playing New Zealand songs.

Exactly what Marian Hobbs had negotiated with the radio broadcasters is not known to me. But suffice to say that in that GPK upstairs room there was unity. David Innes, the RBA CEO, and his board members Brent Impey and John McElhinney, stood there with flutes in their hands. (Not *those* flutes! Sparkling wine!) Arthur and I did the same. Where was the point of difference? The debate? There wasn't one. A truly tangible purpose had been stated: to reach a figure of 20 per cent local content on commercial radio—and it was a real intention. So our Kiwi Music Action Group saw the change from having to leap over hurdles to a joyous diving through hoops of myriad colours. The end of one of the major tunnels had been reached and there was coolness and light.

As the function folded, I descended the stairs to Dominion Road and went and sat in my car. It was full of echoes. And those echoes were attuned to a rhythmic celebration. A race run such that we had all crossed the finish line at the same time. We had all won.

While the political arena was all a-go, in-house APRA matters were also vibrant. In May 2001 the first New Zealand Music Month was held. The t-shirts were red. All metropolitan and regional commercial radio stations were committed and ran interviews, features and competitions, and, most crucially, increased the rotation and exposure of New Zealand songs. The local music scene was alive and kicking, and a greater number of people were getting to hear the amazing work of Kiwi songwriters.

The contrast with those adventurous early Split Enz days was immense. Yes, commercial radio had played New Zealand records in the early '70s. But they were virtually all cover versions of northern hemisphere songs that had been hits over there and not released in New Zealand. It was shabby. Now the tide had turned. And there we were, all priming up the powder and filling the kegs for a 20 per cent quota of New Zealand records on radio.

The same year, 2001, was the seventy-fifth anniversary of the establishment of APRA, and as a salute to our members, new and old, a survey was undertaken. All New Zealand

APRA members were invited to nominate their ten favourite New Zealand songs of the past 75 years. With the average age of members being something like 32 there weren't many songs from the pre-'60s era, but more than 600 members sent in their lists and more than 900 songs were voted for.

When it was totalled and tallied, Wayne Mason's 'Nature' took first place. His band The Fourmyula had hit number one with it in 1970, it had won the Silver Scroll that year, and then it had had a new lease of life in the '90s when Don McGlashan's Mutton Birds released it as a single.

Debbie Little and I arranged to have the top 30 songs made into a two-disc CD compilation. At the 2001 APRA Silver Scroll, the top ten were performed by invited artists, and every person in attendance got a free copy of those discs. The Mutton Birds performed 'Nature' with Wayne Mason joining in—a triumphant moment for that great songwriter. The night was on fire.

Towards the end, Rodney Hewson from Sony Music came up to me. He and his boss Michael Glading had been talking. They thought the CD should be released commercially and they had a title for it—*Nature's Best*.

I said, 'Of course, young man. Do it.' And they did.

The top 30 collection was a supreme array of quality songs. My old friends Tim and Neil Finn, Jordan Luck, Juddsy, the Crocodiles and more were all part of that line-up. It was a glorious moment when I was delivered the *Nature's Best* CD and started playing it. Released in early 2002, *Nature's Best* didn't take long to be a *huge* hit. Eventually it sold more than 150,000 copies; a volume unheard of for a New Zealand music compilation.

What did this mean? I wrote an article talking of this phenomenon. I believed that New Zealanders bought this album through word of mouth. People in the streets were talking about it because it brought to them songs that were a high-class contemporary assembly. Because the songs had been nominated by peer-group songwriters, there wasn't a Top 10 emphasis. Commercial legacy bore no relevance. Sure, songs like The Swingers' 'Counting the Beat', Bic Runga's 'Sway' and 'Don't Dream It's Over' by Crowded House had been hits. But songs like 'She Speeds' by Straitjacket Fits, Darcy Clay's 'Jesus I Was Evil' and Chris Knox's 'Not Given Lightly' hadn't been broadcast on Top 40 radio and they held pride of place on *Nature's Best*. I wrote that the public had finally realised that New Zealand songwriters have a cutting-edge imagination, and this collection had really sunk into New Zealand's psyche.

Shortly after the article was published, I was contacted by the dean of arts of a co-ed Auckland secondary school. He asked me to talk about all this to his year 12 and 13 students— around 250 of them—so I turned up and there they were.

I asked, 'How many of you think you play a sport quite well?' Around a third lifted their hands.

I then asked, 'How many of you think you could write a song?'

Two.

A few months later I was asked by my younger daughter Ruby's primary-school teacher to bring a guitar to school and show them that playing one wasn't rocket science. I did that. I asked them, 'Who of you have parents that can drive a car?' They all put their hands up. I said, 'Playing the guitar is easier than driving a car.' This went down well. I then thought, 'Why not?'

'How many of you play a sport quite well?'

Half put up their hand.

'How many of you think you can write a song?'

All of them put their hand up. *All of them.*

I drove away thinking, 'What happens between eight and eighteen years of age? Why will virtually all those young students lose their self-belief? Is this just simply about the death of imagination? Or is it something else?'

Something had to be done. And I decided to do it. At the right time.

Chapter Twenty-six
Eden Park and a Final Whistle

After Split Enz had played the last date of its US tour on 10 March 1977, at the Ivanhoe Theatre in Chicago, Phil Judd flew to England. On the same day, I flew to Auckland. While Juddsy had officially left the band, I hadn't. I wasn't to know that in four weeks I would.

Tim went to Baltimore with Eddie to write songs. I went to Auckland to find a replacement guitarist for Juddsy. I didn't find one, although I did catch my brother Geoff's band, After Hours, performing with a young Neil Finn and Buster Stiggs in the line-up. Impressive. And then I left for London with their sounds and images in my head. You know these things.

Juddsy, with his wife, Julie, and daughter Amelia, merged into the English countryside. The Kentish village of Rolvenden, in fact. And in a few weeks he had written some songs. One of them was called 'Play It Strange'. This three-minuter was Juddsy writing about himself, in essence, and the notion that the songs he wrote were instinctively oddball and strange, although to him they were perfectly OK. The lyrics were a disguise, about 'others' playing it strange—a busker, a DJ, a teenage band. Out of time. Out of tune. These new songs were looking for a stage.

Once Tim returned to the UK, he and Phil were in contact. The invite was made and Juddsy rejoined Split Enz. The band rehearsed and started playing 'Play It Strange' live. This was around November 1977. But alas, it wasn't too long before Phil and Split Enz parted ways again and 'Play It Strange' went with him, where it wallowed in obscurity. But Bill Moran knew about it.

Bill was and always will be a New Zealand music fan. But he was more than that. He was a super Split Enz fan. He knew all there was to know about Phil Judd. He was also the economic adviser to the then Associate Minister of Finance, Trevor Mallard. In 2001, Bill had arranged a dinner with Mallard and invited a bunch of music industry bods, including me and Arthur Baysting. The idea was to talk about the music industry to Trevor and tell him how it was all going. Well, we started talking about that and quickly got onto rugby.

Mallard was in the Parliamentarians rugby team, and they had won the Parliamentary Rugby World Cup in 1999 in Wales. Bill looked at me. I turned to Mallard.

'Trevor, we'll put together a Musicians rugby team, and we here, right now, challenge you.'

Mallard reached out and shook my hand. *Game on.*

And in September 2001, the Musicians rugby team (including Jordan Luck, Peter Urlich, Malcolm Black, James Reid and me on left wing—the position I played at school) ran onto the hallowed turf of Eden Park to face the Parliamentarians . . . under lights. We were the curtain-raiser to the NPC match Canterbury versus Auckland, and we played twelve minutes a half. I can't begin to tell you how excited we were. Cut to the chase: we beat them 12–10. The game was screened on Sky's Rugby Channel. Stars!

Anyway, back to Bill. Time drifted on, and in early October 2003 Bill rang me as I was ambling down St Benedicts Street in Newton. He had an odd question for me. He asked if I'd heard of gaming societies. I said that I hadn't. I wasn't a gambling man. He explained their existence. How people bet two-dollar coins on what we once all called one-armed bandits. I'd heard of those. And he went on. Gaming societies ran them, and distributed grants out of the profits to the community. Bill suggested that we form a charitable trust and apply for grants.

'Excellent idea, Bill,' I said.

Bill was happy with that response. He then said, 'If we did that, what would the trust do?'

I stood on the footpath as cars swished by. A typical early-summer late morning in St Benedicts Street. The Waitakere Ranges just over there in the west. Cranes dotted on the big city skyline. Every passing car had someone in it, driving it. What were they thinking? They were ripe for a new world. Far and wide. And the young New Zealanders peppered throughout the suburban streets and the country roads? Their reflections suspected that there was a future to be had. Our youth knew it couldn't live in the present. The prophecy of their dreams took shape in the glow of each new dawn. And an enthusiasm was born. These young New Zealanders were gathering their life moments, their revelries, their celebrations, their fears and losses, and all the while were ready for the means to float their stories out into the sky like multicoloured butterflies. And the sooner they were set free, the better. Otherwise time would pass and their imaginations would die at the side of the road. A stifling inertia would fall into their lives.

Bill and I—we could start this thing. What would our charitable trust do?

I had often found myself thinking about those secondary-school students who thought they couldn't write a song. They listen to recorded songs every day of their life. Those songs come beaming at them, and they hold so many in their hearts, where they are emotionally connected to their happiness and peace of mind. So why do so many people *not* write songs? In a society where science, maths and language rule the classroom, songwriting is virtually ignored. It was clear to me. The songwriters I knew well—the Finns, Juddsy, Jordan Luck, Don McGlashan, et al.—had all evolved their songwriting capability outside the educational infrastructure. It wasn't that songwriting was a waste of time. But many educationalists had never written or even *played* an original song. So where to now, St Peter? Time to roll up the sleeves and see what needed to be done to get the beautiful, imaginative craft of songwriting fostered, celebrated and respected in our society.

I had done some investigation. Songwriting was not a subject in New Zealand schools. Nor was it a subject in schools in the UK, the United States, Australia, France, Canada, Italy, Ireland and so on. How many countries are there in the world? What would it take to have it in the school curriculum? And if New Zealand was the only country in the world to have it, so what? Schools have art, they have drama, they have composition. Where is songwriting?

I suggested that the trust ran songwriting competitions in secondary schools.

'Great,' said Bill. 'That's a good start. And I have a name for the trust.'

'What is it, Bill?'

'Play It Strange,' he replied.

It all made perfect sense.

Back at my desk, I found myself deep in thought. It had been a good year. The books showed that APRA New Zealand was now collecting $11 million a year in licensing fees. The members seemed pretty happy. The Labour government was into what we were doing. The APRA Silver Scroll Awards night was monumental in its support, eccentricity and celebration of great New Zealand songs and songwriters. New Zealand Music Month was now a nationwide activity, with its cool logo of concentric rings and t-shirts in a different colour every year. The percentage of New Zealand music on radio was increasing steadily every year, too. (As an aside, from here in the future—it reached 20 per cent after four years, not five.) What was left for me to do?

I thought back to where it had started, eleven years before. APRA New Zealand was sitting quietly at the bottom of the harbour and Brett Cottle had asked me to get it floating and take it out around New Zealand's coastline, scooping songwriters onto its deck. Here, in 2003, we were humming along at a steady speed, with 2000 more songwriters than when we started. It felt like our merry APRA staffers could go anywhere.

The longer I sat in that chair, the more it became real. It was time for me to move on. The Silver Scroll Awards show was a few weeks away. I rang Brett Cottle and told him it would be my last.

At the Silver Scroll Awards in the Auckland Town Hall in mid October 2003, I took the stage for the second and last time. I'd written out some lines. Not many. I thanked a lot of people. Arthur especially . . . and the wonderful Brett Cottle. My fellow staff. And then I thanked *them*—the songwriters. I thanked them all for letting me work for them. It had been an honour and a privilege. And I said:

After all, what is a song? It's a three-minute symphony. The great mystery. A call to arms. The insatiable thirst. The sinking feeling. The winning ticket. The fall from grace. A novel put into three verses, two choruses and a bridge. A hook that is unforgettable. A provocation. It's a plea for common sense, a cry for help, a phantasm, a celebration of love, a tale from Dante's Inferno. It is all these things. And you here in the Auckland Town Hall are the cream of the crop. Thank you.

And then I said, 'A special acknowledgement to you, Brigid. We rode the last eleven years together. And now, we head off into the future, babe.'

My last work day was Friday, 31 October 2003. I don't recall much about it. I guess I was watching the clock. The sun was easing into my office between the Venetian blinds from the west. I thought that I would just leave everything where it was. Our legal officer, Ant Healey, was going to move in to the office on Monday to start his own heady ride as director of operations. I'd hired him six years earlier, not because he was a snazzy lawyer but because he was a Sacred Heart College old boy. A cool pedigree. Would he use the same chair I had? Make coffee at the same time each morning? Pick up the phone when it rang and say, 'Healey!' How different would things be on Monday when I wasn't there? And where would I be?

Eventually it was 5 p.m. I stood up and didn't move. I just started crying. It took a long time for me to stop.

As I said, Bill Moran is very focused on all things Phil Judd. Hence, when on that sunny morning in 2003 he suggested we form a charitable trust, his suggestion of naming it 'Play It Strange' made perfect sense.

At the same time, he suggested we ask Juddsy to be one of our judges. I contacted Phil, who was living in Melbourne, and asked him if he was cool with us naming our trust after his song and if he would be a judge. He agreed to both. So there we were. How to do this thing?

Forming a charitable trust is really just a matter of drawing up a trust deed and having the Charities Commission approve it. This all happened down in Wellington, on Bill's nudging and cajoling a law firm and other relevant people. As this was happening, Bill called me.

'We need trustees and a settlor.'

A settlor? Trustees? Mmm. A settlor to settle things down. Trustees? Trustworthy people, I presumed. Bill suggested Neil Finn as our settlor and he signed on the dotted line. And trustees? He named a few experts from his political neck of the woods. He also suggested I contact Sam Neill, Dave Dobbyn. 'Anyone else?' he asked. I suggested Sean Fitzpatrick. Another

Sacred Heart old boy. What could be better? And all three agreed.

Shortly after this consolidation, Neil Finn and his wife, Sharon, had a bash at the building they had purchased in Newton. Everyone knew it but claimed to have never been to it. It had been a porn-video hire shop.

Anyway, a fair swathe of connected persons gathered on the top floor of this place—soon to be christened Roundhead Studios—and a stage that had been put in was invaded. Neil and Tim were up there, along with Neil's son Elroy on drums and my boy Barney, now thirteen, on electric guitar. I was on bass. We played a few gigantic hits from the Finn repertoire and then climbed back down and kept drinking.

Neil came up to me and asked about Play It Strange—was it going to get underway soon?

I said that we would, and that secondary-school songs would soon be out and about for all to hear. Neil smiled. He said that the building we were in would have recording studios built in it. I said, 'This bodes well.'

Meanwhile, the Charities Commission approved the Play It Strange trust deed application and we existed. Now what? What were we? How did we? Bill and I talked on the phone. I was probably still standing on St Benedicts Street. We needed to have songwriting competition entry forms. And the competition needed prizes. What would they be? And where would I work from?

The home phone rang. It was Neil.

'Mike, where will Play It Strange be based? And who are the staff?'

'I'm the staff and we have nowhere to base ourselves,' I

replied with as much buoyancy as I could. I'm not one to sad-sack a situation.

'I have a room in the new building. You can use that. There's a computer. Desk and stuff. A phone.'

Seven weeks after Play It Strange took its first breath, I settled into Neil's building. The stage we'd played on was gone and a baby grand piano was in its place. The chair I sat on looked out at it. I thought, 'Neil Finn—you are awesome.' (I still think that.)

And I thought about all that lay ahead. It was shrouded in a light fog. OK—so we knew that songwriting didn't exist as a subject in schools. What does? What is a pursuit in schools that has achieved a permanent and highly populated presence? One that is all about participation? That is encouraged, supported and celebrated? I knew the answer to that: rugby.

I met Sean Fitzpatrick. We always met at Kenzie café in Newmarket, and I would always get there before him because he would always try to get there before me and we're competitive.

'Fitz, rugby in schools is a huge thing. From the principal down, it's supported by everybody—parents, too—and it mirrors a school's culture—the drive, the "success" of a school, particularly in its spirit. Yes?'

'Yes,' he replied.

'Now, every day of the year secondary-school students listen to recorded pop songs. Whether on the radio, TV, car stereos, et cetera. It's an omnipresent *need* in their lives. Yes?'

'Yes,' he replied.

'So what we need to do, we Play It Strangers, is work towards songwriting and the recording, performance and propagation of these original songs being like rugby. It's all about participation. You don't study it, you don't talk about it, you just play it. After all, tell me, Fitz—if rugby wasn't played at secondary school, what would the All Blacks look like?'

'There wouldn't be any All Blacks,' he said.

I looked at him.

'This is what you should do,' he said. 'Go to College Sport here in Auckland and ask them how it works with rugby. Then we should do the music version of it.'

Ah, brilliant. So I did.

In essence, rugby in schools is all about making it easy for the players. I knew this. Hey—I'd played rugby every year for Sacred Heart College. The school took the responsibility for putting teams together. Usually they had their own fields, with white lines on them and goalposts, and maybe a few rugby balls, along with coaches and managers. They gave us football shorts, socks and jerseys, of course. The players bought their own boots.

College Sport organised which team played which team. It organised referees and made sure they had whistles. They made sure someone kept the score and that points tables were maintained. And every year it was a smooth operation, with tens of thousands of young New Zealanders taking part.

So let's do that with contemporary music. Smokefree Rockquest had been around since the early '90s, focusing primarily on the live performance of original songs. We would run parallel with them, focusing on songwriting and recording in the studio.

This was the complete package of what needs to be in place for involvement and potential success in the world of contemporary pop music—let's call it rock'n'roll:

1. A song
2. Live performances
3. Studio performances
4. Taking recordings to the marketplace.

I met with Bill again. I outlined all this. He said, 'Let's do it like that.'

We needed a website where songwriters could download entry forms. Prizes? Let's make it that the top twenty songs as judged get to professionally record their song for a CD album at a studio of their choice. We'll pay for the studio time. We'll pay for the CDs. We'll make about 2000 of them, give a pile to each winning writer and give the rest away. One to Helen Clark! The All Blacks! Our trustees! You name it. We'll open a bank account. What will we put in it?

I met Bill again. We talked about gaming societies again. OK, I would write up a document that explained who we were and why we existed—our purpose—how we were looking to fund what we were going to do, and how it would make a difference out there in New Zealand society. I went to a stationer and shuffled through the paper pads. Which one shall I use to write a 'philosophy' of this Play It Strange? A yellow legal one? A blank white block? Newsprint? This thing could be newsworthy. In the end I chose a Croxley 1B4 exercise book, because Sister Aloysius at the Otahuhu convent school told me they were all you needed to be a good boy and not a brazen brat! And I wrote.

PLAY IT STRANGE PHILOSOPHY

The appreciation of song (words and music) is universal. Every single person enjoys songs every day of their lives. In fact, it happens so regularly and in such a way that we don't think about it. But if it were to disappear from our lives, we would soon sense something was very wrong.

The performance and writing of songs, as a natural consequence, can provide huge benefits to many, many people. To witness a child conquering their adversities through the craft of songwriting is a celebration. To hear a class of disadvantaged children playing in a ukulele orchestra is no less so. There is an empowerment. There is a beautiful distillation where a young person's value is realised.

I added more than that. It was bordering on formal, which made me feel uncomfortable. I'd been uncomfortable for most of my life, so I thought 'screw that', and twisted my lithe frame until I was more comfortable. My shoes came off and I pulled off my socks. I threw them all out the window. There was a pamphlet on the charitable status of non-concomitant charitable entities all in cohorts of blue and green; that went over the balustrade too, in an imagined triumphant moment complete with salutes and speeches.

With the document finished and a nice letter out front, I mailed a fairly large swathe of gaming societies to see if they would be interested in making a grant to a charitable trust like ours so we could run a secondary-school songwriting competition in 2004.

I sat in the room Neil had given me. The phone was a beige colour. It had a curly lead. Parking was a pain around

Neil's building, but that didn't worry me as I didn't have a car. The computer was a PC. A PC Direct. Sharon Hunter. Large screen. Monotone letters. It hummed a bit but perhaps that was a good thing. The windows faced north, so I sat there and thought about the winter and how, on sunny days, the room would be warm. Quite often Neil would be on the piano out there in the large main room. I listened intently. To the phone. It was quiet. Neil is a cool piano player, though.

Each day I would check the post-office box. Then I'd return to the office. I'd call a meeting with the three of us: me, myself and I. We seemed to agree on everything, a raft of wonderful imaginings. Then I'd check for phone messages. Listen to Neil play the piano. I started to recognise some melodies. He must have played them before. Was this going to be a cool song for his next album? And then—

RING RING RING.

I picked it up. 'Play It Strange.'

'Ah, Mike Chunn?'

'Yes. It's me.'

'Hi. I'm Sharon Hollis from the Scottwood Trust in Hamilton. I'm their grants manager. I received your document and letter about Play It Strange. It looks very interesting and I'm thinking—would you like to make a formal application for a grant?'

I rang Bill. Joy!

'I'll make the application,' said Bill. And he did. And in March 2004 the Scottwood Trust put $27,500 in our bank account. This was followed by my dear friends at APRA granting us $20,000. And so my salary came into existence!

But I still didn't know how we were going to run the

songwriting competition—or, more to the point, how we were going to pay for the recording sessions of the songs chosen as finalists.

Then Bill called. 'Let's have a launch function.' I, naturally, said, 'Of course.' We booked Neil and Sharon Finn's Tabac bar in the CBD, sent out invites and asked two young artists to perform, to give focus to what we were all about.

It was a highly successful affair, but the one aspect of it that made it very special, with an eye on the future, was that Prime Minister Helen Clark was right there in the front row. I recalled what Michael Higgins had said to me in the APRA office five years earlier:

It is only when the leader of a nation believes in and respects its music and songs that the people will follow.

As the horde dissipated out into Albert Street and beyond, Bill and I stood on the corner, shifting and shuffling in anticipation of a future that needed some major decisions made and major money thrown at it.

'We need funds to record all these songs,' said Bill.

'That is quite true,' I said. And then I had an idea.

'TVNZ,' I said.

Once upon a time, TVNZ used to run telethons to raise money for this, that and the other thing. Split Enz performed on one in 1975, giving New Zealand a first-time look at our zoot suits, tousled and sprayed hair, lipstick and so on. Tim's out-front persona had blossomed into a truly eccentric yet in-control one and we mimed to our single 'Maybe'. As proof of our colourful advancement, Tim's father Dick was fined at his Rotary Club for having a son that looked a 'twit'. Three years later Citizen Band appeared on a telethon and played 'I Feel Good'. Near the end of the song—miming again—we smashed our guitars, echoes of The Who in our minds. The host proclaimed this display to be 'not in the real spirit of Telethon!'

But telethons worked. Money was raised. And what better way to showcase what we were about than having dozens of odd acts charging about on national television? Why not have a telethon for us? Then our brand-new trust wouldn't slide into a deep recession once the money we had banked had slipped away. We could do it in the New Zealand Music Month of May.

I went to TVNZ and met with programme director Tony Holden. I told him all about Play It Strange. He hadn't heard of us. But he listened intently.

'Let's have a telethon in New Zealand Music Month and raise funds for our trust,' I said.

Tony doodled on a pad. Put his pencil down. Picked it up. Chewed the end of it. Put it down. Looked up.

'Let's take 24 hours of TV2 time—from seven p.m. on Saturday, 29 May, to seven p.m. on Sunday, 30 May—and have New Zealand bands and artists performing the entire time at venues in Auckland, Wellington, Christchurch and Dunedin. Andrew Shaw can be the head producer and we'll bring in Dominic Bowden as MC. It needs a good name. What do you want to call it?'

I scanned my frontal lobe for an answer. 'I don't know right now,' I said.

'We'll come up with one,' he said. And they did. Not long

afterwards Tony rang: 'We're calling it *National Anthem*.' And there we were. It had taken about three minutes of negotiation. Why he agreed so readily is one of the great mysteries of life. But it was a sign that New Zealand music had finally arrived.

The simple reality of it swam around in my head. One thing was clear in my mind: Dominic Bowden would be the ideal front person, as he was a Sacred Heart College old boy.

I would be given space by TVNZ in their Hobson Street building for planning the logistics of the *National Anthem* show. I needed someone in our office at Neil's to answer the phone in case it rang again while I was out. And to answer the door that no one had ever knocked on. Or just to listen to Neil playing his baby grand.

I was walking along Parnell Road when I saw Debbie Little on the footpath. I rushed over.

'Debbie, how's it going at APRA?'

'Well, it's pretty much like it was when you left it five months ago.'

'Cool,' I replied. 'Then you should leave it too and come and work with me. We're a charitable trust called Play It Strange.'

'Called what?'

Debbie came up the stairs and into my—our—office a few days later. We were a team again. Now we were going to run songwriting competitions for secondary schools, raise funds with TVNZ's help and just generally kick arse. We could do it. And by the end of it—7 p.m. on Sunday, 30 May—we should have enough cash to do it, too.

I set up my space in the TVNZ building. I brought in Rebecca Caughey—at that time manager of Sara-Jane Auva'a—and my eldest son Nikko to contact and enlist around 120 acts, schedule them in the four centres, and assemble all the technical requirements. And at 7 p.m. on Saturday, 29 May 2004, *National Anthem* kicked off. All other TV2 programming and advertising was cancelled. All the acts played for free, and people could pledge money online.

It was a rock'n'roll masterpiece. The closing act on the Sunday was Dave Dobbyn, whose extraordinary repertoire, stagecraft and persona were the climax of what had been a brilliant musical adventure. New Zealand songs and nothing but New Zealand songs for 24 hours!

Slowly, it all sank in. As I stood on the stage of Auckland's St James at around 4 a.m. watching Subtract tear it up; as I stared at screens beaming performances from across New Zealand—the new, the respected, the bedraggled, the masters, the colourful, the pinnacles. And as I stood in the remote-mixing room where TVNZ directors were shouting, calling, weaving their instructions around New Zealand to floor managers, stage managers and sound mixers, and as act after act strode onto stages with never a missed beat or a dropped chord, I thought of those APRA years when Arthur Baysting did his arithmetic and told me that the percentage of New Zealand music on commercial radio had dropped below 2 per cent. This weekend, on national television, it was a triumphant 100 per cent.

A few weeks later the usually empty post-office box had an envelope in it: a cheque from TVNZ for $60,000. It doesn't sound like much, but it was like a million bucks to us. It was monumental. I could look around for a space of our own, seeing as Neil wanted to turn our room into a demo studio. And we had enough to pay for twenty recording sessions. Having the top twenty songs chosen by the judges recorded in a studio would be a reality.

We hired Phil Moore to do the website. He was onto it. We sought any and all publicity and PR moments to tell everyone about our songwriting competition. We targeted music teachers all over the place. Jordan Luck was rounded up, and he talked about it here, there and everywhere. The Rockshop came on board with cash vouchers for all songwriter finalists. APRA spread the word. And Debbie and I sat in Neil's office waiting for entries to come in.

In the calm of the waiting game we could focus on who was going to judge the songs. We added three names to Phil Judd's: Brooke Fraser, Jordan Luck and Feleti Strickson-Pua from Nesian Mystik. I got in touch with them. They were in.

As had been the case with the Silver Scroll, I would make the judges coffee, provide club sandwiches and add up the marks they gave each song. Easy. Now all we needed were some songs.

Debbie and I looked out the window. The purr of vehicles on Newton Road was quite mesmerising. At times evocative; like mechanical cats stalking humans. We both agreed on that. We also agreed that 'evocative' was a cool word with an intellectual sound. We thought we might try to use it more often.

At times, we talked about where all this might go. We knew songwriting wasn't a subject in schools. And Google had told us that it wasn't a subject in any other country in the world. The nearest thing to it was the subject of 'Composition'.

Instrumental composition. Well, that was cool. But the way we saw it, having Composition but not Songwriting was a bit like having Chemistry but not Physics. You wouldn't not have Physics. So—let's have Songwriting.

How? Well, surely that was first and foremost a political campaign waiting to be launched. To convince everyone from politicians to music teachers to principals to parents and the students themselves. Starting at the top.

I spoke to Bill. He said, 'Let's do year one on the competition and see what impact it has on the secondary schools. We'll just assess what we get and the standard of the songs.'

So I gazed out the window of Neil's room as a helicopter buzzed the traffic and Debbie went to clear the mailbox. Nothing yet.

Then, four days before the competition closed off, Debbie walked in looking like Santa Claus's sister, with a big bag. She up-ended it and dozens of CDs, cassettes and VHS tapes fell out onto the floor. I looked at her.

'I'll draw up a spreadsheet of the entries,' she said. I screamed for joy.

In the end we received 150 songs from all over New Zealand. We started reading the lyric sheets. We played the tracks on those CDs, cassettes and VHS tapes. It was a revelation. We whittled them down to 50, copied those onto CD and gave them to the judges, and three weeks later we all met at the secret Beatles Room above the Rockshop on Karangahape Road for the judging session. I brought lamingtons, asparagus rolls and club sandwiches. There was coffee and tea. This was serious business.

As the judges scrolled through the songs, it was clear that they had all spent some time with them. I watched Juddsy. I watched Bill watching Juddsy. The judges allocated points to each of the songs, and when they were tallied up Bill proclaimed the identities of the twenty songs that would be professionally recorded. First place was 'To An Extent', by Josh Turner from Whakatane High School.

We wrote to all the finalists with the good news. They could contact any recording studio they liked, anywhere in New Zealand, and we would pay $750 for the session—below the usual rate-card, but no studio ever said no. The feedback said it all; they were ecstatic.

Me? I burned the top twenty songs onto a CD and took it out to our cottage at Bethells Beach, and played it over and over. The songs were amazing. The evocation of the worlds of their writers and their day-to-day lives was riveting. And under wild west-coast skies, the truth poured out of those headphones. I would find myself standing motionless, just listening, forgetting to sit down. Our belief in the songwriting talent of young New Zealanders was well founded. They could do it.

These were great songs and, after they'd been recorded, some were catapulted even higher by wonderful vocal performances. Fourteen-year-old Kimbra Johnson, from Hillcrest High School in Hamilton, was one whose confidence and exultation merged with sonic beauty. Today she goes by just her Christian name—Kimbra.

There was one song I would play repeatedly: 'Perfect Love', by Kristy Hanna from Gore High School. Bill concurred and we both still play it to this day.

I never will forget
Your love, amazing love.
And when I fall
I'll be falling at your feet
My perfect love.

Once the tracks were recorded and we had them all mastered, Stebbing Recording Centre (where Astley Shrine was put down on vinyl) was booked for CD manufacture. I wrote an introduction to the CD booklet.

> The impression the Play It Strange team had in the early days of the 2004 songwriting competition was that large numbers of New Zealand school students have great songs in them. The competition was therefore a means to empower them. A call to action.
>
> When I first heard these twenty songs in their finished, mastered form I realised that I had it wrong. It is we, the listeners, who are empowered by the sheer musical prowess and creative excellence. This album is a piece of magic from which there is much to learn.

We sent it out to each of the finalists (they got twenty copies each), every Member of Parliament, and other interested parties. It made a great calling card—I would carry copies of it wherever I went, and dish them out.

At around the same time as our album was heading out, the Vodafone Music Awards were held, which provided a strong increase in local content on commercial radio. The talk about what was 'going on' out there was cool. I wrote an article for *The New Zealand Herald*. People needed to hear about this.

SONGS OF YOUTH

Last week's Vodafone Music Awards highlighted in a celebratory fashion the buoyant state of the industry. Across all genres, New Zealand music is virtually hyperactive and the increasing standards of production, performance and video-making point the way to increasing activity. But the Awards also highlighted the ever-improving songwriting skills of our writers. And that is a crucial point, because songs are the true foundation of our music industry. They underpin every aspect of it. And they stay with us.

The playwright Ben Hecht said—'Old songs are more than tunes. They are little houses in which our hearts once lived.' That's why we hold onto them. And they burn more brightly as each year passes. And we draw from them a liberty, an escape knowing that what we feel is true. They are not like anything else.

So what is a song? It is a unique construction.

First we have the music. What is that? Vibrations? Yes—but so much more. Music is a mystery. How can three notes in a row and at a certain tempo bring cheers from a crowd of thousands as they recognise the melody? (Dave Dobbyn's 'Loyal' is a good example.) No one knows. And we will never know. But we understand the abstract effect and we rejoice in the huge emotion that melodies in music bring us. We might be catapulted back in time; transported to other places; we might feel better than we did. There is excitement—a rare emotion in everyday life. There is alchemy in music.

Then we have the lyrics.

Words to songs are generally rhyming verse unless you are talking about Paul Simon's 'America', which doesn't have one rhyme in it. Rhymes are the hook of lyrics and the beautiful, concise language therein allows us to see landscapes of the mind rather than mere thoughts. A great lyric is sheer magic in its ability to offer fulfilment, solace or resonance in a quick three-minute burst.

Now put these words to music and you have the perfect mode of expression in the abstract and the intellectual. A unique construction. So how prevalent is songwriting? Do many New Zealanders exercise their minds with this special pursuit? Very few . . . but more than we think.

Some one hundred and fifty songs have been written and recently entered by New Zealand secondary school students in the Play It Strange songwriting competition. And it is interesting to note that of the 188 students who wrote or co-wrote these songs, 60 per cent are studying music for NCEA. That leaves 40 per cent who aren't.

We all see the ambition and spontaneity that permeates great sport. So too does the creative urge rely on such factors. It is a hugely complementary activity to life in those formative years. And the more it happens, the more those who perhaps have never grasped the true worth of creative expression might embrace this new world.

One thing is certainly clear now. This song competition

has drawn songs from every corner of New Zealand; from Kerikeri to Katikati, Golden Bay to Gore. Sung onto the most decrepit ghetto-blasters or recorded in sophisticated school recording studios. Like a horde of diaries flung open, these songs are an extraordinary parade of the thoughts of youth. A roller-coaster ride for the listener. And it's an even match. Great music. And—all the more difficult to do well—great lyrics. Let them speak for themselves.

Ten squares in boxes march across my page
Regular, angular—containing my rage
Sam George-Allen, 'Far Too Often'

So do you want to be a fireman?
Yeah me too, it's all I want to do
And I want to have a cool car
And a cool guitar, and be a rock-star, yeah
Jeff Parsons, 'Enthusiastic'

I am the daughter of pain
My reflection dances in fire
My skin is as blue as rain
My mouth breathes liar
Jennifer Williams, 'Daughter'

A night of restless sleep subsides, and the ants awake once more
'Just a worker' he tells himself, as his six feet hit the floor
Jeremy and Steven Hay, 'The Human Colony'

The Vodafone Music Awards portrayed a music industry blessed with a confidence it hasn't known for many years. But more than that—they come at a time when the whole of New Zealand is knowing and enjoying the huge variety and breadth of excellence in our own repertoire. In essence, New Zealand music is riding high.

Commercial radio is close to playing 20 per cent New Zealand music and the record charts are rippled with local artists. So where are we heading?

Well, if the quality of songs entered in the Play It Strange song competition is indicative of the current state of teenage creative talent, then we are in for an era of original music like we have never seen before.

We kept on giving that first album away. A number of music teachers asked for copies. Out they went. And we rolled into another year.

In 2005, the Scottwood Trust made a grant that allowed us to record 30 songs. We posted the entry form online and by mid July we closed off with around 175 songs. And we started the process again. We read the lyric sheets first, then moved on to the entry recordings. We were now certain that lyrics and music should be judged equally. And we officially ignored the quality of recording and performance. After all, this was a songwriting competition. Words and music.

We gathered again in the Beatles Room above the Rockshop and the orderly business of judgement began. The top 30 songs were chosen, we wrote to all those songwriters and said, 'Go hither and record these songs.' They did, and we mastered the album and made 3000 CDs.

Once again I lived with those songs for many days. Playing them over and over again. Some of the lyrical journeys had me frozen. This from Kirsten Taylor from Rotorua Girls' High School titled 'Change The Script'.

> *You locked me in the dressing room*
> *To change the script*
> *Sentenced me to a new story line*
> *Like I'm a convict*

Another, Claire Duncan from Auckland's Lynfield College, made the album with her song 'Summer's Lament'. A short while after we'd written to all the writers who were recording for the album, Jordan Luck and I were invited to Lynfield to talk to the Year 12 and 13 students taking music. In we went.

I said, 'Is there a student here by the name of Claire Duncan?'

A hand went up very slowly in the far corner of the room.

Jordan asked, 'How many of you know that Claire is going to be on the Play It Strange album this year?'

From what I remember, no one put up their hand. Jordan picked up his guitar.

'Claire,' he said. 'Come on up the front here and sing them your song.' And she did. She sat on a chair and held the guitar like a weapon. She sang her evocative song 'Summer's Lament' not only to them but *at* them.

> *Summer time embraces*
> *It's too late to make amends*
> *I miss your pretty face*

But I'm tired of waiting for a friend . . .
But then it's alright
To lie alone

And then she straightened up. Stared out at the students sitting in silence. Paused . . . and sang the coda.

And if you need a friend
Try being one
And if you need a friend
Try being one

I sensed that curling wave of her future coming alive and crashing down on us all. The lyric pinned us to our seats, and the music in its gentle, haunting nature gave us, the listeners, a perfect path to journey on.

Claire recorded the track at Goodshirt's Royal Studio. When she left school she began recording under the moniker Dear Time's Waste. She was away.

In 2006, with sustained funding from the Scottwood Trust, we launched our third songwriting competition. Our shift from Neil and Sharon Finn's Roundhead Studios found us in new premises down by the railway lines in Parnell. Again, it was just one room, but Debbie and I had been together ten years on the trot and had almost reached the stage where we didn't need to talk to each other.

There was a peaceful regime in that room. Occasionally the phone would ring. We'd look at it and wonder. I thought of Alexander Graham Bell. Debbie would have thought of changing the ring to a more gentle, sonorous tone. Neither she nor I would have known how to do that. There was a third Play It Stranger in the room by then. A finance manager: Damask Neal. She would put debit on the left and credit on the right. Or maybe the other way around.

And once again, in mid July—bags of cassettes, CDs and the odd video poured out of the post-office box. Around 190 songs in total.

The lyric sheets were read. I picked one up. It was titled 'Angel', by fourteen-year-old Shorale Ong of Howick College.

> *I know a lady*
> *that's sweeter than a baby*
> *but unwanted by her own.*
> *She's kind and she's caring*
> *But the hurt that she's bearing*
> *Is also cutting me . . .*
> *I'm still surprised*
> *And questioning why*
> *They wouldn't want an angel by their side.*

I noticed a paragraph at the bottom of the page. Shorale had written: 'This song is a plea to my mother and father to stop treating my grandmother, who lives with us, so badly.'

I took her CD, played it with headphones on and cried.

A few weeks later, Shorale was in Platform Studios recording the song for the album. I opened the door to the control room and there was her father sitting on the couch. We looked at each other in silence. His face softened and his eyes narrowed. In that silence I believe he was saying, 'I will be a better man.'

When the CDs were manufactured at Stebbings I took a pile around to their home in Dannemora, which was such a new suburb that the maps were flipped back to front and I got very lost. Pre Siri and Google Maps! Was this an allegory for my future? Searching brand-new streets in topsy-turvy suburbs so that I could deliver CDs of extraordinary songs to young songwriters? Looking for letterboxes. Streets named after famous golfers. And wide, mown berms that could be used as cricket pitches. Eventually I knocked on the right door, 30 minutes late, and Shorale's mother opened it.

'Come in, Mr Chunn,' she said, 'and meet the grandmother who this song is about.'

Chapter Twenty-seven
Achievement Standards and the Jacinda Effect

I n 2007, the New Zealand Music Hall of Fame Awards were introduced as a joint initiative by APRA and RIANZ. I liked that idea. Fame. A truly integral part of rock'n'roll life. All those faces and voices, eyes fixed on futures and audiences swaying as if they'd all been seduced by the words and music. You could see it all around you—year after year. Let's make it permanent in our memories.

APRA hosted the inaugural award induction as part of its annual Silver Scroll Awards function, and I was asked to give the speech that introduced this very first Hall of Fame inductee. It was going to be a surprise. I liked that, too. Let's lead them to the water. So I took the Auckland Town Hall stage and went to the microphone. I looked around. Just over there—that's where Paul McCartney stood. He'd played a Hofner bass that night back in 1964. It had flatwound strings. I paused, briefly but long enough to hear his bass lines still echoing in that long, timeless room. That euphoric space that I once called a part of my world. Why not call it that again?

Here is what I said.

Hello, old friends. I am here to announce the first inductee into the New Zealand Music Hall of Fame. Is it a he? A she? Or a they? I cannot say just yet.

I thought—seeing as this is the first one!—perhaps this is the ideal opportunity to philosophise on fame. What is it? Why is it? What makes someone famous in the sense of their musical effect?

I was sitting with my dad and I said to him, 'I'm doing this speechy thing and I'm thinking of "describing" fame.' And I paused—like I do—expecting him to give me the answer. He said, 'Fame is like greatness, really. Shakespeare comes in handy. "Some are born great, some achieve greatness and some have greatness thrust upon them".'

This person or group who will be inducted tonight— where do they fit?

Tonight's inductee was born great. He/she/they have a true musical creativity that transcends normal life. A creative urge that sails in from other planets, slips over the horizon in dreams and proffers lines of wisdom and hooks destined for instant memory.

BUT!

This inductee has achieved greatness. He/she/they have toiled, slaved, bowed, scraped, climbed, sustained, overwhelmed and raised a sword high into the air. In that battle of the wills and against this—at times—barbed-wire industry of ours, he/she/they have conquered through a fierce, magnificent will.

BUT also!

This inductee has had greatness thrust upon them. I first saw this artist perform his/her/their songs on a stage over 25 years ago. Every single pair of eyes in the room was fixed on the stage and never wavered.

He/she/they have a unique connection with the audience, where long arms reach out from the stage and envelop everyone in the room no matter how cavernous it is. Every punter on the floor or in the circles believes—rightly so—that they have been drawn close to the heart of this artist. That they are loved by this person.

And this is only achieved when he/she/they have a humility quite profound. When they wish for all their fellow humans to walk the same paths, drink the same beer and hum the same tunes as them. Greatness quite simply falls upon them as a natural consequence.

There are very, very few people like this special man.

And at this point, what better way to highlight the life, times and the love that we all have for this inaugural inductee to the New Zealand Music Hall of Fame than to stand up and celebrate that codger—

Whose name is: Jordan Luck.

Jordan walked up onstage and we looked each other in the eye. We embraced. He stood back; we fixed eyes again. His weren't so different from when I'd first seen them in 1982 at the Hillsborough Tavern in Christchurch. Those eyes were still throwing out beams and relishing a moment of ascension. He was New Zealand's first inductee into the Music Hall of Fame. We all knew it was the right choice. He was quietly swirling in a shower of applause. We all loved that man. Still do.

By 2008 we had major funding from the Perry Foundation in Hamilton (into which the Scottwood Trust had merged) and were able to record even more songs for the annual Play It Strange album. And, as with each preceding year, more songs came in. We had our panel pick 42 to be recorded in professional studios.

One of them was 'Lasts Forever' by Graham Candy, who attended Rangitoto College in Auckland. He was recording the track at Stebbings, so I dropped in. Here was this lithe, smiling, deeply exuberant lad with a voice like a bird. He was always moving. Shifting. Literally. I was very taken.

'Graham—so, you take music at school?'

'Ah, no, I don't.'

'So where did this song come from?'

Graham prepared himself. He had penetrating eyes. He told his story.

'I don't take the subject of music. I'm a ballroom dancer. Southern hemisphere champion, actually. Our whole family dances. And this had led to my playing the lead role in all the Rangitoto College stage productions. So I learned to sing and act along with that.

'Well, one day a classmate, Alex, said he was going to enter the Play It Strange songwriting competition and he said I should too. I said, "I'd better learn an instrument. I'd better buy one." So Alex and I went to the Rockshop in K Road and I said to him, "I'll walk in with my eyes closed—you make sure I don't crash into anything and the first guitar I touch, I'll buy. Then I'll go learn how to play it and write a song."'

That's exactly what he had done. He bought the pink Ovation guitar that he touched first and then cornered a guitar teacher, who first taught him the chord of E major like all good guitar teachers do! His teacher suggested that if you move that E major chord around different frets you can build up a song that way. (For an example of this, listen to the opening lines of the verses of 'Waterloo Sunset' by The Kinks.) Graham Candy and his E major chord took flight— that chord became a ballroom dance in its own right—and Graham's song 'Lasts Forever' came to be. And here it was going down on a digital desk at the Stebbing Recording Centre.

This kid had something. I kept in touch. He was deeply motivated by the discovery of his songwriting ability and songs poured out of him. He thought, 'I'll form a band.' And he did. They were called The Lost Boys. They entered the New Zealand Battle of the Bands competition and reached the national final, at the Kings Arms in Newton. I was there, along with his mother and girlfriend and God knows who else.

They took the stage. To this day I have never seen such youthful mastery of the lead singer role. Graham spun, twirled, catapulted and slid all over that stage. Ballroom dancing, acrobatics, singing, songwriting and a hyperactive mind all merged into this powerhouse entity.

They didn't win. But something else was just round the corner.

Some time later, I was contacted by Rachel Watson, an artist manager. She had a friend called Matt Mueller who ran a music label, Crazy Planet Records, in Berlin. He was on the lookout for New Zealand singer/songwriter talent. He had an appealing lack of presumption for a northern hemisphere music-biz bod. He smiled a lot. He was enthusiastic. But he was serious about the purpose of his trip Down Under. I knew exactly what to say.

'Matt, you need to hear Graham Candy.'

Matt made moves and saw Graham performing at the Portland Public House in Kingsland. He was impressed, and when I spoke to him a day or two later he said, 'I want Graham to come to Berlin and record for my label.'

'And . . .?' I asked.

'He seems a bit unsure about it.'

I rang Graham. 'Drag your sorry arse to Chapel Bar on Ponsonby Road right now, Mr Candy,' and he did.

I bought a large pizza and lots of beer and said to him, 'You *have* to go to Berlin.' We said other things but I kept repeating it. Berlin was *so* where he should be.

Graham flew to Berlin in 2013, where he dug in, wrote songs and recorded. Within a year, he sang lead vocals on a German Top 10 track—Alle Farben's 'She Moves'—and took to stages here, there and everywhere. Now, every time I see on his Instagram page a vast festival crowd going ecstatic with an enthusiasm that is so addictive it moves you, I think back to the Kings Arms.

In 2009, I was in conversation with Delysse Glynn, head of music at my old stamping ground Sacred Heart College. She was talking to me about how my ambition to have songwriting as an achievement standard should start with my meeting the new vice-CEO of the New Zealand Qualifications Authority (NZQA), Bali Haque.

I contacted Bali, who agreed to meet me. He walked into

a meeting room at NZQA with an air of genteel authenticity. He *looked* the part. I'd failed to do my usual background checks (before I meet someone, I usually do some investigation to find out where they're coming from), but I sensed they were unnecessary. We would just wing it. So I reached into my haversack and took out a copy of each CD we had made so far, from the first in 2004 to the most recent in 2008. And I laid them out in a row in front of him.

'Bali, all these songs are written by secondary-school students in New Zealand. Do you think there could be a way in which they could earn NCEA credits for writing them?'

He looked up at me, devoid of any bureaucratic impatience. He looked back at the CDs.

'I can't see why not,' he said. This was blissful.

The next thing, probably a few weeks later, Brent Logan from NZQA walked into the Play It Strange office looking happy. 'Well, that wasn't an easy thing to pull off, but we got it.' The NZQA would accept songs as legitimate musical pieces in the achievement standard called Composition.

Just to give you the background: for many decades, music students could take Composition, which required the writing of a musical work (with no words). One of the principal components was the 'notation'—the written musical representation—what people like me call a score or a manuscript or a bunch of crotchets and quavers. We knew the percentage of songwriters entering our competition who didn't take music as a school subject (40 per cent, remember?). And the feedback we got from some of those songwriters was that they didn't want to learn how to write scores, et cetera. They just wanted to record their songs.

From now on, the NZQA would accept a *recording* of a song as sufficient 'notation' in the Composition achievement standard. Here was the rub: there was still no focus at all on the lyrics of the song. But it certainly led to more songs being entered in our competition, now called the Lion Foundation Songwriting Competition thanks to Lion's generous grants each year.

Not long after my meeting with Brent Logan, I was invited to the Ministry for Culture and Heritage in Wellington to talk about Play It Strange. In I go and there's CEO Lewis Holden and three of his team. Lewis said (as I recall), 'OK, Mike, what's Play It Strange all about?'

I repeated my Bali Haque move—now refined, like I was the man with the golden arm. I could spin out the CDs in perfectly aligned rows and in chronological order. Their bright colours floating.

I told the four of them pretty much everything I've already told you, dear reader. How songwriting should be in the curriculum, how we need funds to maintain our operation and pay for recording studios, and so on. The essence of their response was an indication that they would look at some way of supporting us financially. One of them said, 'I'm pretty sure we have a spare salary that we're not using, so perhaps we could put that to good use.'

I thanked them for their consideration and left.

About two months later I was in a bar and happened upon an acquaintance who was also a Ministry for Culture and Heritage person. I hadn't heard from the ministry. I investigated. 'Do you know anything about discussions re. ministry funds for Play It Strange?'

'They decided against making any grant, as you might then expect to get the same year after year.'

That was the end of that. I sat in my car. The new album of songs was in my CD player. I started playing it. I thought about the NZQA and how they had massaged the system to allow songs to be assessed in the subject of Composition. The music was the total focus of it; the lyrics were ignored. I found myself thinking, 'This isn't right.' Lyrics are a major component of a song. The listening public judge them equally with the music. And as each year had brought more and more songs to us we had realised the power of the songwriters' stories.

Gareth Malan was a songwriter from Havelock North High School. He was on the 2009 CD with his song 'Carry Me Home'. I turned it up.

> *On a broad back*
> *We carry our honour*
> *And in the heart:*
> *A love for the brother*
> *And in our eyes*
> *We see that crime*
> *That takes us from*
> *One another*
> *How can one life,*
> *I just don't understand*
> *And how can he be*
> *So quickly taken*
> *By the man . . . by the man*
> *With his black heart of stone?*
> *Carry me home.*

Gareth wrote the song after the murder in 2009 of Mark McCutcheon in central Hawke's Bay. McCutcheon had intervened when a man began abusing and assaulting his own girlfriend in a tavern carpark. McCutcheon threatened to get his rifle from his ute if the man and his two mates did not leave. One of them ran to McCutcheon and knifed him. McCutcheon attempted to drive home but was found dead in his ute early the next morning, a few kilometres from the tavern.

I joined the stage with Gareth when he and eight of his classmates performed the song at a Halberg Trust fund-raising dinner in Napier. As it finished, the whole room rose to their feet and the ovation was long and sustained. Gareth could have submitted 'Carry Me Home' for the Composition achievement standard but the words would have been ignored. I thought, 'That's appalling.' And I thought some more.

A short while later I was rung by Wayne Senior, who has a Master of Arts (Music) from the Waikato Institute of Technology (Wintec), as well as having done about ten thousand other things in all facets of the world of music. He told me he had Professor Pat Pattison, Lecturer in Lyric Writing and Poetry at the Berklee College of Music in Boston, Massachusetts, in his apartment.

'Mike, Pat is giving a lyric-writing seminar at Wintec tomorrow and I'm tied up. Would you be able to give him a lift to Hamilton?'

Lyric writing!? *Holy moly.*

'Of course,' I said. And the next morning, Pat and I drove off to Hamilton.

In a word, Pat's seminar to Wintec students was

riveting—a deep insight into the world of lyric writing. For a few years, every time Pat came to New Zealand to give that Wintec seminar, I would drive him down. We talked and talked and talked, mainly about lyrics but also about the Boston Red Sox, about whom he is also passionate. One time we were driving and I was playing the latest Lion Foundation album from our glorious pool of songwriting competition finalists.

'Mike, you know what I think? Your competition isn't about who wins. And it's not about those songs that get to go to pro studios and be placed on the album. How many songs were entered in this year's competition?'

'Two hundred and sixty.'

'What really matters here is that 260 songs are started by young songwriters. And then they are finished. The student then records the song, writes out the lyrics and sends all that to you, where they are read and listened to by strangers. If you didn't run that competition, I would imagine that at least half of those songs that are started would never be finished.'

Brilliant.

To this day Pat and I meet up and I wallow in his lyric wisdom. These days he gives lyric masterclasses to secondary-school songwriters. Play It Strange hosts them.

And then, in 2011, I met Jacinda Ardern.

I was in Landreth & Co café on Ponsonby Road—alone, as I frequently like to be. Yes, I people-watch. Their graces, their bad habits. The colour of their socks, the patterns on their shirts and the scuffs on their shoes. How'd they get there? I imagine how they would all react if Maria

Schryvers walked in, sat at a piano and performed her song 'Let Me Go'. It'd be the same as when I heard her sing it in a small hall in Whangarei. Riveted. Stranded, really, in the knowledge of how such a traumatic time for her and her friends could be so beautifully remembered and, in its recording, recalled forever. Or what if it was David Afoa from Manurewa High School walking in? Miles from home. It would be the same as when I heard him sing at one of our concerts. People around me weeping. Here? No different. The café would go deeply quiet, with all the red eyes on him as he sang 'Beautiful Life'.

> *Mama asked me about my life*
> *What's going on inside*
> *I said 'Mother, mother no.*
> *Please don't cry.'*
> *After I realised*
> *Why mama cared so much*
> *I said 'Mother, mother no.*
> *Hear me out.'*
> *Beautiful Life, listen I am coming*
> *Beautiful Life, can't you hear my cry*
> *I said Beautiful Life*
> *Never letting you go.*

'Mike!' It was Barb Ward. I'd met her a few years earlier, at the home she and her partner, Chris Knox, inhabited in West Lynn. I'd had $3000 in cash and was dropping it off to Chris. He had just won the APRA Silver Scroll for his song 'My Only Friend', and I thought, 'Well, we could mail him a cheque.

But far more exciting to get it in folding.' So I arranged it. He's cool. He deserved folding.

'Mike,' said Barb, 'I'd like to introduce you to someone.'

I went over, sat down and was introduced to Jacinda Ardern from the Labour Party, then in Opposition. Barb was playing an active part in Labour Party machinations then. (Still does!)

We all talked. I talked about Play It Strange. Jacinda listened. She talked about politics. I listened. She told me she was going to contest the Central Auckland seat in a few months and she would be having a launch function soon.

Not long afterwards we met again and she asked me if we could arrange for a couple of Play It Strange songwriters to perform at that launch. I said, 'Of course', and in a small building above the shores of Cox's Creek in Ponsonby, Graham Candy and Avalon Hewitt sang their songs in support of Jacinda's launch event.

Watching her watching them was a revelation. Watching and listening to her was a revelation full-stop. There was insight and warmth and a celebration of who and where she was. Who we all were and how she fitted in with this new generation of songs and performances where words and music merged into song—and we could discern their stories, their journeys.

I went outside, above the water's edge. A quiet moment of reflection in the late-afternoon sun. I walked back in and asked her if she, as Labour Spokesperson for Youth Affairs, would like to present the Peace Song award at our annual awards show later in the year. (We had various awards, including best song and best lyrics.) She said yes immediately, and so it came to be.

In late November 2011, at the Backbeat bar above the K Road Rockshop, we gathered for the Play It Strange awards show. I was MC, so off I went.

'Dear everybody, to present the next award—the Auckland region Peace Song award—please welcome to the stage Jacinda Ardern from the Labour Party, who will be prime minister before she's forty.'

Jacinda walked up to the stage and with a big smile said to me, 'That's a big ask, Mike.'

I said, 'You're right.' So I looked out at the very attentive crowd and said, 'Please welcome to the stage Jacinda Ardern who will be prime minister before she's forty and—' I turned to her—'and on that I bet two dollars.' She shook my hand and the deal was made.

The next day I went driving. I listened to the mastered tracks from the 2011 album. There was wonderful, evocative music. Composition. But there were also profoundly insightful, expressive lyrics. They were going to be ignored. How could they be? Here are a few of the lyrics I heard.

Maria Schryvers, who I mentioned before, was from Nelson. A classmate of hers was dying in hospital, and Maria and her friends would visit her. Maria quoted her friend in the title of her song from that year, 'Let Me Go'.

> *It seems, it was only yesterday*
> *We were making our mistakes*
> *And soaking up the rain*
> *It seems, it was only yesterday*
> *I was speaking out your name*
> *And the only noise was praying*

And I hear her singing
'If you love me, let me go.'
I wish, you could have one more chance
One more day to say goodbye

Seventeen-year-old Eliette Boumeester, a student at Westlake Girls' High in Auckland, had a rare, life-threatening disease, Guillain-Barré syndrome. She was able to see and hear but couldn't move any part of her body. Eventually she pulled through, and wrote a beautiful song called 'Believe'.

I feel cold, I feel numb
I feel nothing
I hear voices all the time
And I see you by my side
I see you standing there
Tears are running
Like a ghost the shadows call me
I won't let this take me over
And I believe in angels . . .

Fletcher Mills, a Wellington College sixteen-year-old, wrote 'The City' after watching coverage of the Christchurch earthquake on television.

Rocks come falling barely missing
The people down below
And I can't even help them
And I can only scream

Debris and dust stings my eyes
As tears mix them in
A broken face
That screams again

But no one
No one
Can hear me (x 2)

And then I played the past winners of our competition, from 2004 onwards. In 2006, fourteen-year-old Annah Mac, who was in Year 10 at St Hilda's Collegiate in Dunedin, won our Lion Foundation Songwriting Competition with a song she had written when she was thirteen. It was called 'Blue Butterfly'. With a number of years' experience performing live with her younger sisters at country and folk festivals around New Zealand, Annah performed 'Blue Butterfly' at the Play It Strange award show and you could have heard a pin drop.

Well walk on in
Yeah, I see you standing there
But I won't let that interfere
With what I'm doing

The next year Annah entered again, and her song 'Home' (also written when she was thirteen) was picked for third place. I introduced her to Professor Pat Pattison and he was hugely impressed with her. He funded Annah's attendance at a week-long seminar and series of recording workshops in Nashville,

Tennessee, and she became a skilled recording artist during this time. On returning to New Zealand and now sixteen years old, Annah was approached by Sony Music and offered a recording contract based on the extraordinary number of songs she had written and recorded as demos. Sony hired US producer Brady Blade, who had recorded Brooke Fraser, and the album *Little Stranger* was put down. One of the songs, 'Girl in Stilettos', was released by Sony as a single and reached number two on the New Zealand singles charts. The video has had close to 500,000 views on YouTube.

Annah did a national tour and Sony continued to release singles. Now in her mid 20s, with a strong and settled relationship, Annah no longer seeks the bright lights but continues writing, recording and performing live shows, which has set her on the path of a life that she has found deeply rewarding and satisfying.

A short while after the 2011 awards I got an email from Cynthia Orr. Cynthia was National English Coordinator in the Faculty of Education at the University of Auckland. We met and talked. Cynthia knew of songs being eligible for the Composition achievement standard, and she thought that, while lyrics couldn't be part of that assessment, why didn't we have a look at including them in the creative writing environment in the subject of English?

'Of course,' I said.

Cynthia asked that I email her the last five lyrics that had won our David Richwhite Lyric of the Year Award, and she would have them assessed against English creative writing protocols. And that's what happened. I emailed her the five sets of lyrics, which had been picked as Lyrics of the Year by people like writer Emily Perkins, musician Don McGlashan and poet Jenny Bornholdt. About a fortnight later we met again.

Cynthia advised me that all five lyrics had been rated as Not Achieved. She held a steady, nondescript look on her face but slight trembles gave her away. I asked how that had happened.

Cynthia said that they had failed because each line is meant to start with a capital letter and there was bad punctuation and, not only that, lines were often repeated. I thought about that. Dave Dobbyn sings 'Ya ya ya ya ya' many times in Th' Dudes song 'Bliss'. If he'd been at school that song lyric would have been Not Achieved. *Humbug.*

I said, 'Well, instead of having English teachers assess lyrics, why doesn't Play It Strange handle the assessment of lyrics for those songwriters who ask us to?' And so that came to be. We added to the entry forms online: 'If you tick this box we will assess your lyrics against the Creative Writing requirements for NCEA.' That seemed simple enough.

However, I then went to see Barbara Bristow, who was a team leader at NZQA, about this lyric-assessment thing. Barbara is cool. I'd met her a few times before. What was her spin?

Barbara got right to it. She asked that we abandon our handling of the assessment of lyrics of songs. I didn't ask for details. It was clear to me that we had travelled down a thorny, stressful road and it was time to pull over.

I said, 'I hear you.'

Then I picked up an A4 piece of paper, took one of her pencils and wrote in Very Large Letters across it:

SONGWRITING

'That's what should be in the curriculum,' I said.

'You're the only one talking about it, Mike. You need to find some teachers who are on your wavelength and lobby as a team.'

I sat back in my chair. Her office didn't have windows, as I recall. But the chair was comfortable. It wasn't leather or anything flash, but it had give and a springy sense. The sort of chair you'd find for visitors at Paul McCartney's holiday home. I thought for a second or two about asking her how that might work, this gathering of a cohort of songwriting-focused music teachers. Was it all about the Ministry of Education? Or was it the Minister of Education? What's the real difference? Maybe there was a huge gulf between them. Images flooded back: Arthur Baysting tackling MPs in the Beehive corridors, on the rampage for music quotas. Maybe I could grab some music teachers and do all that like he did? Maybe.

I looked at Barbara. She had that 'You are going to get there, Mike, but it may not be today' look on her face. I kissed her on the cheek and slipped away.

With our funding on a gentle rise thanks to other grants and philanthropic entities, we were able to record 49 songs in 2012. As we dived into the world of listening to the entries, as usual pleasantly shocked at their excellence, I wrote to the Minister of Education, Hekia Parata, to see what we might unearth. It was very clear to me now: songwriting *had* to be in the curriculum! Hekia didn't reply.

A few months later, I was asked by NZQA if I would be on a panel to assess the application of the Music and Audio Institute of New Zealand (MAINZ) for accreditation of their proposed Bachelor of Musical Arts degree. 'Of course,' I said.

The panel convened. The chairperson was Colin Knox. I knew that name—Auckland Regional Authority CEO some time back. A name that bounced around in the fourth estate. He was hugely impressive. A man who knew how to chair a roundtable of odd-bods. Also on the panel was Trevor Thwaites, from the University of Auckland's School of Curriculum and Pedagogy. He's a drummer. Played for many years all over the place.

Now, as we all know, drummers and bass players are joined at the hip. We smiled at each other knowingly, and at the end of the first day a group of us went and had a beer. We talked about rhythm sections. We talked about music education. We talked about the state of things. Things go up, things go down. We were on a similar wavelength. We were children of the stage.

When the final day at MAINZ was over and we had approved the degree, the panellists floated away. Colin Knox remained. He came up to me and said, 'What worries me about graduates with this degree is who is going to employ them?'

I said, 'No one will employ them. They will be starting their own business. They will form their own groups; go solo; do duets where all the decisions are their own. Their name, the songs they write, their membership, their characters, their schedule of live shows, their recording plans, their identity.

They will gather their own forces and charge on, Colin. It requires strength, energy, discipline, imagination, creative energy, musical talent, stagecraft, tenacity and the building of human relationships at every step of the way. And it all starts with songwriting.'

Colin looked at me for some time.

'I understand,' he said.

A few months later I was at MAINZ talking to the dean there, Harry Lyon—of Hello Sailor fame—and we started discussing songwriting in schools. How it was an 'isn't'. Harry said, 'If you want to see it happen, you need to talk to Trevor Thwaites.' Ah. I could see ducks lining up. Scrolling along the sideshow of life, poised to be popped over by BB gun pellets.

So I suggested that Harry, Trevor and I meet up and drink beer. And we did and the drummer and bass player talked about rhythm sections and songwriting in the curriculum and I asked Trevor if we could meet specifically on the songwriting thing. He said, 'Sure.'

In time, we met at The Cavalier pub on Ponsonby's College Hill, just a stone's throw from Jacinda Ardern's offices. I told Trevor what Barbara Bristow had said. I asked if he would help lobby for songwriting in the curriculum. He said, 'Let's get a group together and we'll thrash it out.' And we talked some more about rhythm sections. How could we not?

A few months later I met Trevor, Jeni Little (HOD Music at Green Bay High School) and Tim Randle (HOD Music at Manurewa High School), with Delysse Glynn (now national music moderator for NZQA) as an informal cajoler, at the Cav. We talked about songwriting in the curriculum. What would it take to get it in? What processes were involved? Who needed prodding?

Trevor came up with the plan. First, he went out on the Musicnet—a music teachers' email group with hundreds of subscribers—and sought feedback on the idea of a songwriting achievement standard. The response was pretty supportive.

Then the paperwork. In essence a 'draft achievement' would be drawn up that would go along the same lines as Composition, except it would mention 'words and music' not just 'music'. The 'right' person at the Ministry of Education would then be approached to see if they could, well . . . push it through. And that's exactly what happened.

Ministry of Education chap Geoff Gibbs received the draft achievement standard for Songwriting at Level 3. He went back to Trevor with a 'Looks OK'.

I met Trevor at the Cav. 'Trevor, what happens now?'

'We wait.' So we waited.

Quite some months went by, until the day came when Trevor beckoned me back to the Cav. 'Geoff has shaped up the draft and he'll be sending it out for feedback from music teachers and a few others.'

I thought, 'Okey-dokey. What if they don't want it?' I booked a flight to Wellington to see Geoff Gibbs.

Geoff was devoid of fidgets, blinks, twitching and all that other stuff that can sometimes inhabit bureaucratic environments. He was cool.

'Geoff—you've got the draft out for feedback, comments,

et cetera. Can the teachers and school administrations kill it?'

'No,' he said.

And at the end of November 2016, the Ministry of Education announced the implementation of Achievement Standard 91849—Songwriting at Level 3. Words and Music. Songwriting was in the school curriculum.

I was in Alphabet café in Parnell when the email came through. I ordered a 187 ml bottle of Brut sparkling wine, poured it and drank it. And—as you would expect—I wept.

After the $2 bet with Jacinda Ardern in 2011, we had met every year in December to drink wine and shoot the breeze. The first time was 2012 and we met at Dida's Wine Lounge, a stone's throw (in the other direction from the Cav) from her electorate office on College Hill. Jacinda was aware of the campaign for songwriting to be in the curriculum and was very supportive.

That was also the year that my father, Jerry, passed away. We talked about that, and I told her how Jerry used to drive my youngest brother to school when he was nine years old while playing the Split Enz album *Mental Notes* on the car cassette player, back in 1975. Jerry was very taken with Phil Judd's lyrics, a favourite being 'Time for a Change'.

After Jacinda and I sloped off into the Auckland traffic, I went home and took a book from the shelf. It was *Essays* by Hilaire Belloc, and on the first page Jerry had put his signature and a date, 1969. There was a birthday card inside, marking a particular page which Jerry had opened and read to me back in 1975 after one of Split Enz's triumphant Auckland Town Hall concerts.

Write a good song and the tune leaps up to meet it out of nothingness. It clothes itself with tune, and once so clothed it continues on through, eternally young, always smiling, and always ready with strong hands for mankind. On this account every man who has written a song can be certain that he has done good; any man who has continually sung them can be certain that he has lived and has communicated life to others.

It is the best of all trades, to make songs, and the second best to sing them.

On 19 October 2017, Winston Peters announced that he and his New Zealand First party would form a coalition government with the Labour and Green parties. Jacinda would be prime minister at the age of 37. I learned of this from a text to me by Debbie Little. It was in the evening, and I was sitting alone in a café on Dominion Road, people-watching.

I immediately texted Jacinda and congratulated her. A short while later she replied: 'Thank you so much!!!! Thank you for always believing in me. And I think I just lost a bet with you?'

Epilogue

And so it comes to be.

The world will always fuel its revolutions, its evolution, with the words and music of its people. I was destined to know that and to evolve with them, those tunes and stories of hope, love, regret, loss and so much more, all through that small world; me, a child with expectation and marvel as my daily bread . . . and so much more.

I was there. That curtain, that ancient curtain, lifted and there I was on a stage. And the future unfolded. And I started walking on and on and on. One step at a time. And everywhere I turned, everything I saw: all those exploding images of wonder and instinctive responses of defence; the impact of joy upon the soul and love in its buoyancy of the heart; the flight from terror and the embrace of our fellow humans. The kaleidoscope of life in its psychedelic colours and dark, insidious corners. The deep, sinking stealth and the towering assault on the senses. They arrived as I walked on. One step at a time.

The main street of Otahuhu remains. The school has a playground and the lunchtime noises are of the same midsummer pitch and flight from boredom. It was just a few years ago that my dear school friend Jim Skinner and I walked onto that playground and played one last game of marbles. And now he has passed away. His Alzheimer's tore his beaming swarm of excitement from him and he fell to the ground.

Sacred Heart College has harboured my two younger sons, Barney and Johnny, for seven years each. The assembly hall with the scuffed and roughed-up wooden stage saw Tim Finn and me and a pile of others walk on one last time, in 2014. We called the show 'The Last Riot in the Old School Block'. As we blasted through 'Six Months in a Leaky Boat', I watched Tim throw himself out to the crowd and I saw their eyes, en masse, relish his prowess. It was a look I'd seen many times before. Around the world. Although as time wore on my agoraphobia bleached my dizzy view. The spell of our Split Enz adventure flew away from me and found me lying on a Holiday Inn bed with an invisible, leaden blanket of confusion and misery suffocating me, leaving me behind and alone as I grappled with the mysterious magnet of Auckland city: the retreat. The heavy wooden door with its spiral staircase that I realised I was too scared to climb, so I watched others—my teenage friends, the musicians I used to call my own—scale heights I had only dreamed of and never got to. That one last time I watched the velvet curtain fall, that ancient curtain, and I was in the dark. So I left the stage, that stage I could be happy on, that stage that mothered me but from which I would be relentlessly tossed amid such an inferno of fear that I stopped and stood still. I walked out into the crowd. I watched and witnessed.

If I couldn't play the beautiful, vivid songs of those who asked me to share the stage with them, I would find a way to remain in their vicinity, with responsibilities and a purpose such that the words and music of the great inventors of song could be an integral part of my life. And that came to be, and my days were filled with wonder and reason and I charged into each new day, each new world, with my smiles and heeded calls and a challenge to be achieved. It was glorious. And so it will remain. It will be glorious.

To witness, know and believe in the voices, the songs, of our fellow citizens. To love their words and music. To believe them, to believe in them. To follow them down the road in a train of shared celebration. Fists in the air. Feet stamping. We can do that. You and me. We must do that.

And as the curtain, the ancient curtain, rises on each new arrival from that distant, luminous place, bless this world we are in.

AUTHOR PHOTOGRAPH BY JOSEF SCOTT

Mike Chunn is a music legend who has been involved at almost every level of the New Zealand music industry for decades. Along with Tim Finn and Phil Judd, he was a founding member of Split Enz, playing the bass on their first three albums. While he loved the stage, life on the road was a different story: unbeknown to his bandmates, he suffered frequent panic attacks and debilitating anxiety, triggered every time he left Auckland. After five years he reluctantly left the band.

In 1977, Mike co-founded Citizen Band with his brother Geoffrey, but left that band after three years for the same reason. It wasn't until 1981 that he discovered the name of his illness: the phobic disorder agoraphobia.

Mike went on to become general manager of Mushroom Records NZ, signing up artists DD Smash and Dance Exponents; later he was general manager at Sony Music Publishing NZ. From 1991 to 2003, he was the Director of NZ Operations for APRA, where he was instrumental in setting up New Zealand Music Month—an integral factor in Kiwi music gaining airtime on commercial radio.

In 2004, Mike co-founded Play It Strange, a highly respected and successful charitable trust that supports young New Zealanders in their songwriting ambitions. He is currently CEO of this trust.

Mike was awarded the Companion of the New Zealand Order of Merit for services to music and men's mental health in 2013. He is also an observer trustee of the Sir John Kirwan Foundation. He lives in Auckland.